D0073190

FAMILY SECRETS
AND THE PSYCHOANALYSIS OF NARRATIVE

FAMILY SECRETS

AND THE PSYCHOANALYSIS OF NARRATIVE

Esther Rashkin

PRINCETON UNIVERSITY PRESS PRINCETON, NEW JERSEY

Published by Princeton University Press, 41 William Street,
Princeton, New Jersey 08540
In the United Kingdom: Princeton University Press, Oxford

Library of Congress Cataloging-in-Publication Data

Rashkin, Esther, 1951–
Family secrets and the psychoanalysis of narrative / Esther Rashkin
p. cm.
Includes bibliographical references and index.
ISBN 0-691-06951-4
1. Short stories, American—History and criticism—Theory, etc.
2. Short stories, English—History and criticism—Theory, etc.
3. Short stories, French—History and criticism—Theory, etc.
4. Psychoanalysis and literature. 5. Secrecy in literature
6. Family in literature. 7. Narration (Rhetoric) I. Title.
PS374.P7R37 1992
809.3'9353—dc20 92-4682 CIP

This book has been composed in Adobe Palatino

Princeton University Press books are printed
on acid-free paper and meet the guidelines
for permanence and durability of the Committee
on Production Guidelines for Book Longevity
of the Council on Library Resources

Printed in the United States of America

1 3 5 7 9 10 8 6 4 2

In memory of my mother

Rien ne pèse tant qu'un secret . . .
(La Fontaine)

Contents

Acknowledgments

PARTS of this book have appeared, in altered form, in essays published elsewhere. A slightly different version of chapter 1 appeared as "Tools for a New Psychoanalytic Literary Criticism: The works of Abraham and Torok," in *Diacritics* 18, no. 4 (Winter 1988). A very different version of chapter 3 was first published as "Secret Crimes, Haunted Signs: Villiers's *L'Intersigne*," in *The Stanford French Review* (published by Anma Libri) 6, no. 1 (Spring 1982) and was revised for publication as "Le signe enterré dans *L'Intersigne* de Villiers de l'Isle-Adam," in *Cahiers Confrontation*, no. 18 (Fall 1987). It was further revised for inclusion here. Chapter 4 first appeared as "Signes cryptés, rimes dorées: *Facino Cane* de Balzac," in *Cahiers Confrontation*, no. 8 (Fall 1982); it was significantly altered and published as "Phantom Legacies: Balzac's *Facino Cane*," in *Romanic Review* 80, no. 4 (November 1989). Copyright by the Trustees of Columbia University in the City of New York. Chapter 5 was first published as "A Spectacle of Haunting: James's *The Jolly Corner*," in *The Oxford Literary Review* 12, nos. 1–2 (1990). I am grateful to the publishers for permission to reprint.

I am also grateful to the National Endowment for the Humanities for a Fellowship that allowed me to devote a year of uninterrupted work to this project.

This book could not have been written without the intellectual stimulus, critical commentaries, and warm, generous, sustained encouragement provided by many friends and colleagues. I would especially like to thank Colette Gaudin, Vivian Kogan, David Sices, Jacqueline Sices, John Lyons, Debbie Garretson, Nancy Frankenberry, Laurence Davies, Karen Edwards, Anthony Fothergill, Susan Harding, Nicholas Rand, and Maria Torok. I am also indebted to my literature students over the years whose mixture of enthusiasm and skepticism in the face of some of the ideas elaborated in this study has kept me mindful of the need for analytic rigor and of the pedagogical demands of literary interpretation. Finally, I would like to express my deep appreciation to Deborah Porter and Martha Helfer for their help proofreading, to Lauren Lepow for her intelligent and very careful copyediting, and to my editor, Robert Brown, for his attentiveness and good-humored support.

Note on Documentation

FOR the reader's convenience, page references to primary texts in each chapter appear throughout in parentheses following quotations. All italics and translations are my own, unless stated otherwise. *The Oxford English Dictionary*, cited as *OED*, and *Le Grand Robert de la langue française*, 2d edition (1985), hereafter cited as *Robert*, are used to confirm the common usage of a word at the time it was employed in a text and are most frequently cited because they provide dates and examples of usage for references. Also used for corroboration is *Webster's New International Dictionary of the English Language*, 2d edition, unabridged (1949), cited as *Webster's*. *The American Heritage Dictionary* (1985), *The Collins English Dictionary*, 2d edition (1986), and the *Larousse de la langue française* (1979) have also been used to confirm word usage, although they are not cited. All references to Freud's works are cited, by volume and page number, from *The Standard Edition of the Complete Psychological Works of Sigmund Freud*, 24 vols., trans. James Strachey (London: Hogarth, 1955).

FAMILY SECRETS
AND THE PSYCHOANALYSIS OF NARRATIVE

Introduction

Character Analysis, Unspeakable Secrets, and the Formation of Narrative

THIS BOOK is a study of the haunting effects of family secrets on characters in narrative. It grew out of an interest in the psychoanalytic study of fictional personae in works of literature. Over the years, the field of character analysis has entertained a variety of theories and methodologies that have been invented and applied to texts in order to account for the actions and speech of their protagonists. The analytic approach I delineate and whose implications I explore in this book is markedly different from these previous perspectives and is even more at odds with recent attempts to bracket or debunk such undertakings. It has nevertheless been informed to some degree by all the principal critical stances toward interpreting characters in narrative. It is thus indebted to the debate and innovation that have preceded it just as it aims to contribute a new line of inquiry, both theoretical and methodological, to character analysis and to psychoanalytic literary criticism in general.

Historically, psychoanalytic critics have sought to describe the dynamics of repression and thereby explain the underlying signification of manifest elements in a text. Freudian approaches have often relied on the theory of the "return of the repressed" to interpret characters' expressions of love, hate, guilt, ambivalence, and fear as manifestations of buried or repressed conflicts between instinctual desires and societal prohibitions. Ego-psychology, object-relations theories, archetypal theory, and reader-response criticism have explored different models of psychic organization, shifting the emphasis from Oedipal to pre-Oedipal dynamics of development or from the manifestations and vicissitudes of infantile desire to the formation and maintenance of identity, self, societal norms and classifications, or the reader's own fantasies.[1] Despite their widely divergent theoretical underpinnings and practical applications, these reading approaches all pay heed to an array of rhetorical and grammatical mechanisms by which signification, interpersonal relationships, and societal codes are disguised, camouflaged, transformed, and displaced in and through a text. A large part of my research has been devoted to the related but somewhat different problem of assessing the precise manner in which such rhetorical and grammatical mechanisms resist understanding and to finding ways of surmounting the obstacles they pose to interpretation.

In the course of doing so, I have encountered rhetorical modes of hiding and concealment previously unknown to literary analysis. *Symbol* and *cryptonymy* are two such modes discovered by the French psychoanalysts Nicolas Abraham and Maria Torok, who explored their significance for the theory and practice of psychoanalysis and for the elaboration of certain philosophical and aesthetic concepts. Abraham and Torok's writings, especially their discussion of *secrets,* have had an important impact on my examination of the problems of character motivation, textuality, and the formation of narratives in nineteenth- and early twentieth-century literature.

This study is concerned with setting forth a new approach to analyzing certain literary works organized by the inscription within them of a particular kind of secret. It does not treat secrets in the sense of pieces of information or gossip passed on confidentially from one person to another to the exclusion of a third. Nor does it concern an act or event involving one or more persons that is kept from everyone else or willfully covered up. My interest, in short, is not with secrets explicitly identified as such, as one finds in *The Scarlet Letter*, *Benito Cereno,* and *What Maisie Knew.* By "secret" I mean a situation or drama that is transmitted without being stated and without the sender's or receiver's awareness of its transmission.

This is clearly distinct from the kinds of secrets parents regularly keep from their children (minor medical problems, sexual habits, or the contents of a will, for example) to preserve their privacy or keep peace in a family. At stake here is an interpersonal drama, experienced as too shameful to be articulated, which must be kept silent. The reasons for which it is shameful are not always revealed by the text. Neither can it be assumed that overwhelming shame is innately present in or automatically attached to any particular event or experience. Secrets of illegitimacy, a parent's imprisonment, a suicide, or a sexual molestation can be and frequently are brought out in the open where their psychic charge may be reduced and ultimately dissipated. While these dramas may still evoke feelings of shame or embarrassment once revealed, such effects are quite distinct from the psychic turmoil produced in both the sender and the receiver when these and similarly charged secrets are kept concealed by the former and then tacitly passed on to the latter.[2]

The configuration in which a shameful, unspeakable secret is silently transmitted to someone else in whom it lodges is called a *phantom.* It was discovered by Nicolas Abraham in response to certain patients encountered in his clinical practice and was elaborated upon in his and

Maria Torok's writings on the metapsychology of secrets. One of my book's aims is to explore the theoretical and interpretive implications this configuration holds for the study of narrative literature. In conjunction with this endeavor my analyses depart significantly from Abraham and Torok's quite logical clinical emphasis on identifying phantoms as sources of psychopathology potentially susceptible to therapeutic treatment. My focus is instead on examining how phantoms can be concealed rhetorically and linguistically within literature, how their concealed presence can be detected and exposed as the driving force behind the actions and discourse of certain fictive characters, and how the analysis of the modes and processes of their concealment makes possible the articulation of a new approach to literary character analysis and a new theory of narrative generation.

My project thus directly engages the debate concerning the relationship between literary analysis and psychoanalysis. Literary analysis, as it will emerge from this study, is interested in identifying and reading the traces or effects of a drama that has been inscribed in a narrative but is not readily visible within it. From a methodological point of view this means that the linguistic elements of the text are considered to be incomplete and need to be joined with their missing complements, whose traces are embedded in the text. This union of complements enables the reader to perceive or conjecture a concealed drama in the family history of the character that occurred, in most cases, prior to the events of the narrative. The result of this approach is a reconsideration of extant conceptions of narrative limits and textual boundaries and a rethinking of the notion of textual origins.

This inquiry also engages the long-standing debate concerning the legitimacy of analyzing the behavior and motivation of fictional characters. My training in the close reading of literary works and my interest in exposing textual complexity and interpreting the enigmas posed by various narratives have drawn me to explore the divergent positions of this issue. It has become apparent to me that, despite their substantial theoretical and practical differences, all those who have addressed the question of character analysis—from partisans of New Criticism to those aligned with deconstruction, from orthodox Freudians to post-Freudian Lacanians—implicitly agree that literary texts worthy of interpretation have a level of complexity that is not readily apparent and that their visible elements are signs, semes, codes, signifiers, traces, or symptoms of something yet to be revealed. The thrust of my research for this book has been to identify visible elements of selected narratives as symptoms or "symbols" that point to unspeakable family dramas cryptically inscribed within them. In the process of reconstituting these dramas from their textual traces, I show how the motivating forces behind the puzzling, seemingly incongruous behavior and speech of the characters in these narratives can be determined, and how the generative force of the narratives themselves can be revealed.

Structuralism, represented by critics such as Roland Barthes, Tzvetan Todorov, Vladimir Propp, and A. J. Greimas, has largely rejected the legitimacy of character analysis, stressing instead the systems of codes, conventions, and signs that traverse characters and define the roles or functions they assume. As Jonathan Culler has noted, structuralism considers the conception of characters as "richly delineated autonomous wholes, clearly distinguished from others by physical and psychological characteristics . . . , a myth."[3] Although my work is at odds with this view and with structuralism's dependence on underlying formal systems of oppositions for evaluating a text's conformity to predetermined literary expectations, conventions, and modes of organization, it shares structuralism's larger interest in textual tension and ambiguity and in the possibility of locating principles of coherence that might account for these effects.

While deconstructive criticism has tended to dismantle the notion of the fictive character into what Peter Brooks calls "an effect of textual codes, a kind of thematic mirage,"[4] my approach to character analysis shares deconstruction's concern with pushing aside the apparent meaning of the text and unveiling the rhetorical strategies by which that meaning is undermined or deferred. It branches off from deconstruction's concentration on elaborating how signification is rendered undecidable or unavailable in a text by focusing on *why* signification has been made unavailable. This entails showing how the processes by which coherence is obstructed can themselves be interpreted in certain texts to reveal unspeakable dramas concealed within the narratives.

Lacanian interpretations of literature have by and large transmuted the question of character analysis into an analysis of the subject as an effect of language or of the signifier. The Lacanian emphasis on the relationship between psychoanalysis and language, on the production of signifying chains, and on the rhetorical mechanisms by which language distorts, condenses, and displaces meaning are pertinent for any psychoanalytic literary critic. My tracing of the incongruous behavior of characters in texts to concealed family dramas, however, hinges on a view of the subject's relationship to the signifier different from Lacan's. The elaboration of the mechanisms by which these dramas are concealed also diverges from Lacanian modes of analysis, since these mechanisms reach beyond the scope of known rhetorical strategies based on distortion, condensation, and displacement and offer an alternative to the preeminence of metaphor and metonymy in Lacanian theory. One of the major implications of this inquiry is to question the legitimacy of relying on the infinitude of the signifying chain and on the primacy of the phallus in the formation of the subject as heuristic principles.

A primary argument forwarded by those disagreeing with the appropriateness of analyzing characters in literature has been the impossibility of reconstructing a character's past when it is not explicitly present in the text. Meredith Skura, for one, has argued that retracing a hidden past is solely the domain of clinical psychoanalysis which, in treating the human mind, deals with experiences "less coherently organized and less comprehensible than even the most horrible and irrational passions in any poetic schema. . . . The analyst," she contends, "always deals with more of the mind than does either the poet or the theoretician. . . . Like the poet, the analyst asks about a character's unacknowledged motives; but unlike the poet, he traces these back to other thoughts, other experiences, other contexts, which gave rise to motives and give them their only meaning. What is unique about psychoanalysis is that it not simply identifies strange behavior but also locates a source for behavior in something besides current experience. . . . [T]he characters [in Shakespeare's plays] have objective correlatives for their behavior. The play's world explains . . . what the characters do. . . . The explanation lies in the context, not in some additional unseen shaper of the will, and certainly not in offstage, never-mentioned past events."[5]

Readers themselves can decide whether, in light of my analyses, the characters depicted by Joseph Conrad, Auguste de Villiers de l'Isle-Adam, Honoré de Balzac, Henry James, and Edgar Allan Poe are more coherently organized, comprehensible and rational than human patients encountered and described by clinical psychoanalysis.[6] On the other hand, the objection to seeking the cause of a fictive character's behavior in unseen, never-mentioned past events can be addressed at this juncture because it is, I think, based on a fallacious assumption. It presumes that talking about a fictive character's past means treating that character as human and his or her past as "real." If this were my project such an objection would be justified. My enterprise, however, is different. The past dramas I reconstruct from short stories and to which I trace characters' behavior have the same fictional status as the characters themselves. Both the "life" of the character as it is presented in the text and the past I conjecture are fictive, which is not to say fictitious. The familial dramas that can be reconstituted as motive forces in each story are not without textual basis but are inscribed and readable in the narrative. It is thus not a question of inventing a false, fantasized past for a character but of understanding that the text, in each instance, calls upon the reader to expand its apparent parameters to include scenarios that are rhetorically, semantically, phonemically, cryptonymically, and symbolically inscribed within it. These dramas, while predating the events of the text, have no reality outside the limits of the text. Such limits, however, have to be construed as extending beyond their readily visible borders. The task of the reader is to redraw these boundaries, which, we will see, are not static but move constantly outward.

Shoshana Felman has addressed the question of the text's limits and the problematic relationship between literature and psychoanalysis in her introduction to *Literature and Psychoanalysis—The Question of Reading: Otherwise.*[7] In a now-classic argument, Felman states succinctly and eloquently that the traditional hierarchy in which psychoanalysis is presumed to have mastery and explanatory power over literature elides the specificity of literature. She proposes that the task of the literary critic is "to engage in a real *dialogue* between literature and psychoanalysis, as between two different bodies of language and between two different modes of knowledge."[8] She goes on to argue that the way to discover what literature might have to teach us about psychoanalysis is to view the relationship of the two in terms of mutual implication rather than of one-sided application.

While the questions she and I pose in analyzing a text are somewhat different, Felman's emphasis on the need to avoid the application of psychoanalysis to literature is in my view indisputable. Her contention that literature has a great deal to teach us about psychoanalysis and that it is essential to establish and maintain an open exchange or dialogue between these two realms is equally valid. One goal of my book is to contribute to the ongoing and mutually beneficial dialogue between literature and psychoanalysis through an inquiry into the relationship between the transmission of family secrets, the analysis of fictional characters, and the generation of narrative. A specific result of this inquiry will be to shift the terms and implications of this dialogue from considering literature and psychoanalysis as two different bodies of language and two different modes of knowledge to viewing literary analysis and psychoanalysis as two different contexts for the same mode of interpretation. This shift will, in turn, open the way to articulating the heretofore unrecognized commentaries, tacitly offered by certain fictional texts, on the nature and workings of the psyche and on the relationship between psychic drama and the formation of literary narrative.

The study begins with a preliminary statement of my methodology and a comparative analysis of those metapsychological and interpretive theories of Freud, Lacan, and Abraham and Torok that have particular relevance for psychoanalytic literary criticism. Although interest in the writings of Abraham and Torok continues to grow, their psychoanalytic concepts are still not widely known in the English-speaking community. Chapter 1 is thus also intended as an expository introduction to selected aspects of the analysts' work, specifically to the theories of the phantom, cryptonymy, symbol, symbolic operation, trauma, and anasemia. It also begins to suggest how these concepts, if considered in conjunction with specific works of literature, may be viewed as fundamental components of the literary and not just the psychoanalytic realm.

The readings of five short stories that follow explore the ramifications, for the analysis of character, narrative structure, and narrative generation, of the concealment of an unspeakable secret within a work of fiction. Joseph Conrad's *The Secret Sharer*, in chapter 2, introduces the kinds of textual problems potentially generated by the haunting presence of a phantom in a narrative. Although a secret, unspeakable family drama can be sketched from traces within the text, the details of this drama can be only partially reconstituted. The specificity of Conrad's text is shown to lie rather in its function as an allegory of the phantom structure. The captain's obsessive insistence that he shares a secret with Leggatt, his allusions to doubling, uncanniness, and ghosts, and his willingness to risk his crew and career by recklessly maneuvering his ship are explained as symptoms that tacitly speak of his inability to share a secret that haunts him. His first-person account thereby emerges as a narrative driven by the phantom lodged within him, and as an implicit commentary on the potential link between phantomatic secrets, the generative force of narrative, and the formation of allegory in literature.

Chapter 3, on Auguste de Villiers de l'Isle-Adam's *L'intersigne*, explores how hallucinations and altered states of mind, typically associated with literature of the "fantastic," can be linked to the perturbing yet unseen presence of a phantom. The unfolding of the narrative is exposed as the cryptic story of the inception of a secret and of its mute transmission between two characters. The protagonist's reciting of the narrative is revealed to be a symptom generated by the secret that has been transmitted to him without his knowledge and that he carries within him. The demonstration of the psychic complexity of Villiers's work, which has traditionally been assigned only marginal status in literary history, also contributes a different perspective to the recently begun reassessment of his importance to the development of occult literature in the nineteenth century and to the beginnings of science fiction.

The fourth chapter, on Honoré de Balzac's *Facino Cane*, expands upon the possible modes by which a secret can be transmitted silently and by which a narrative can emerge from such a transmission. It examines how the unspoken transmission of a drama of illegitimacy and its unknowing retransmission can be connected to the obsessive and self-destructive behavior of the title character. At the same time it reveals that a phantom can "peregrinate" in several directions and inhabit strangers as well as family members. The richness of Balzac's text also provides an occasion to outline readings of it inspired by Freudian and Lacanian theory and to compare their specific results and implications for interpretation with those produced by a reading informed by the theory of the phantom.

The increasing complexity of the texts under study and of the forms by which phantom structures may manifest themselves and propel narratives is pursued in Henry James's *The Jolly Corner*. The reading exposes the protagonist's bizarre quest to confront his "alter ego" as an unwitting reenactment of a drama of adultery that has been transmitted to him through several generations of his family. The questions of why the story had to be written in the third person and what the text suggests might be meant by a "psychotic narrative" are addressed. So too are the implications for textual analysis of the possibility that a narrative may contain several discourses, belonging to several different characters, all of which are conflated and cryptically articulated in a single character's speech and behavior. The delineation of the effects of a transgenerational haunting and of the main protagonist's unrecognized staging of the complex and traumatic scenario at its source also leads to an inquiry into the possible analytic role played by another fictional character in the narrative and, ultimately, into the role of the reader as analyst.

Chapter 6, on Edgar Allan Poe's *The Fall of the House of Usher*, recapitulates and expands upon the previously seen aspects of secret transmissions and the haunting effects of phantoms in a narrative explicitly concerned with madness and mental distress. It addresses the questions of why a given drama must be transformed into a secret, how the secret is formed, and to what extent transgenerational haunting can determine the destiny of an entire family line. The function of the reader as analyst or "exorcist" is further investigated, as is the issue of how a text can implicitly demand that its apparent limits be extended and can suggest the direction in which they be redrawn. The chapter also discusses a deconstructive reading of Poe's text in order to delineate, within a specific context, some of the principal differences between the interpretive results of this methodology and those of my own. The book ends with a discussion of the implications of the interpretive approach I have elaborated for the analysis of fictional characters, family histories in literature, and the motive force of narratives.

Throughout the book, my readings reflect upon and offer a new vantage point from which to consider such problems as the dynamics of collective concealment, the relationship between an encrypted secret and the generation of narrative, the difficulty of defining a text's limits when it includes other apparently self-contained texts, the manner in which textual fragments can both conceal and reveal a family history, and the forces that make a character create her- or himself as an enigma that obstructs interpretation. My concentration on these issues and the specific nature of my methodology are not meant to suggest that the tales I have treated cannot be considered from other critical perspectives. The intrinsic richness of all the stories I analyze is such that they can sustain varied interpretations informed by diverse theories and methodologies. My readings are sustained by specific questions concerning character motivation, secrets, and the production of narrative that have been opened in scope by my encounter with concepts such as the phantom and cryptonymy and have been altered and augmented by my work on the texts themselves. These readings neither exhaust the texts' possibilities nor claim to account for every narrative element others have treated. By the same token they treat problematic aspects of the narratives that have until now never been addressed.

The very close textual analysis I perform and my concerns with family histories and character motivation may at times give readers the impression that they are reading case studies. In *Studies on Hysteria,* Freud noted a parallel effect: "[I]t still strikes me myself as strange that the case histories I write should read like short stories. . . . I must console myself with the reflection that the nature of the subject is evidently responsible for this. . . ."[9] The stories I have chosen to interpret are in my view detailed descriptions of psychic states of distress that contain the traces of the hidden dramas of their origins. As such they afford an occasion not only to demonstrate how such dramas can be reconstituted but to write down the steps of the literary-analytic process necessary to do so. For this reason, my interpretations have a narrative style, a beginning and an end, which may resemble that of case studies or even detective stories. This resemblance is not without its own significance and suggests that my critical readings may themselves be construed as commentaries on the nature of literary criticism: as readings that enact the idea that literary analysis, in its simplest terms, is, as Freud observed of his case histories, a matter of telling tales, of spinning out stories about others' stories.

This book did not begin as a study of family secrets and phantoms but as a project on the "uncanny." My preliminary research in this area and my encounter with the works of Abraham and Torok led me to conclude that the uncanny was part of the larger topic of secrets. It became clear that processes of concealment lay behind the uncanny effects in the texts I had chosen to study. My selection of these texts was quite deliberate. From the outset, I was interested in narratives that posed enigmas or problems related to the psychological states typically found in works classified as fantastic, uncanny, gothic, and occult. I sought texts that not only gave the reader a sense of their complexity and mystery but that gave the impression that they also contained keys or codes for unlocking these mysteries.

The interpretive experience was nonetheless one of discovery and surprise. For although I suspected that each of the texts had to do with keeping something hidden or obscured, I did not know when I chose them that they would all turn out to contain phantoms. In fact, I did not know what a phantom was when I selected all but one of the tales, having not yet studied Abraham and Torok's work. I also had no inkling that the secrets in the texts were all family secrets or that four of the five had to do with illegitimacy. This mixture of ignorance and intuition had the methodological result that my reading process was essentially constituted by the texts themselves: by the way in which their secret dramas slowly emerged, and by what this emergence itself led me to conclude about the problems of textuality and interpretation.

Not all texts have phantoms. Those that do do not all involve families or illegitimacy. The results of this study are nonetheless perhaps an indication of how frequently unspeakable family secrets, phantom structures, and concealed bastards may be found in nineteenth- and early twentieth-century literature. One aim of this book is to encourage further research in this domain in order to determine whether, as I suspect, other texts by the authors here treated and other authors of this period share these preoccupations—and why. (The specificity of pre-Freudian literature and the effects of the American and French Revolutions on the development of narrative would certainly be relevant areas of inquiry in this context.) Another aim of this study is to invite investigation into whether phantom structures and unspeakable family secrets can be found, as the discussion of *Hamlet* in chapter 1 appears to confirm, in literature from other periods and genres. A further goal is to raise questions and provoke debate concerning the concepts of haunting, ghosts, fiction, secrets, the text, and literary analysis elaborated herein. This study does not aim to define these concepts or propose conclusive statements about their meaning or vicissitudes. Its intent rather is to show how existing perspectives on them may be altered and expanded. In this same spirit my project seeks to contribute to ongoing discussions of the works of Conrad, Villiers de l'Isle-Adam, Balzac, James, and Poe as well as to the increasingly frequent reassessments of other authors typically associated with the uncanny, the occult, the fantastic, and the supernatural.

CHAPTER 1

For a New Psychoanalytic Literary Criticism

THE WORKS OF ABRAHAM AND TOROK

FOR THE LAST twenty-five years the link between literature and psychoanalysis has been the subject of an energetic and at times impassioned debate that no well-informed literary scholar has been able to ignore. Sigmund Freud and Jacques Lacan are the two major figures whose works have articulated the terms of this debate: the problematic relationship between psychic structures and textual structures, between the language of the mind and the language of the poetic work. With the publication in France in 1976 of *Le verbier de l'homme aux loups*,[1] the first volume of the collected writings of Nicolas Abraham and Maria Torok, two new voices joined this debate. Having taken degrees from the Sorbonne in philosophy and clinical psychology, respectively, Abraham and Torok became psychoanalysts in the mid-1950s and began publishing articles on metapsychology, the phenomenology of poetics, and the theory of translation in a variety of French journals. Not until their reopening of Freud's celebrated analysis of the Wolf Man, however, did their work catch the attention of the larger French psychoanalytic, philosophical, and literary communities. The recent publication in translation of the *The Wolf Man's Magic Word: A Cryptonymy*[2] and of several essays from the second volume of their writings, *L'écorce et le noyau* (*The Shell and the Kernel*),[3] has brought Abraham and Torok to the attention of increasing numbers of English-speaking scholars and clinicians.

Abraham and Torok did not conceive their theories as a response to others but as an internally coherent system of thought that grew out of their clinical experience and philosophical reflections. The purpose of this chapter is to consider their conceptual system within the history of ideas. It aims specifically to examine the potential significance, for the study of literature, of the analysts' theories of the dual unity, the phantom, secrets, cryptonymy, and symbol. To this end, I will begin by situating Abraham and Torok's work within the context of Freudian and Lacanian theory. My intent here is not to provide exhaustive summaries of Freud's and Lacan's writings. Nor is it to do a "Freud-on-Freud" or "Lacan-on-Lacan" reading that would show how one of their texts diverges rhetorically from itself or "self-deconstructs." I propose rather a comparative analysis of those developmental and psycholinguistic aspects of Freud's and Lacan's work that have relevance for Abraham and Torok's project, by virtue of either their convergence with it or their divergence from it. This will lead to a preliminary exposition of the implications, for the study of narrative, of extending into the literary-analytic realm certain concepts articulated by Abraham and Torok. The chapter will conclude with a brief précis of the cogent similarities and differences between their project and mine.[4]

FREUD, LACAN, ABRAHAM AND TOROK: VIEWS OF PSYCHIC DEVELOPMENT

The Oedipal Scenario

The centrality of the Oedipus complex to Freud's concept of human development cannot be overstated and bears recalling for the sake of the analysis that follows. Freud considered this complex to be universal and ineluctably traumatic for all individuals. According to this phylogenetic view, a child matures into an adult as the result of conflictual encounters between instinctual drives and the necessities and prohibitions of external reality. In the course of this maturation, the child passes through a series of overlapping stages of psychosexual organization. In the oral stage, the nurturing relationship with the mother takes on a libidinal or erotogenic dimension as pleasure is associated with the mouth and sucking the breast. Upon the child's entering the anal stage, the orally oriented drives are repressed and redirected to activities of defecation and retention. The ensuing phallic stage sees a further repression and libidinal shift to the (male) genitals and an emerging perception of the two sexes as differentiated by virtue of the presence or absence of the penis. This discovery of sexual difference coincides with the onset of the Oedipus complex and the actualizing of a fear Freud deemed to be universal: the threat of castration by the rival father as punishment for the (male) child's instinctual and incestuous desire for the mother. The successful outcome of the Oedipus complex is contingent upon the repression of this desire for the mother. This enables the child to disengage libidinally from the mother and to identify with the father, who is no longer perceived as a rival but as a model of the man the child will someday become. The unconscious as a repository of repressed wishes is organized at this moment in terms of this identification with the parent of the same sex and the prohibition against incest. The superego, the agency of conscience and moral and cultural law and authority, also takes shape at this time.[5]

The Imaginary and the Symbolic

Lacan's conception of the Oedipus complex differs from Freud's most notably for its emphasis on language and on the subject's position in society as a function of language. Informed primarily by the linguistic theories of Ferdinand de Saussure, the structural anthropology of Claude Lévi-Strauss, G.F.W. Hegel's dialectics of the subject, and the phenomenological writings of Martin Heidegger, Lacan views the pre-Oedipal stages as part of one structuring system called the Imaginary. The Imaginary is a prelinguistic state in which the child exists in an equivalent or "metaphoric" relationship with the mother, misapprehending in her image a reflection of its own (illusory) plenitude and self-identity. Organizing this realm of fiction is the "Desire of the Mother," a formulation signifying the child's desire to be united with the mother in a satisfying, fusional rapport, and the desire to be the object the mother lacks and desires above all else: the phallus.

The child's recognition of the father as a symbol of the law prohibiting incest shatters this dyadic mirror structure by inserting a third element into the equation. The Name-of-the-Father (*le-Nom-du-père*), meaning both the father as a "name" (*nom*) or figure of language and as the "No" (*non* is homophonous with *nom*) or agency of interdiction threatening castration, comes between the child and its desire (to be the phallus) of the mother. The child represses this desire, as well as the threat now associated with it embodied in the name and the "no" of the father, and thereby enters language, the realm of the Symbolic. Where before (illusory) meaning and fullness appeared there is only lack, a world of "empty" language in which signification is an effect of the difference between signifiers. Henceforth the child's desire of the mother will be mediated by a potentially infinite chain of signifiers—linked to each other by what Lacan calls metonymy—all functioning as substitutes or metaphors of the absent and irretrievable phallus. The phallus or "privileged signifier"[6] has been pushed below the bar of repression. This bar, which in Saussure's algorithm signaled a correspondence between signifier and signified, represents for Lacan the insurmountable barrier between the chain of intertwined signifiers above it and the fixed, identifiable meanings or signifieds below it. The child, as a subject in language and as subject to language, is itself split by this bar, marked by the irreducible lack at the core of its existence and by its radical otherness to itself. It can never know or grasp what is below the bar—the unconscious and signification—except as missed understanding, missed signification, and the fictions of the conscious.[7]

The Dual Unity

Abraham and Torok's view of psychic maturation and of the signification of the Oedipus complex differs markedly from both Freud's and Lacan's. In general terms, Abraham and Torok reject the accepted universality of the stratification of childhood development, be it sexual or linguistic, as the organizing principle for the practice and theory of psychoanalysis and as an explanation of psychic conflicts. They also do not accept as axiomatic that a particular event is traumatic for all individuals or that a given moral system can legitimately serve as the a priori determinant of what does or does not cause trauma. This means the analysts reject the Freudian concept of the Oedipus complex (and its Lacanian correlative of the Imaginary/Symbolic) as an inevitable drama, central to all psychic development, born of the ineluctable conflict between the desire for incest and the societal prohibition against it.

Abraham and Torok propose instead that human existence be understood in terms of a process of "individuation." They contend that psychic development is potentially nonlinear, and that in certain cases it is constituted by specific influences *outside* the individual's immediate or lived experience. In this view, a patient's symptoms can be attributed to something other than a fixation at a particular stage of development producing, for example, an unresolved Oedipus complex or an inability to pass from the "Imaginary" into the "Symbolic."[8] Within this wider optic they also conceive of the mechanisms of symptom-formation as potentially more varied and complex than Freudian processes such as condensation and displacement and their Lacanian equivalents of metaphor and metonymy, generally associated with the "return of the repressed."[9]

At the core of this new perspective is the concept of the "dual unity."[10] Informed in part by Sandor Ferenczi's theory of "bio-analysis" and by Imre Hermann's notion of "filial instinct,"[11] Abraham and Torok conceive of the individual as literally an "in-dividual," as an un-divided entity gradually defined by a constant process of differentiation or "division" from a more primary union: the mother. The crucial moment in this process is the child's discovery of the power of the word. Prior to this the child exists in an undifferentiated state within the mother's world. The mother is everything for the child: "amnion, warmth, nourishment, mainstay, body, cry, desire, rage, joy, fear, yes, no, you, me, object and project."[12] With no conscious or unconscious of its own other than the mother's, the child perceives the mother's words, gestures, and physical attributes without distinguishing between the mother's conscious and unconscious intent or charge. The discovery of the word occurs when the child detaches the mother's words—what Abraham and Torok call the "pieces-of-the-mother" (*bouts-de-mère*)—from her person and uses them to designate "objective events," that is, "events unbound by the mother's unconscious."[13]

Abraham and Torok point to the fort/da game recounted in Freud's *Beyond the Pleasure Principle* as a model of this process. When the child makes a word—"o-o-o-o" (*fort* = gone, over there)—coincide with the event of the mother's absence, it detaches that word from the mother and her unconscious. The almost magical coincidence of word and thing marks the moment at which the child realizes the repression of the mother's unconscious as the Core or Kernel of its own. This repression signals in turn a split in the psychic topology of the child, which gradually transforms itself into an internal duality between Unconscious and Ego, Kernel and Shell.[14]

These events constitute the beginning of the child's emergence as an individual, as separate from the mother. The child is by no means rid of the maternal unconscious, however. As the verbal pieces-of-the-mother are disengaged from the mother's person, the unconscious charge or affect bound to the word is transmitted into the child's speech. The maternal unconscious becomes part of the child's language. Communicated without ever having been spoken, it resides as a silent presence within the newly formed unconscious of the child. As the child matures, it will add its own repressions—produced by its own lived experiences—to this central core. Its Ego will simultaneously expand to accommodate new introjections. The child will still carry with it, however, part of the mother, a reminder of the prior union from which it issued.[15]

The child, in Abraham and Torok's terminology, is thus always in a "symbolic" relationship with the mother. It exists by virtue of the negation of a previous unity, by implicitly repeating, "not the mother, not the absent member of a prior union whose trace I bear." For Abraham and Torok, being is only possible in this symbolic mode. (The concepts of "symbol" and "symbolic operation" will be elaborated more fully later in the chapter.) We are all, to use their invented locution, *mutilés de mère* or "mother-amputees" (rhymes with the common French expression *mutilés de guerre*: "war-amputees" or "war-invalids"). We are all veterans of a process of cutting ourselves off from the mother-child union that precedes our emergence as individuals. And we all carry within us the vestige of the lost appendage from which we have been severed.[16]

A crucial distinction between Abraham and Torok's view of human development and that of Freud and Lacan may be drawn at this point. The process just outlined of the individual's detachment from the mother is not determined by any specific instincts or prohibitions. It follows no preprogrammed sequence of drives and repressions, as one finds organizing Freud's oral, anal, phallic, and Oedipal stages. Nor does it hinge on one privileged desire and repression—that of the phallus—as for Lacan. According to Abraham and Torok, there are no general principles of being. Everyone creates being for her- or himself. Every child's emergence as an individual is distinctive, constituted by repressions of uniquely charged pieces-of-the-mother, each bearing affects specifically related to the singular circumstances and psychic traumas of the mother's life. Moreover, since every mother is also the child of another mother, she must herself be understood as always already carrying the contents of another's unconscious. This is why Abraham refers to the dual unity as the "*genealogical* concept par excellence."[17] We are all the psychic products of our infinitely regressive family histories. We all recapitulate, in our individual, ontogenetic work of being, the phylogeny of our ancestors' sagas, all the while expanding these sagas with the stuff of our own lives.[18]

OEDIPAL MYTH

The Lie of Incest

The status of the Oedipus complex and its role in psychic maturation can be understood in view of the noninstinctual, ontogenetic organization of the dual unity. Simply stated, Abraham and Torok believe that if such a complex does in fact exist, it is to be construed as a strategic lie offered by the child to the mother. This radical idea issues from their definition of myth, outlined in the essay, "The Shell and the Kernel":

> [M]yths are efficient ways of speaking by means of which some situation or other comes about and is maintained. We know how: by carrying out, by means of their manifest content, the repression of their latent content. The myth then points up a gap in [our] communication with the Unconscious. If it offers understanding, it does so much less by what it says than

> by what it does not say, by its blanks, its intonations, its disguises. An instrument of repression, the myth serves also as a vehicle for the symbolic return of the repressed. Any study of myths, whether ethnological or psychoanalytical, should take this aspect into account. (26)

Myths are vehicles of repression, "collective imaginary objectifications" (25) of various metapsychological relationships between, for example, the Unconscious and the Conscious, the Ego and external objects, and the Child and the Mother. What must be read in myths is the silence or lacuna in their story, the gap in their speech that points to hidden and unspoken contents.

Considered in these terms, the Oedipus complex is the metapsychological myth par excellence. It is a discourse, addressed to the mother by the male child during the process of separation, that uses the lie of incest desire and the implied threat of castration by the father to reassure the mother of the child's love:

> [I]s not the intention [of the child] always to speak to [the mother] of another object than herself, in this instance the father, in order to let her know, in accord with the contingency of the operative code, that she will not be abandoned in favor of this third party? Is this not, by the same token, already to introduce this third party into the maternal relation, to introduce it in the mode of denegation, to be sure, but all the while foreshadowing an imminent detachment from her? (27)

The desire for incest and its prohibition is "a 'story' that the child 'tells' himself . . . in accordance with the contingencies of the cultural codes already in force" (26). It is an "alibi" (27), readily available in our society in which some form of incest prohibition reigns, that the child uses as a salve to soothe the mother for her imminent loss. Having successfully introjected the maternal Shell and appropriated as its own all that the mother is able to give it (amnion, warmth, nourishment), the child now redirects the work of introjection toward everything beyond this world, to "the whole of social life, represented by the 'non-mother,' whatever form the non-mother may take—which is to say, in our civilization, the person of the father" (27). The Oedipal fantasy, the idea of incest and its prohibition, the fear of castration, and the wish to kill the father are all part of the cultural vocabulary, implicitly offered to the child, from which it invents its own way of reassuring the mother of its faithfulness while pursuing a more or less smooth detachment from her. To take literally the child's discourse as a desire for incest is thus to be "duped by a child theory" (27) or a "pseudology" (27). It is to mistake the manifest content of a myth for its latent content, the disguise for the metapsychological reality.[19]

This conception of the Oedipus complex explains why Abraham, in the only explicit reference to Lacan in his and Torok's writings, suggests that the "Lacanian error consists in placing 'castration' at the origin of language when it is only its universal *content*."[20] Castration is the manifest content, furnished by society, which the child uses as an excuse to detach itself from the mother. It is a convenient, double-edged fiction that allows the child to reiterate its affective connection with the mother—"I am threatened by castration because I love you"—while reorienting its assimilative energies toward the world of the non-mother.[21]

The Child Gives Birth—to Itself

This new perspective on castration and the Oedipus complex underscores another of the major metapsychological disparities separating Abraham and Torok from Freud and Lacan. Abraham and Torok's view of psychic development is not phallocentric. It does not hinge on the incest/castration conflict or on the presence or absence of the phallus, either as the mark of sexual difference or as the signifier of the lack constitutive of the subject, to explain the child's maturation into adulthood. While the authors concur that the child in the Oedipus complex may exhibit a mixture of loving and hostile wishes toward its parents that can in some instances assume a violent cast, they do not attribute such wishes to a universal instinctual desire for the mother or a passion for the phallus, but rather to the vicissitudes of playing out the incest pseudology. They also reject the axiom that the fear of castration is necessary to explain the child's separation from the mother.

This last point is central to Freud's and Lacan's systems. In both, the mother is implicitly identified as the obstacle to the child's maturation, as a potentially unhealthy and delusional attachment—either libidinal or Imaginary—that must be transcended. The father is represented as the child's "savior," as the one who, by threatening castration, comes between the mother and the child and ruptures their union, allowing proper development to continue. While it is true Lacan shifts the emphasis in the dynamic from the instinctual to the linguistic realm, the endemic phallocentrism of the system remains. It may be argued, moreover, that the "passion of the signifier"[22] at the core of his rereading of Freud is essentially a transcription of Freud's instinct theory, with one key difference. Where Freud poses the desire for incest as one motor (albeit, the central one) of human psychic development, Lacan posits the desire of the phallus as the sole motivating force for the subject. The subject for Lacan lives exclusively for the passion of the phallus, for the (object of) desire of the mother. The interdiction of this desire by the father as figure of the Law paves the way for separation from the mother and entry into the Symbolic.[23]

For Abraham and Torok, the child's relationship to the mother in the dual unity is not construed as a passing phase to "get beyond" or as a deceptive, imaginary fiction to be transcended in "the name of the father." It is a dyadic structure that allows the individual to "give birth to itself" psychically by gradually differentiating itself from the mother and becoming "not mother." At the same time, it is a vehicle of transmission through which the emerging individual receives as its own its family history. The mother is not necessarily an obstacle to development, nor the object of incestuous desire. Neither is she a lack to be filled by the child as phallus. By virtue of a separation that is never quite completed, the mother provides the child with the possibility of gradually becoming an individual. Whereas for both Freud and Lacan the child's conflict is between the desire for union (incest) and the impossibility of that union (enforced by the father's threat of castration), Abraham and Torok begin with the premise—based on the life-situation—that the mother-child union already exists. They explain the child's conflict in terms of the desire to remain faithful to the mother in an (obsolete) state of indifferentiation and the desire for detachment from the mother in a forward-looking quest for individuality.

UNSPEAKABLE SECRETS, PSYCHIC HISTORY, AND THE PHANTOM OF HAMLET

The implications of the dual unity for psychoanalytic theory and practice are numerous. On the most immediate level, this concept calls into question the validity of identifying Oedipal dramas as latent structures central to mental organization with explanatory or heuristic power. It also suggests the need to reevaluate the legitimacy of hermeneutic models based on instinct-theory, prohibitions, and the phallus. At the same time, the dual unity serves as a theoretical stepping-stone toward a new metapsychological concept whose potential for interpreting incongruous behavior has only recently begun to be realized.

The theory of the *phantom* was conceived by Abraham as what might be called a pathological corollary to the dual unity.[24] It offered a partial response to his and Torok's dissatisfaction with the inadequacy of morally determined, stratified, phallocentrically oriented epistemologies to account for a certain order of symptoms prevalent in numbers of their patients. The concept of the phantom allowed them to explain how influences outside an individual's lived experience can determine her or his psychic development. It does this by linking certain states of mental disarray, hitherto resistant to analysis, to the concealment of a secret. For Freud psychopathology occurs when sexually oriented drives and fantasies are blocked or when a trauma (in the form of an actual seduction or molestation) intrudes upon the normal course of infantile development; for Lacan illness is explained in terms of a failure to assimilate lack as the core of subjectivity. Abraham and Torok propose that symptoms can occur when a shameful and therefore unspeakable experience must be barred from consciousness or simply "kept secret." This idea offers an alternative to the view that the Oedipus complex, patricidal fantasies, fear of castration, and penis envy are inescapable components in the etiology of neurosis. It also introduces, via the concept of "transgenerational haunting," a novel perspective on the potential configurations of psychic history and on their role in pathogenic processes and symptom-formation.

The idea that an individual's behavior might be traced to a secret kept by a family member in another generation is crucial to this study. From a methodological perspective it implies a shift in the analytic process, which does not aim to link an individual's symptoms with his or her unconscious (understood as a repository of repressed wishes) but to trace these symptoms to an unspeakable drama in the family's history. As a first step in elaborating how such an analytic inquiry might proceed and what it might mean for the study of literary works, I would like to discuss a text situated at the critical vortex of literature and psychoanalysis: Nicolas Abraham's last work, a treatment of *Hamlet*.

Abraham's Hamlet

"The Phantom of Hamlet or The Sixth Act: Preceded by the Intermission of 'Truth,' "[25] completed in 1975 shortly before Abraham's death, is a fiction created in decasyllabic verse as an addition to Shakespeare's tragedy. In it, Abraham suggests in allusive, poetic language the reason for Hamlet's indecision to take revenge on Claudius for murdering his father. It is not essential to summarize here everything conveyed in *The Sixth Act* concerning the motives and actions of the play's characters. My aim is rather to expose and comment on Abraham's conjecture that a phantom haunts Hamlet and that the concealment of a family secret generates this phantom. The organic relationship between Abraham's theory of the symbol (alluded to in the preceding discussion of the dual unity) and *The Sixth Act* can then be elucidated. Explaining how symbols in Shakespeare's text point to an obstacle to Hamlet's existence and how this obstacle prevents him from becoming a self-contained individual will provide some insight into why the phantom may be considered what I have termed a pathological corollary of the dual unity. It will also offer a launching point for studying the interpretive concept of *cryptonymy*.

Abraham's *Sixth Act* is particularly conducive to such an elaboration because it treats the literary work whose principal character has probably been subjected to more psychoanalytic inquiry and character analysis than any other in literature. It also invites theoretical and practical comparisons with Ernest Jones's quintessential Freudian interpretation of *Hamlet* and with Lacan's less frequently studied analysis of the play.[26] The contention that an unspoken family secret causes Hamlet's puzzling behavior, moreover, offers a logical and suggestive point of departure for a study devoted to a new way of interpreting the behavior of characters in fiction and to the means by which texts made enigmatic, if not illegible, by the mute presence of secrets may be explained.

Abraham begins by seizing on what the critical tradition surrounding *Hamlet* has long recognized as the difficulty of the play: the enigmatic nature of Hamlet's doubt, the lack of anything within the play to explain adequately his hesitation, despite the command of his father's ghost, to take revenge on Claudius. As T. S. Eliot stated in his well-known essay, there is no "objective correlative" for Hamlet's behavior. "Hamlet is dominated by an emotion which is inexpressible, because it is in *excess* of the facts as they appear."[27] The result, according to Abraham, is that the play has produced a disarray or illness in the public, a "neurosis" of sorts, caused by the haunting influence on the characters of an element missing from it. Abraham's intention is to "cure" the audience of this malady by supplying the missing fragment, by reconstructing a hidden drama, different from the one given in the play and unknown to almost all of its characters, that in effect "completes" the play. He does this by reinterpreting the role of the Ghost—generally recognized by critics as the perturbing element for Hamlet—as the mute carrier of a secret concerning King Hamlet. To reveal what this secret is, Abraham must first find a way to get beyond the enigma-laden silence, left by the corpses littering the stage at the final curtain, to the question of Hamlet's indecision. He therefore resurrects Hamlet, invites the Ghost to make an encore appearance, and assigns young Fortinbras the analytic function of the listener who knows nothing but is ready and eager to learn.

Through the ensuing exchange among Hamlet, Horatio, young Fortinbras, and the Ghost, Abraham conjectures a scene that must have occurred prior to the events of the play. He proposes that the duel alluded to by Horatio (1.1) between King Hamlet and King Fortinbras was rigged and that King Hamlet, realizing that Gertrude (not yet his wife) was in love with Fortinbras, killed the Norwegian ruler with a poisoned sword. Abraham suggests further that Polonius provided the poison for the sword. This scene, Abraham maintains, constitutes the secret of the play (and is shared by the Ghost and Polonius); it haunts Hamlet and accounts for his puzzling behavior. Moreover, Abraham sees Laertes as betraying, by his actions, his father's identity as a secret poisoner: Laertes duels with Hamlet and kills him with a poisoned sword. The enigma of Hamlet's hesitation to kill his father's assassin is also dissolved by this final scene of dueling, which is understood by Abraham as a reenactment of the murder of King Fortinbras. If Hamlet is unable to act on the Ghost's command for revenge, Abraham suggests, it is because he is haunted by the Ghost's undivulged secret of murder. Hamlet's indecision toward killing Claudius, even after Claudius's guilt has been proven, testifies to the presence of some influence, unavailable to Hamlet, that perturbs his behavior and interferes with what should by all accounts be a clear course of action.

Jones's Hamlet

Ernest Jones, in his *Hamlet and Oedipus*,[28] has already considered Hamlet's indecision as a symptom worthy of psychoanalysis. His interpretation focuses on explaining Hamlet in terms of the Freudian theory of the Oedipus complex: the desire for the mother and the wish to kill the father.

> Of the infantile jealousies the most important, and the one with which we are here occupied, is that experienced by a boy towards his father . . . when the latter disturbs, as he necessarily must, his enjoyment of his mother's exclusive affection. This feeling is the deepest source of the world-old conflict between father and son, between the younger and the older generation, the favourite theme of so many poets and writers, the central *motif* of most mythologies and religions. (75–76; Jones's italics)

The Oedipal model has to be adapted somewhat to the specific situation in Hamlet because, in the play, the father has already been killed by Claudius. Jones therefore concludes that the reason for Hamlet's reluctance to obey his dead father's command to avenge his murder is

Hamlet's secret gratitude to Claudius for having murdered the father. "The call of duty to kill his stepfather cannot be obeyed because it links itself with the unconscious call of his nature to kill his mother's husband" (90). What we see in Hamlet, Jones extrapolates, is a conscious loyalty to the dead father in conflict with the fulfillment of Hamlet's unconscious wish to see his father dead. Jones thus identifies the two elements of Hamlet's indecision and terms them a conflict resulting in a neurosis.

Lacan's Hamlet

In "Desire and the Interpretation of Desire in *Hamlet*" (1959),[29] Lacan too diagnoses Hamlet to be suffering from a neurosis caused by an Oedipal drama. Lacan displaces the play's dynamic, however, from the realm of instinctual incest desire and its prohibition to the "dialectic of desire" at the core of the Imaginary/Symbolic topology.[30] To put it simply (which is always a risky endeavor where Lacan is concerned), the tragedy of Hamlet lies in his inability to repress lack, that is, the phallus as signifier of lack. Hamlet is fixed in the Imaginary register, incapable—until the very end of the play—of committing the act that would pave the way for him "to be" as a subject-in-lack within the Symbolic.

Lacan's analysis hinges on identifying Claudius as the usurper of Hamlet's desire, not just of the throne. Prior to King Hamlet's death, Hamlet exists in an Imaginary relationship with his mother, defined by the desire of the mother (that is, to be the phallus of the mother). Whereas in *Oedipus Rex* the father's death opens the way for the son to fulfill this desire, Claudius's marriage to Gertrude forecloses this possibility because Claudius comes to embody the phallus.[31] As a result, Hamlet shifts his desire from the mother to Claudius and identifies with the latter as phallus. Still in the Imaginary, Hamlet is suspended in what Lacan calls "the hour of the other" (*l'heure de l'autre*), a formula whose homophone *leurre de l'autre* (the trap or illusion of the other) underscores the delusional, fictitious equivalency of Hamlet's identification with the other as phallus.[32] This narcissistic identification is for Lacan the root of Hamlet's dilemma of being and the cause of his hesitation to kill Claudius. To strike at Claudius would mean to strike at Hamlet's own (illusory) self-image. Hamlet's query, "To be or not to be," is for Lacan the expression of this dilemma: if he does not kill Claudius he can continue to be (as an illusion); if he kills Claudius he himself will die.

Hamlet's rupture of his delusional rapport with Claudius is made possible by his duel with Laertes, who serves as Hamlet's foil in a duplication of the latter's Imaginary relationship with his stepfather. Viewed by Lacan as Hamlet's perfect "double" ("Desire in *Hamlet*," 31), Laertes allows Hamlet to play out the murder/suicide drama essential to his entry into the Symbolic.[33] When Hamlet is pricked by Laertes' poisoned sword, he receives from the other his identity as a subject marked by death and by the phallus as signifier of lack. (Lacan identifies Laertes' foil with the phallus.)[34] Delivered from all narcissistic attachments, Hamlet leaves the Imaginary, the "hour" (*l'heure*) or trap (*leurre*) of the other, and enters the Symbolic, the "hour of his destruction" (25). No longer bound by his identification with Claudius, Hamlet is finally free (if only for an instant) to accomplish the task that has until now been impossible. "The presence of [Laertes as] customized double will permit [Hamlet], at least for a moment, to hold up his end of the human wager: in that moment, he, too, will be a man. But . . . the phallus . . . will be able to appear only with the disappearance of the subject himself" (34). Hamlet is able to strike Claudius (the phallus) only at the instant he has himself received the phallus as the mark of his own loss as subject; he is able to become a man only at the moment of his death.

Hamlet is thus for Lacan the tragedy of a man who must die in order to be; who is doomed always to ask the Imaginary question, "To be or not to be the phallus?" and who, only at the moment of death, (implicitly) poses the ultimate and essential Symbolic question: "To have or not to have the phallus?" Hamlet's ability finally to avenge his father's murder is understood by Lacan as his tacit response to this question, as his recognition of the absence of the phallus as constitutive of his being in the world and of his identity as a subject-in-lack.

The Phantom

In contrast to both Jones and Lacan, who locate within Hamlet the conflict giving rise to his indecision, Abraham identifies the cause of indecision and situates it outside of Hamlet. For Abraham, Hamlet's oscillation is not the neurotic symptom of a conflict between the conscious and the unconscious. Nor is it the result of an inability to repress the phallus as signifier of lack. It is the effect of a conscious lie perpetrated by someone other than Hamlet. The indecision plaguing Hamlet is shown to result from the father's (the Ghost's) willful manipulation of his son. From a methodological point of view, Abraham's analysis of *Hamlet* treats the conflict implied by indecision as the apparent meaning of the play. His conjecture of the Ghost's machinations dissolves the issue of indecision and locates a form of discontinuity, in an untruth beyond Hamlet, that is not a conflict. In terms of psychoanalytic literary theory, Abraham's text implies that a specific causative agent can be found to explain the enigmatic behavior of a fictional character. The metapsychological concept of the *phantom* serves Abraham as an instrument for identifying this agent.

The critical tradition surrounding *Hamlet*, which has accepted at face value the "truth" of the dead king's information (his murder by Claudius), has at its center the common notion of the ghost as a regretted presence and avenger. According to this view, the King returns to unveil the secret of his murder by Claudius and, through the act of revenge he demands of Hamlet, to "even the score" and thereby appease (somewhat) Hamlet's pain at his loss. To explain Hamlet's enigmatic behavior, Abraham redefines the notion of secret. A secret, he proposes, can be something transmitted without being stated.[35] King Hamlet is the carrier of a secret that never appears in the play: his own murderous duel with King Fortinbras, an event that he has never divulged but has taken with him to the grave. This unstated event is "in excess" of the drama's action (although its traces can be read within the play) and returns to perturb and haunt Hamlet in the form of what Abraham calls a ghost or phantom:

> Should a child have parents "with secrets," . . . the child will receive from them a gap in the unconscious, an unknown, unrecognized knowledge—a *nescience*. . . .
>
> The buried speech of the parent will be (a) dead (gap) without a burial place in the child. This unknown phantom returns from the unconscious to haunt its host and may lead to phobias, madness, and obsessions. Its effect can persist through several generations and determine the fate of an entire family line.[36]

To say that Hamlet is haunted by a phantom or ghost is to say he is haunted by someone else's secret, by the silence erected around the foul deed committed by his father. The phantom is thus a formation totally outside any developmental view of human behavior. It holds the individual within a group dynamic constituted by a specific familial (and sometimes extrafamilial) topology that prevents the individual from living life as her or his own. The phantom may therefore be understood as a pathological or "diseased" form of the dual unity: it occurs when the child's normal processes of individuation or separation from the parent are hindered by the presence of a gap or lacuna within the parent's speech. The unspeakable secret suspended within the adult is transmitted silently to the child in "undigested" form and lodges within his or her mental topography as an unmarked tomb of inaccessible knowledge. Its presence there holds the child (later the adult) in a pathogenic dual union with the parent, in a silent partnership dedicated to preserving the secret intact. The child's unwitting involvement in this mute pact interferes with the psychic processes leading to successful introjection and inhibits its emergence as an autonomous subject.

The symptoms displayed by an individual haunted by a phantom lie beyond the scope of any hermeneutic theory or tool previously offered by psychoanalysis. This is because the processes of symptom-formation associated with the phantom differ from the mechanism known as the return of the repressed. What returns to haunt is the "unsaid" and "unsayable" of *an other*. The silence, gap, or secret in the speech of someone else "speaks," in the manner of a ventriloquist, through the words and acts (readable as words) of the subject.

> The imaginings coming from the presence of a stranger [within the subject's own mental topography] have nothing to do with fantasy strictly speaking. They neither preserve a topographical status quo nor announce a shift in it. Instead, by their gratuitousness in relation to the subject, they create the impression of surrealistic flights of fancy or of *oulipo*-like verbal feats.[37]

To distinguish the mode of symptom-formation at work in the phantom, Abraham and Torok use the term "preservative repression" (*refoulement conservateur*)[38] to contrast with the Freudian concept of "dynamic repression." This invented locution conveys the custodial status of the haunted individual, whose symptoms are unrelated to his or her own lived experience and are produced outside the recognized mechanisms of active repression. It also points to the inherent driving force of the phantom: the desire of the parent—and of the child, in their dual union—to guard or "preserve" a secret intact.

Before I elaborate the implications of the theory of the phantom, it is important to clarify a potential source of confusion concerning its formation. In the essays "Notes on the Phantom," "Notes from the Seminar on the Dual Unity and the Phantom," and "A Story of Fear. The Phobic Symptom: Return of the Repressed or Return of the Phantom?" in *L'écorce*, Abraham and Torok explain that the secret transmitted into the child's unconscious, which returns to haunt, first undergoes a form of repression, exerted upon it by the parent, and becomes lodged in the parent's unconscious.

> The phantom is a formation of the unconscious that has never been conscious—for good reason. It passes—in a way yet to be determined—from the parent's unconscious into the child's. (*Phantom*, 289)

In her addendum to "Notes from the Seminar on the Dual Unity," Torok makes clear that the initial repression of the secret is not dynamic but preservative and that it results in the formation of a *crypt*: of a "false unconscious," lodged within the Ego, in which the parent buries alive a secret so shameful that it must be concealed from the parent's own awareness. Torok thus explicitly links the conceptualization of phantomatic haunting with her and Abraham's previous discovery, in the Wolf Man, of the hitherto unknown psychic topology of the crypt.

> The work of haunting can only be understood . . . in each case where the psychic apparatus of the [parent] includes a crypt. [The intrapsychic reality] of the child born of a cryptophore [a carrier of a crypt] . . . will symbolize with the encrypted reality of the [parent]. The [child's] "reality" . . . will have one single peculiarity: it will function in relation to a vital intersubjective drama located *"elsewhere,"* in a *"beyond the self,"* in the crypt of the [parent], and it will provoke, as a result, the playing out of a repetitive and lethal scene in the [child] who suffers the effects of haunting. (*Dual Unity*, 421–23; Torok's italics)

Now the idea that the formation of a phantom is contingent upon the transmission, into the child's unconscious, of a silence sealed within a crypt in the parent is significantly altered by Abraham's reading of *Hamlet* just discussed. In *The Sixth Act*, young Hamlet is understood to be the victim of the willful manipulation and conscious lie perpetrated by his father in order to conceal the latter's murderous duel with King Fortinbras:

> The "secret" revealed by Hamlet's "phantom" . . . masks another secret, this one genuine and truthful but resulting from an infamy which the father, unbeknownst to his son, *has on his conscience*. . . . [W]hat returns to haunt [Hamlet] . . . is the thing "phantomized" during the preceding generation, "phantomized" because it was *unspeakable in words*, because it had to be *wrapped in silence*. (*The Sixth Act*, 3–4)

King Hamlet is not a cryptophore. His guilty conscience compels him to conceal the truth of his crime from others but not from himself. He does not exert a repression upon the drama of murder but simply removes it from speech, "wraps it in silence." It is this silence that is "phantomized," transmitted unwittingly to Hamlet as a gap in his unconscious that will perturb his behavior.

The Sixth Act has thus to be read as an implicit modification of the theoretical elaborations on the phantom contained in the essays that precede it. It opens a new perspective on the etiology of this psychic structure, broadening its scope to include the transmission of an unspeakable secret that has been consciously—not just unconsciously—

concealed by a parent and transmitted silently into a child's unconscious. This conceptual shift implies in turn a significant extension of the analytic and hermeneutic potential of the phantom and, as this study will demonstrate, of the kinds of literary narratives that can be understood as organized or propelled by transgenerational haunting.[39]

IMPLICATIONS OF THE PHANTOM: THE OTHER, THE UNCANNY, THE DEATH INSTINCT, TRANSFERENCE

The implications of the phantom are far-reaching, on both a theoretical and a practical level. On the one hand, the phantom allows us to view in a new light various psychoanalytic, philosophical, and literary concepts. It permits us to speak of the "other," for example, not as a capitalized, general philosophical notion, which it is for Hegel and Lacan, but as a specific, nameable entity. The "other" situated beyond the subject and affecting his or her existence need not be identified with the Phallus, the Law, Death, or the Father. While in certain cases the person actively concealing a secret may indeed be the father, this is by no means universally true. Neither can it be systematically assumed that the father in such instances functions as a correlative of castration or patriarchal law. He is to be understood as an identifiable member of a particular family whose secret and whose reason for keeping a secret are determined by a specific psychic constellation. By the same token, the effect on those to whom he transmits the secret—as well as their identity (whether child, grandchild, nephew, niece, or nonrelative)—cannot be predetermined or predicted according to any behavioral or metapsychological model.

Within the literary and psychoanalytic domains, the phantom provides a new vantage point from which to consider the effect Freud called "the uncanny" (*unheimliche*). In saying that the person haunted by a phantom is inhabited by a *nescience*, by an "unknown knowledge" that can be transmitted or passed down through an entire family line or community, Abraham offers a definition of the uncanny different from Freud's.[40] He suggests that the psychological effect of something seeming familiar and strange at the same time can be explained through the specific configuration in which something is unknown (*unheimlich*) to the subject in one generation and secretly "known" or "within the family or house" (literally *heimlich*) in the preceding one.[41]

On a metapsychological level, the phantom provides a way of reassessing the rather enigmatic and highly controversial theory of the death instinct proposed by Freud in *Beyond the Pleasure Principle*.

> [T]he work of the phantom coincides in every respect with Freud's description of the death instinct. First of all, it has no energy of its own; it cannot be "abreacted," merely designated. Second, it pursues in silence its work of disarray. Let us add that the phantom is sustained by secreted words, invisible gnomes whose aim is to wreak havoc, from within the unconscious, in the coherence of logical progression. Finally, it gives rise to endless repetition and, more often than not, eludes rationalization.[42]

Abraham's observation suggests that at least certain instances of repetitive, obsessive behavior may be attributed to the haunting effects of a phantom. This should not be entirely surprising in view of the earlier discussion of the dual unity in which the fort/da game—emblematic, for Freud, of the compulsion to repeat—was identified as a model of the process by which the child assumes the parent's unconscious as his or her own in the course of individuation, and in view of the "pathological" relationship noted between the dual unity and the phantom. Freud himself lends credence to the hypothesis of a link between the death instinct and the phantom when, in *Beyond the Pleasure Principle,* he associates unexplainable repetition phenomena with "possession by some 'daemonic' power."[43] Several texts in this study provide material from which to expand upon this link and to explore the connection between a fictional character's apparently inexplicable, obsessive behavior, her or his sensations of being possessed by demons or ghosts, and the presence of a phantom within a literary narrative.[44]

In the area of clinical technique, the phantom's radical heterogeneity to the subject's own topography and the subject's unwitting but relentless efforts to guard intact the secret she or he harbors pose certain obstacles to analysis. One of these involves the dynamic of transference.

> The special difficulty of these analyses lies in the patient's horror at violating a parent's or a family's guarded secrets, even though the secret's text and content are inscribed within the unconscious. The horror of transgressing, in the strict sense of the term, is compounded by the risk of undermining the fictitious yet necessary integrity of the parental figure in question.[45]

Effecting transference in the presence of a phantom is all the more challenging since the playing out or actualization of the internal drama must occur not between the analyst and the patient, as is usually the case, but between the analyst and the patient's ancestor (or whoever else may have originated the secret). At stake for the analyst is assuring that the individual "on the couch," metapsychologically speaking, is the one responsible for the formation of the phantom. Outlandish as it may seem, this often means analyzing, via the mediating presence of the patient, someone who is long since deceased:

> [T]he phantom . . . may . . . be deconstructed by analytic construction, though only by fostering the impression that the patient has in fact not been the subject of the analysis. It is understandable that, in contrast to other cases, this type of work requires a genuine partnership between patient and analyst: all the more so since the construction arrived at in this way bears no direct relation to the patient's own topography but concerns someone else's.[46]

Given the focus of this study, it may seem incongruous to speak of transference, traditionally considered a purely clinical aspect of psychoanalysis. The role of the analyst is nonetheless staged, under various guises, in numerous literary works, as some of my interpretations (particularly of James's *The Jolly Corner* and Poe's *The Fall of the House of Usher*) will demonstrate. These stagings take on added significance in the presence of the phantom since this psychic configuration erects enigmas to analysis beyond the grasp of established analytic theory and technique. Dissolving these enigmas implies learning a new way of listening to language.

Abraham alludes to this when he describes the phantom as "sustained by secreted words, invisible gnomes whose aim is to wreak havoc, from within the unconscious, in the coherence of logical progression," and as "obstruct[ing] our perception of words as implicitly referring to their unconscious portion."[47] Analyzing a phantom implies understanding how words can be stripped of a crucial portion of their signification and how coherence can be reestablished in the face of apparent enigma and discontinuity. Proposing a theory of the phantom is thus contingent upon an expanded conception of the rhetorical possibilities of language and of the ways in which intelligibility may be denied. The articulation of such a conception constitutes for the literary critic one of the most suggestive aspects of Abraham and Torok's contribution to analytic theory. I would like now to turn to their theory of cryptonymy, to indicate how it differs from Freud's and Lacan's approaches to interpretation, and to indicate some of its implications for the analysis of narrative.

CRYPTONYMY: A RHETORIC OF HIDING

In contradistinction to most contemporary theoretical currents concerned with demonstrating how meaning may be distorted, displaced, deferred, or denied in the various processes of its generation and reception, Abraham and Torok's emphasis is on determining how meaning that has already been obstructed or aborted can be reconstituted and made intelligible from the traces left by its apparent disappearance. Their emphasis, in other words, is on establishing how particular systems of signification have been prevented from coming into being and on identifying, in the language and behavior (translatable into language) of a patient, the mechanisms of concealment and dissembling that thwart readability.

One such mechanism frequently (although not always) at work is *cryptonymy*. Just as a phantom carries a secret, so words, Abraham and Torok propose, can themselves be carriers of veiled lexical relationships. A word can be a *cryptonym*, literally a "word that hides." This concept is explained in *The Wolf Man's Magic Word*. While describing their search for the unutterable words hidden within the Wolf Man's language, Abraham and Torok outline techniques of psychoanalysis distinct from the Freudian and Lacanian emphasis on displacement, distortion, condensation, and the signifying chain:

> [I]n order to reach the sought-after key word, we had to move across the signifieds and search for semantic displacements. The key word, no doubt unutterable for some reason, and unknown for the moment, would have to be polysemic, expressing multiple meanings through a single phonetic structure. One of these would remain shrouded, but the other, or several other meanings . . . would be stated through distinct phonetic structures, that is, through synonyms. To make our conversations about this easier, we would call them *cryptonyms* (words that hide) because of their allusion to a foreign and arcane meaning. We also wanted to set them apart from simple metonymic displacement. (18; Abraham and Torok's italics)

A specific example may be helpful to explain the operations described here and to suggest their significance from the perspective of literary analysis. Let us imagine a story concerned with delivering letters, sending parcels, and receiving dispatches. A linguistic aspect of the story is that the word "post" (or any form of it such as post office or postbox) is never once mentioned. Analysis reveals that this is because the word "pillar," whose synonym is "post," is a word that has been hidden because of its connection to some unspeakable drama. (Such a drama might involve the theft of money that has been concealed in a hollowed-out wood pillar, to invent just one of an infinite number of possibilities.) What has happened is that "pillar" has undergone a double and unstated transformation. First, it has become its synonym "post." "Post," the synonym of "pillar," has then been transmuted in the story into its homonym "post," with its set of entirely different associations: letters, dispatches, stamps, parcels. These words are the "words that hide," the *cryptonyms* of the secret word "pillar." Each one carries secreted within it, through a process of lexical and phonetic *encrypting* that elides the meaning of "post" (as "pillar"), the word that cannot be said: "pillar." The story thus becomes a dictionary of the different associations of "post"—but without its meaning "pillar." "Letters," "parcels," and "stamps" are what circulate in the tale, to the exclusion of "post," which otherwise would suggest "pillar."

Freud's Theory of Reading

Freud never articulated any theory or analytic technique such as cryptonymy. There are nevertheless certain affinities between Abraham and Torok's concept of lexical encrypting and the reading methods Freud proposed in some of his earlier writings. In *Studies on Hysteria* (1895), for example, Freud showed how specific psychic structures may be converted into linguistic phenomena, and how somatic symptoms can be read as the literalization of a figurative form of speech. In the case of Elisabeth von R., he linked his patient's recurrent leg pain and partial paralysis to an unresolved conflict between her erotic desire for a young man (and later for her brother-in-law) and her moral obligation to "stand by" her ill father (and later her dying sister). He then "read" Elisabeth's symptoms as the physical expression of her repressed thought: I cannot "take a single step forward"[48] in my life to escape my paralyzing family situation.

In *The Interpretation of Dreams* (1900), Freud pursued and expanded this reading method and made explicit one of the major implications of the *Studies on Hysteria*. Symptoms (or dream elements), he maintained, cannot be interpreted in terms of a universal key or code book but are to be understood as carrying specific meanings particular to each individual: "My procedure is not so convenient as the popular decoding method which translates any given piece of a dream's content by a fixed key. I, on the contrary, am prepared to find that the same piece of content may conceal a different meaning when it occurs in various people or in various contexts."[49] The different ways in which these meanings may be concealed are elaborated in chapter 6 on "The Dream-Work," where Freud states that dreams are structured like rebuses or hieroglyphics and employ a variety of linguistic procedures, such as rhyming, synonymy, and interlinguistic substitution, to disguise their signification.

There can be no question that Abraham and Torok found inspiration in the theory of reading Freud expounds in these and other writings (which include the case of Katarina in *Studies on Hysteria*, the study of Jensen's *Gradiva* [vol. 9], and portions of *The Psychopathology of Everyday Life* [vol. 6] and *Jokes and Their Relation to the Unconscious* [vol. 8]). They part company with Freud when he describes his practice of dream interpretation, which, paradoxically, involves the creation of his own "dream-book" consisting of a predetermined system of symbolic equations through which certain images or words are automatically understood to represent specific objects, such as male or female genitalia. (See especially, in *The Interpretation of Dreams*, chapter 5, section D, "Typical Dreams," and chapter 6, sections E through I, "Representation by Symbols," "Some Further Typical Dreams," "Absurd Dreams," etc.) This puzzling circumstance in which Freud practices an interpretive technique at odds with his interpretive theory is rendered even more mystifying by what may be called Freud's own brush with cryptonymy.

In delineating the discoveries that led to their analysis of the Wolf Man and the development of the concept of cryptonymy, Abraham and Torok refer to Freud's essay "Fetishism." They note that the ex-patient Freud describes as "a young man [who] had exalted a certain sort of 'shine on the nose' into a fetishistic precondition [and who] had been brought up in an English nursery but had later come to Germany, where he forgot his mother-tongue almost completely," could be none other than the Wolf Man.[50] Acknowledging that Freud's jottings regarding his ex-patient's use of the English language paved the way for their multilingual approach to interpreting the Wolf Man's dreams and symptoms, Abraham and Torok continue their quotation from the essay, adding a revealing footnote: "The fetish, which originated from his earliest childhood, had to be understood in *English*, not German [our emphasis]. The 'shine on the nose' (in German *'Glanz auf der Nase'*)—was in reality a *'glance* at the nose' [*Blick auf die Nase, Blick* = glance: *Glanz*]. The nose was thus the fetish, which, incidentally, he endowed at will with the luminous shine which was not perceptible to others (*Standard Edition*, vol. 21, p. 152)." The footnote to this passage asks: "Why stop midway and leave untranslated the German word *Nase*, nose = (he) knows. The unexpected result of this restoration will be clear shortly" (*The Wolf Man*, 120). The unexpected result is the authors' discovery that *Nase* is a cryptonym of "(he) knows" and refers to the scene of testimony in which the Wolf Man is called upon to say whether or not he saw his father seduce his sister. Recognizing Freud's analytic acumen in hearing the interlinguistic rhyme between *Glanz* and "glance," Abraham and Torok ask why Freud short-circuits the insightful methodological approach he himself begins to establish.[51]

Cryptonymy and Lacan's Signifying Chain

To the extent that Jacques Lacan has continued the Freudian emphasis on language and has furthered this tradition by placing language at the center of his entire project, he too shares a certain affinity with Abraham and Torok. The authors' discovery of cryptonymy, however, allows the literary analyst to go beyond the Lacanian notion of the signifying chain and the metonymic and homophonic devices used to establish it.[52] A Lacanian reading of the story recounted earlier might see "letters," "stamps," and "parcels" as signifiers all pointing to "mail," then hear the signifier "mail" as a homophonic play on "male." This would be interpreted as a metonymy of the phallus. The reading would thus rebound, from pillar to post, as it were, without any end point other than the phallus, castration, or death as the signifying lack that circulates in the text and out of which the text, as a sequence of empty signifiers, is produced. The signifying chain is inexorable in its arrival at the phallus or its substitutes. It does not allow us to stop at any one signifier to read through it the secreted word or semantic element in place of which it might be circulating. It does not allow us to read in "letters," "stamps," "parcels" and the further associations "mail" and "male" the hidden drama of "pillar."

In a cryptonymic reading we may stop at a signifier if we can determine what it hides, how it hides it, and what drama might be linked to its process of hiding. "The signified is not secondary," Abraham has written. "From the [assigning of one specific] signified results the cutting off of the signifier from [its] drama."[53] From the assigning to "post" of the sense "mail" results the cutting off of the signifier "post" from its other potential signified "pillar." The task of the reader is to find in the signifiers "letters," "parcels," and "dispatches" the trace of the hidden drama of "pillar." It may thereby be revealed that "letters," "parcels," "dispatches," and the like can *mean* or intend "pillar" by the tacit mediation of "post." The notion of a signifying chain as constituted by a potentially infinite sequence of empty signifiers is put into question.

The divergence between cryptonymy and the infinite deferral of signifiers can be restated in terms of the bar Lacan places between the chain of signifiers above it and the stable, identifiable signifieds or meanings below. In "The Agency of the Letter in the Unconscious or Reason since Freud," ("L'instance de la lettre dans l'inconscient ou la raison depuis Freud"),[54] Lacan states that the bar in his formula does not merely separate signifier from signified but that it "insists on meaning," preventing its emergence except as lack or difference. For

Lacan, the bar is the sign of the repression upon the phallus that infinitely defers signification. In contradistinction to this view, Abraham and Torok's theory of cryptonymy construes the bar or sign of repression as an object of investigation that gives itself to be read. Cryptonymy does this by revealing that the repression exerted by the bar can be exerted not merely on thoughts, reminiscences, and images but on the word itself. This discovery, elaborated in *The Wolf Man's Magic Word*, marks a major departure from Freudian and Lacanian theory:

> [In cryptonymy] it is not a situation *including* words that becomes repressed; the words are not dragged into repression by a situation. Rather, *the words themselves, expressing desire, are deemed to be generators of a situation that must be avoided and voided retroactively*. In this case, and only in this case, can we understand that repression may be carried out on the word, . . . and that the return of the repressed cannot have at its disposal even the tortuous paths of metonymic displacement. For this to occur, a catastrophic situation has to have been created precisely by words. (20; Abraham and Torok's italics)

The Lacanian bar which insists upon meaning and prevents its emergence is for Abraham and Torok an obstacle to intelligibility that, when analyzed in terms of the processes of cryptonymy, can be rendered intelligible. The bar is understood as having been created to defy cognition, as resulting from a verbal procedure whose purpose is to keep concealed an unspeakable lexical association. Cryptonymic analysis can therefore be said to recognize the proliferation of the signifying chain while providing a means for understanding how a particular signified has been severed from that chain. What is obstructed or barred in cryptonymy is not "meaning," in any traditional sense of the term, but a connection, situation, or drama that resists meaning or intelligibility. We might say, in more concrete terms, that the word "pillar" is not the meaning of our story about letters and dispatches. Rather it is part and parcel—a lexical parcel—of a drama that (for reasons as yet unknown) must be kept secret.[55]

While Abraham and Torok would thus commend Lacan for placing emphasis on language and on the signifying chain and would acknowledge the inspiration he has provided for literary analysis, they would contest the notions of the arbitrariness of the signifier and the indefinite sliding of signifiers over inaccessible signifieds. They do not view the inaccessibility of signification and its infinite deferral as ontological givens. They propose rather that the proliferation of signifiers and the hiding of particular signifieds is necessitated by a specific topology that, while resistant to understanding, can nevertheless be read.

SYMBOL AND INTERPRETATION

Crucial to appreciating the discovery of cryptonymy and to elaborating its potential for psychoanalytic literary interpretation are the concepts of symbol and symbolic operation. The following passages, from works spanning Abraham and Torok's collaboration ("The Symbol or Beyond Phenomena" [1961][56] and *The Wolf Man's Magic Word* [1976]), constitute two statements on the analytic functioning of the symbol.

> We are used to treating symbols like archaeologists who attempt to decipher the written documents of an unknown language. What is given is "something" with a meaning. Many of us live with the convenient misconception that in order to decipher [the document] it is sufficient to add meaning to the "thing" or the hieroglyphs.... Yet in so doing [we] merely convert one system of symbols into another and this latter system still stops short of laying open its secret. Actually, the reading of a symbolic text cannot be content with registering one-to-one equivalence between two terms. The work of deciphering will be completed only if we restore the entire circuit of functions involving a multiplicity of subjects and in which the symbol-thing is simply a relay....
>
> Here a first distinction must be made between, on the one hand, the symbol-thing considered as a hieroglyph or symbolic text—the *lifeless symbol*—and, on the other hand, the symbol included in a process, the *symbol in operation*, endowed with meaning and implying concrete subjects, together considered a functioning unit. *To interpret a symbol consists in converting the symbol-thing into an operating symbol.* A *thing* must never be taken as the symbol of another thing. (*Symbol*, 26–27; Abraham's italics)[57]

An analogy may help explain the implications of this passage and of Abraham's choice of the word "symbol," already heavily determined within psychoanalytic and literary theory. For the Greeks, the *symbolon* was a piece of pottery or earthenware that was broken in two prior to someone's (usually a warrior's) voyage. One of the two pieces remained at the site of departure while the other was carried by the traveler and "voyaged" with him. Upon his return (often many years later), the traveler's piece of pottery served as a sign of recognition and as proof of his identity when it was rejoined with its complement. The word "symbol" referred to each of the two pieces individually as well as to the act of putting the two pieces together (from the Greek *symballo* = to put together). An initial statement of Abraham's theory of the symbol can be extrapolated from these two meanings. When we read a text we read its symbols. We read fragments of semantic or phonetic elements that, if joined to their missing parts, would signify something (a drama, scene, or simply a lexical or phonetic element) that must for some reason be kept hidden or out of circulation.

> Whereas normally we are given meanings, the analyst is given symbols. Symbols are data that are missing an as yet undetermined part, but that can, in principle, be determined. The special aim of . . . listening is to find the symbol's complement, recovering it from indeterminacy. . . . [T]heoretical efforts have [long] been aimed at finding rules that will permit us to find the unknown missing complement, in other words, the fragment that "symbolizes with"—or, we might say, that "co-symbolizes." (*The Wolf Man*, 79)

The task of interpretation is to make sense of symbol fragments or "broken symbols"[58] by reconnecting them with their absent complements. An extension of my analogy will show that the key for doing this is contained within the symbol itself. One could understand "symbol" in Abraham and Torok's sense as referring not only to the two pottery fragments and their union but also to the jagged edge of each fragment, which meshes with the edge of the other, and to the displacement of the "voyaging" fragment. The multiple operations necessary to bring the two fragments together would be called *symbolization* or the *symbolic operation*. The shape and pattern of the jagged edge of the piece of pottery reveal the direction or "sense" in which it must be held to fit its complement; they allow us to reconstruct what that complement might look like. Similarly each symbol contains the lines or traces of the direction or sense of its "voyage" or displacement from its other half. It thereby permits us to retrace that voyage and reconstruct the complement or *co-symbol* from which it has been split.

An example from Abraham's "sixth act" to Shakespeare's *Hamlet* illustrates how such a symbolic operation might function. One of the elements in *Hamlet* to which Abraham implicitly refers, and that may be seen as one basis for his conjecture of Polonius's role in the duel between King Hamlet and King Fortinbras (involving the former's poisoning of the latter), is the fact that Ophelia drowns wreathed in plants, among them "dead men's fingers":

> Therewith fantastic garlands did she make
> Of crowflowers, nettles, daisies, and long purples
> That liberal shepherds give a grosser name,
> But our cold maids do dead men's fingers call them.
>
> (*Hamlet* 4.7.166–69)

Abraham would suggest that this conjunction of plants and death points to an earlier reference in the play to a deadly plant: hebona, from which comes the poison poured into King Hamlet's ear. Linked to poisoning and following, as it does, Hamlet's murder of Polonius, Shakespeare's reference to "dead men's fingers" would point for Abraham to a link in the play between poisoning and Polonius, Ophelia's father. The mention of "dead men's fingers," in other words, functions as a symbol. It is part of a system of traces that emerges from the text in which the elements chosen by Ophelia to accompany her death may be interpreted as fragments of a more complete drama in which Polonius's role as poisoner in King Hamlet's rigged duel is revealed.

Reading, for Abraham, is the reading of such traces. It is the deciphering of the inscriptions left by the voyage, displacement, or *differement*[59] of the symbol, and the retracing of the steps or operations constituting that voyage. To read or interpret is therefore not a matter of attaching meaning to a signifying element but of carrying the symbol back to the place of its co-symbol. For this reason Abraham calls the reunion of the two co-symbols a *metaphor*[60] and the process of interpretation a process of *metaphorization*. Interpretation, in other words, does not consist in answering the questions, What are the symbols of the text? or What do these symbols mean? It consists in trying to resolve the enigma: How and with what does something symbolize? What constitutes the text's symbolic operation?

Interpretation, it must be added, is posited as an infinite process, since the operation of the symbol is itself infinite. "What is symbolized is always the symbol of something symbolized earlier" (*Symbol*, 34). To join a symbol with its complement is to encounter, in this union, another symbol itself separated from its own complement. Abraham and Torok's analysis of the Wolf Man may be seen as a concrete example of the infinitude of the interpretive process. Their analysis is based on retracing the displacement of the symbol fragments manifested in the Wolf Man's dreams, nasal infections, choice of profession, and so forth back to a traumatic scene of witnessing in which, as a young boy, he was obliged to deny having seen his father seduce his daughter (the Wolf Man's sister). Near the end of their study, Abraham and Torok raise the question: "Could the analysis have gone further?" If so, they respond, it "would have had to extend to the paternal grandparents, and even to the great-grandparents, so that the Wolf Man could be situated within the [entire] libidinal lineage from which he was descended" (*The Wolf Man*, 75–76). The resolution they offer of the enigma posed by the Wolf Man's symptoms is not construed as absolute; the resolution itself can potentially be traced to yet another trauma in the preceding generation. While Abraham and Torok have reconstituted a scene of witnessing they consider generative of the Wolf Man's entire life, the question of why the seduction of the daughter by the father (about which the Wolf Man was called upon to give testimony) occurred in the first place still remains unanswered. The solution to this enigma would potentially bring to light another trauma whose existence, despite the absence of available textual evidence, must be conjectured.

SYMBOLIC OPERATION, TRAUMA, AND ANASEMIA

Symbol and the Origin of Being

The example of the Wolf Man, whose life Abraham and Torok compare to the creation of a living poem composed of symbols, suggests the nature of the link, alluded to earlier, between Abraham's poetic "sixth act" to *Hamlet* and his theory of the symbol. To demonstrate this link and to explore its implications for psychoanalytic literary criticism, a delineation of Abraham's philosophical grounding of the symbolic operation, elaborated in chapters 2 and 3 of "The Symbol or Beyond Phenomena," will be helpful.

In "The Archaeology of the Symbol" and "The Genesis of Symbolic Structure," Abraham returns to the basics of physics and to the dyadic structure of the atom to describe the origin of being (not just of the subject) as a symbolic operation involving the constant oscillation between a negative and a positive pole:

> ... *being* ... *is only possible in a symbolic mode*. In formal terms one can say: A *is* A only if one can somehow say that A *implies* B in the form of *not*, that is, if A symbolizes *with* B. (*Symbol*, 38; Abraham's italics here and below)

A can only be A by saying "not B," not the other. Being A thus implies B in the form of a negation. It requires that A symbolize with B in its absence:

> It is clear that the single symbol alone is not sufficient for being. . . . To say that A corresponds to B signifies that it is not closed in upon itself but is in some sense *in communication* with B. *For A to be A and not B it must itself accomplish this act of discrimination.* Such is its symbolizing operation. (*Symbol*, 38)

The origin of being is a communication or co-symbolizing between two entities constituted by mutual negation, that is, by repeatedly articulating their difference from one another:

> *Being ... consists in the indefinitely repeated affirmation of its otherness.* (*Symbol*, 38)

Abraham's "archaeology of being" does not end here. He postulates that, if the origin of being is grounded in the otherness or difference of a perpetual symbolic operation, at the origin of the symbolic operation itself is "*the impossibility of being* or . . . *active nonbeing tending toward being*" (*Symbol*, 37). The symbolic operation is thus understood by Abraham as a response to the blockage of being; as the means by which nonbeing is transcended, that is, an obstacle surmounted.

It is precisely at this point that Abraham's *Sixth Act* may be seen as a continuation or complement of his treatise on the symbol. As was noted earlier, his conjecture of a drama of murder perpetrated by King Hamlet and lying beyond Prince Hamlet's awareness makes visible the reason for Hamlet's indecision or "madness of doubt." The theory of the symbol enables us to recast this formulation and interpret what is called indecision or hesitation as an obstacle to being that exists by virtue of a phantom. "To be or not to be"—that *is* the question for Hamlet. Abraham's *Sixth Act*, I would propose, restates the question in terms of a transgenerational haunting and offers an alternative to Hamlet's tragic response. It implicitly asks: What would it take to remove the obstacle to Hamlet's being and to reinstate the possibility of his existence? *The Sixth Act* responds by situating the origin of Hamlet's behavior in a blockage to being generated by a lie, beyond his lived experience, that haunts him. It brings forth this unspoken drama, whose traces are readable in the play, and "exorcises" its haunting effect, thereby removing Hamlet's "madness of doubt" and reinstating the possibility for Hamlet to be.

Trauma and Anasemia

In psychoanalytic terms, Abraham and Torok call an obstacle or blockage to being a "trauma" or "catastrophe."[61] An event too painful to be absorbed by the ego whose stability it would threaten, trauma drives the individual to speak and behave in ways that simultaneously conceal and reveal their catastrophic source. Implicit in this view is the idea that the content of an event does not in itself classify it as traumatic. The manner in which the event is "lived" or experienced psychically by an individual renders it a trauma. This perspective removes trauma from external moral or ethical taxonomies to situate it as a function of the specific mental configuration and psychic history of an individual. Abraham's comment on a clinical case of haunting produced by the concealment of an illegitimate birth underscores this point: "[W]hat our subject does not know, what must be covered with the veil of modesty [is] the fact that his father is a bastard. . . . *An insignificant fact in itself,* had it not led to a secret pain in the father and to his constructing an entire family romance about his aristocratic origins. . . ."[62] Illegitimacy "in itself" is "insignificant"; its traumatic effect is attributable not to its nonconformity to an aprioristic moral or behavioral code but to an internal source or "founding silence" (*Shell,* 19) (here unspecified) that causes the father to experience the illegitimacy as acutely painful and prevents him from putting it into words, thereby evacuating or "exorcising" it.

The process of discovering why the father experiences this illegitimacy (not necessarily all illegitimacy) as traumatic and conceals it as a secret is called by Abraham and Torok *anasemia.* This analytic methodology consists in a constant movement "back up toward" (from the Greek *ana*) successively earlier sources of signification (*semia*) that lie beyond perception. It aims to reconstruct the (theoretically) infinite regression of signifying sources or "transphenomena"[63] that cause an experience to become traumatic and that trigger the creation of symbols as means of transcending it. This explains in part why Abraham and Torok speak of anasemia as the complement of symbol and why they consider these two structures to be the organizing principles of psychoanalysis to which "all authentic psychoanalytic concepts may be reduced" (*Shell,* 21). Anasemia allows them to construe an individual's existence as constituted by the constant creation of symbols in response to traumas. It enables them to read these symbols—and thus the individual's life—as a series of telltale symptoms that tacitly speak of their founding silence beyond perception.

Within the context of Abraham and Torok's overall psychoanalytic project, anasemia refers to the process of interrogating all established metapsychological theories as symbols or traces of an apparently missing beyond or signifying source. Capitalization is the strategic ploy the analysts use to bracket the present, concrete significations of terms such as Drive, Instinct, Castration, Phallus, Pleasure, Anxiety, Shell, Kernel, Mother, Child and to suggest that these terms be "de-signified," that is, stripped of their common sense and reinserted within the symbolic operation whose retracing would give voice to their founding silence. By capitalizing Pleasure, for example, Abraham and Torok tacitly ask: What can such a concept signify if pain is sometimes a source of pleasure and pleasure can also mean suffering? A similar anasemic inquiry of Drive led to the discovery that, in certain instances, what pushes or drives someone to do something is a silence in the speech of someone else. The psychic configuration of the phantom emerged as one of the signifying sources or transphenomena of the Freudian theory of Drive.[64]

Character Analysis and the Interpretation of Narrative

The readings of five short stories that follow are informed by the theories of anasemia, symbol, cryptonymy, and the phantom. In the process of extending these analytic concepts into the literary realm, however, my project departs from Abraham and Torok's with respect to its aims and results. The purpose of my readings is to demonstrate how and why it is possible to treat the "lives" of certain fictional characters as narratives—composed of symbols—of the traumas they have surmounted. This signifies that behavior and speech manifested in certain texts may be construed as the means by which fictive characters recreate themselves as "other," symbolically telling the tale of what and why they could not be. Although not real, these characters are no longer considered merely effects of systems of codes, conventions, signs, or functions. They are viewed as animated ciphers of concealed "life-sagas" whose peripeties, vicissitudes, and driving forces can, theoretically, be determined. What emerges is an alternative to structuralist and poststructuralist views of literary character analysis as a delusional or impossible undertaking.

The unifying feature of the stories I treat is the fact that the secrets within them are all structured as phantoms. The catastrophe motivating a character's behavior can be shown in each text to have been experienced by someone else, who transformed the event into a secret and transmitted it transgenerationally, binding its recipient in an unspoken, unrecognized pact of collective concealment. This common thread does not in any sense represent the signification or "meaning" of the texts. Nor does the fact that the phantomatic secret transmitted in four of the five tales involves an affair and an illegitimate offspring represent their "content." If the intent of my analyses were to reveal this, there would be no need for further discussion. On the contrary, my readings are concerned with elaborating the specific way in which a fictive character's existence can be understood to be propelled by the haunting presence of a secret beyond her or his awareness, and with exposing the precise manner in which this secret determines and drives the structure and formation of the narrative itself. One result of this inquiry is a new view of subjectivity in fiction, a view that construes a subject's sense of alienation, ex-centricity, or otherness not as an ontological given but as potentially the result of being "possessed" by a phantom.

The theory of the phantom is thus not used here as a heuristic model that can be "applied" to a text as a prescriptive paradigm for interpreting characters' speech or behavior. It is considered a conceptual option that allows the reader to imagine the possibility—to be verified or dismissed in the process of uncovering the specific structures of organization and coherence obscured by each text's linguistic elements—that a fictive character in a narrative may have a (fictive) past which, while not apparent, is inscribed hermetically within the narrative. My study, conducted with this option in mind and aided by hermeneutic concepts new to literary analysis such as cryptonymy and symbol, ultimately aims to shed light on literature's until now unrecognized preoccupation with the relationship among psychic history, family history, and character analysis. It also provides a new perspective on the potential connection between hidden family sagas and the genesis of narrative, between the textual manifestations of a concealed "metapsychological reality" propelling a character and the notion of textual "authorship."

This last point is a crucial result of my project. The readings that follow demonstrate how the incongruous speech and behavior of the texts' protagonists can be traced in each instance to the disturbing yet unrecognized workings of a secret they carry within them. Establishing the cause of these verbal and behavioral phenomena—which constitute the very material of the narratives and which range from the captain's fantasies of sharing a secret (*The Secret Sharer*), Xavier's hallucinations (*L'intersigne*), and Facino Cane's obsessive pursuit of gold to Spencer Brydon's quest for his alter ego (*The Jolly Corner*) and Madeline and Roderick Usher's acute physical and mental suffering (*The Fall of the House of Usher*)—leads to the conclusion that the existence of the narratives themselves is contingent upon the secrets embedded within them. Each story emerges as the telltale saga of an unspeakable drama the story conceals within itself as its own propulsive force. Existing conceptions of the origin or "author" of texts have thus to be enlarged to account for these instances in which a text's secret is also its generative agent. Poststructuralist perspectives that conceive of the author as a fictional entity must also be expanded to include the possibility that such an entity may assume the form of a secret a text encrypts within itself.

The idea that a text can contain its own "author" means that certain texts exist in what may be called a "textual dual unity." They function as their own "secret sharers," as partners in a pact of collective concealment they form with themselves. Considering the theory of the dual unity within the literary domain in turn invites an expansion of previous conceptions of intertextuality. *Transtextuality* is the term I propose for the specific kind of intertextual relationship at work in narratives organized by phantoms. Transtextuality refers to the situation in which a narrative and its intertexts—identifiable from the textual entities, fragments, or allusions the narrative contains—complement, inform, and interpret one another across a fissure or gap in the transmission of a family history. This fissure, formed by the silence wrapped around an unspeakable drama, divides the visible narrative from the prior drama that, although not readily accessible, grounds the narrative's existence. Reading these intertexts means recognizing their status as *transtexts*, as encoded bits or pieces broken off from the trauma suffered and silenced by someone in the narrative's prehistory, and whose content and effects have been transmitted transgenerationally as cryptic lexical parcels of an unutterable tale.

Precisely how transtextuality and textual dual unities manifest themselves in literary works will be seen most clearly in the analysis of *The Fall of the House of Usher*, although these concepts are at work to some degree in all the tales in this study. Examining how transtextuality functions and how a text can be perceived as its own secret sharer, carrying inscribed within it the missing complement from which it has been cut off, will also lead to a reconsideration of the rapport between text and reader. As the analyses evolve, it will become increasingly apparent that the reader's charge in confronting phantom-texts involves reconstructing and "completing" a narrative that has become estranged from its generative source and hence from itself. Understanding that this "completion" can never be fully achieved—and elucidating the reasons why not—will reveal a new way of construing the notion of the infinitude of the reading process. It will also bring into relief the pivotal function of the symbolic operation for analyzing the formation and evolution of literary history.

While departing from Abraham and Torok's primarily clinically and philosophically oriented work to emphasize the theoretical and interpretive implications of some of their conceptual discoveries for literary analysis, my readings of tales by Conrad, Villiers, Balzac, James, and Poe also diverge methodologically from Abraham's treatment of a literary text, his reading of *Hamlet*. *The Phantom of Hamlet or The Sixth Act* combines poetic creation with interpretation to produce a work of psychoanalytic imagination. Although Abraham's conjecture of a rigged duel between Kings Hamlet and Fortinbras and of Polonius's role as poisoner is based on symbol fragments contained in Shakespeare's play, he also imagines events that may have occurred prior to the play but whose traces are not inscribed in the text. Abraham's contention that Hamlet is the child of Gertrude and King Fortinbras, to cite one example, is not grounded in textual evidence from the drama but meshes psychoanalytic imagination with a theoretically plausible extrapolation of events consistent with the tragedy.

My analyses, by contrast, are not poetic fictions but reconstructions of obscured family histories whose telltale traces are all inscribed and readable within the narratives. The readings eschew poetic license and imaginative extrapolation. They rely for their legitimacy and authority on a rigorous attention to textual detail and on the substantial accumulation of internally coherent elements contained within each narrative. In this respect, my interpretations differ from Abraham's treatment of *Hamlet* by demonstrating that certain fictional works are as responsive to textually grounded, textually delimited anasemic analysis as the accounts of patients in the clinic. They illustrate that fictive tales and their personae can exhibit the same (or even a greater) degree of internal disarray as certain patients, and that they can express (however cryptically) a demand to be read and analyzed in terms of their specific narrative elements with as much force—and, at times, with as much pathos—as those on the analyst's couch.

The interpretations in this study also diverge from Abraham's *Sixth Act* in that they are concerned as much with delineating the step-by-step process of analysis as they are with unveiling its outcome. They have no curative or therapeutic intent; they are aimed rather at articulating strategies for explaining the apparently incongruous or enigmatic behavior of characters in certain narratives as symbols or symptoms of secrets formed in response to catastrophic experiences. The initial step of each analysis therefore consists in establishing that a narrative is in fact concerned with the state (or states) of a character's mental disequilibrium. This means elucidating precisely how one recognizes the aberrant elements of a fictive character's speech and actions, and how one identifies and reestablishes the links that connect them.

The reading process I delineate in this study may therefore be viewed as a kind of "archaeology" in which buried fragments of infinitely regressive and symptomatic family histories are disinterred and used to reconstruct unspeakable sagas concealed in the past. While the result of this process is in each case a unified, cohesive interpretation, the resolutions I propose to the enigmas posed by the texts make no claim to exclusiveness or to exhausting the narratives. Nor do they deny the discontinuity of the texts or aim to recover their meaning or essence. My methodology aims rather to uncover, in certain narratives, principles of coherence that allow us to explain why something had to be concealed or rendered unintelligible, how it was made to resist intelligibility, and how its resistance can itself be read. My approach is not concerned with defining a theory of reading or with "curing" a text or its characters. It instead views the text as a "text in distress," and it seeks to show how, unaware of its own hidden secret, the text calls upon the reader to hear and understand that to which it and its characters are deaf.

The analyses I present thus invite reflection upon the nature of the interpretive process itself as it evolves between reader and text. One result of this reflection is the articulation of a distinct alternative to previous psychoanalytic and poststructuralist approaches to narrative analysis. Another result is the ability to open, within literary studies, a new perspective on fiction and readability and on the interrelation of psychic drama and narrative: a perspective that construes characters in certain texts as emissaries of unspoken sagas, emissaries whose words and actions can be heard to tell the secret history generating their existence—and the existence of their narratives themselves.

CHAPTER 2

The Ghost of a Secret

PSYCHOANALYTIC ALLEGORY IN JOSEPH CONRAD'S *THE SECRET SHARER*

> The task . . . is to hold up . . . the rescued fragment before all eyes. . . . It is to show its vibration, its colour, its form; and through its movement, its form, and its colour, reveal the substance of its truth—disclose its inspiring secret. . . .
> (Preface, *The Nigger of the "Narcissus"*)

IF THERE IS an obvious choice for inclusion in a study of secrets it would seem to be Joseph Conrad's *The Secret Sharer* (1909–1910).[1] The idea that something is kept hidden is inscribed throughout the tale, even if the precise content of the secret and the identity of the characters involved in its concealment are open to debate. At the same time, the story's references to ghostly apparitions, haunting, and uncanniness, elements traditionally viewed as signs of mental perturbation, suggest its appropriateness for a psychoanalytically oriented inquiry. The tale has in fact served as something of a Rorschach for myriad psychoanalytic interpretations, which have focused primarily on the problems of doubling, identity, and hidden drives and desires. A brief résumé of the plot confirms that these issues are indeed legitimate ones worthy of consideration, although one may take exception to the specific approaches previously used to address them or to the conclusions drawn from their analysis.

The story begins, following a brief preamble, when a newly appointed captain, who has been standing watch alone, spots a man hanging on to the side ladder of his ship. Leggatt, chief mate of the *Sephora*, climbs aboard, introduces himself, and recounts to the captain how, in trying to save his ship from disaster during a violent storm, he struck a recalcitrant sailor and killed him in the ensuing struggle. To escape incarceration aboard the *Sephora* and the murder trial facing him back on land, he jumped overboard and swam toward one of the small islands in the Gulf of Siam. Upon seeing the lights of the ship in the distance he decided to head for it. The captain, who is unnamed in the text and narrates the tale, responds by telling Leggatt to slip down into his stateroom.

The remainder of the story describes the captain's awkward maneuvering as he tries to keep Leggatt concealed in his cabin. With his ship resting at anchor awaiting sufficient wind to start its voyage back to England, he divides his day between trying to maintain a calm appearance as commander of his vessel and keeping hidden the man he repeatedly calls his "double," "other self," and "secret sharer" of his life. When a search party from the *Sephora,* headed by its captain Archbold, comes looking for Leggatt, the tension of the situation seems to get the better of the captain; he recklessly invites Archbold to look into his stateroom, counting on Leggatt to conceal himself in a recessed part of the room. In another close shave, the captain nearly loses his composure when the steward enters his cabin unannounced to fetch his rain gear. At night, Leggatt and the captain whisper together side by side, joined in what the captain calls their "secret partnership."

Following his near detection by the steward, Leggatt tells the captain to maroon him on one of the islands off the coast. At first adamantly opposed to the idea, the captain reluctantly agrees. The following night he orders the ship toward shore, ostensibly in search of the land breezes. As the ship shaves the land closer and closer and the crew grows anxious with the looming danger, Leggatt slips out of the cabin and over the side. With his vessel on the brink of disaster, the captain suddenly remembers that he is unfamiliar with her handling. As he stands helplessly on deck, staring at the still water for a sign that the ship has turned, he sees floating on the surface the hat he gave Leggatt to wear for protection from the sun. With this "saving mark" as a reference point to gage the ship's progress, he orders the helm shifted. The vessel, to his and the crew's relief, comes about, and the captain—no longer thinking of Leggatt, who has swum off to start a new life—feels suddenly possessed of knowledge and joined in a silent communion with his ship.

Although the bibliography on *The Secret Sharer* is extensive, the vast majority of critics have concentrated on two principal questions implicitly raised by the title: who is the secret sharer and what does he share? Despite their divergent theoretical and methodological approaches, critics generally agree that the title refers to Leggatt and that he shares or embodies some part of the captain.[2] Two issues have been left largely unaddressed by these responses. Identifying Leggatt as the title character does not take into account the inherent contradiction between the idea of sharing, which by definition involves at least two people, and the title's singular noun "sharer." If Leggatt shares something in secret with the captain, the captain must also be considered a secret sharer. One could expect a narrative about such a relationship to be called *The Secret Sharers*. At the same time, identifying Leggatt as the "secret sharer" leaves unresolved the grammatical ambiguity of the title, which can refer either to a sharer who is kept secret ("secret" read as the adjectival modifier of the noun "sharer") or to a secret that is shared ("secret" read as part of the compound noun "secret sharer"). While some readers have conflated these two possibilities, interpreting the title to mean "The secret (or hidden) sharer of a secret," its polysemy and potentially misleading nature remain issues for inquiry.[3]

My reading of Conrad's story takes as its point of departure the ambiguity of the title and aims to account for it by investigating Leggatt's function in the narrative with respect to the captain. The analysis operates from the hypothesis that the text's title may be in the singular because the secret sharing in the narrative is itself "singular" or one-sided, which is to say nonexistent. It proceeds to show that there is in fact no secret shared in *The Secret Sharer*. The apparent rapport of doubling and sharing between the captain and Leggatt is explained instead as a symptom of the captain's haunting by a phantom, by the silent transmission to him of someone else's unspeakable secret. The text itself can then be understood as an allegory of the psychoanalytic configuration specific to the phantom.

Proposing that a phantom is at play in a text entitled *The Secret Sharer* may elicit surprise not only because this psychic formation is, by definition, generated by the inability to state or share a secret, but because such an idea contradicts virtually all previous interpretations of the story, which generally concur in viewing the two protagonists as sharing something they (knowingly or unknowingly) hold or conceal between them. The idea becomes less startling if we recall the preceding discussion of Nicolas Abraham's "sixth act" to *Hamlet*, in chapter 1,[4] in which a nearly identical and widely accepted view concerning a secret apparently held in concert by two characters was put into question and, through analysis informed by the idea of the phantom, revealed to be based on a subterfuge or "false secret" designed to conceal a genuine, unspoken, and unshared one.

This does not mean to imply that Leggatt's function in Conrad's tale is identical or even similar to that of King Hamlet's ghost in Shakespeare's tragedy. All the same, several elements in *The Secret Sharer*, notably the captain's insistent references to Leggatt as "a ghost" (660, 671, 687), a "ghastly . . . mystery" (655), and a "cadaverous . . . corpse" (654), who seems to have "risen from the bottom of the sea" (655) to provoke in him "uncanny" (662) feelings of "haunt[ing]" (686), do resonate with the underlying drama of haunting found in *Hamlet*.[5] While the mere mention of terms such as "ghost," "haunted," "mystery," and "uncanny" can never be assumed to signal the presence of a phantom, their juxtaposition with the narrative's themes of concealment, secrets, and whispered or muted communication encourages the hypothesis that the captain's unsettled feelings and discomposed behavior may be related to his haunting by a secret transmitted to him without his knowledge. What appears to be shared in secret between Leggatt and the captain may be (as in *Hamlet*) only a false secret or symptom camouflaging a genuine, unspoken one whose content, the text's title notwithstanding, is never shared.

1

The text's preamble suggests itself as a starting point for testing this hypothesis. Some critics have interpreted the passage as a "dreamscape," reflecting the captain's quest for self-awareness, or as a figure of his inner journey toward psychological maturity.[6] Others have tended to dismiss the passage as a flaw in the narrative, claiming that its elements are only tenuously related to the remainder of the tale. The captain's insistent description of mysterious divisions, deceptive unions, incompleteness, and the difficulty of clearly perceiving things nearby raises another possibility: the preamble may reflect his separation or alienation from something as yet unnamed that is nevertheless close to him:

> On my right hand there were lines of fishing stakes resembling a mysterious system of half-submerged bamboo fences, incomprehensible in its division of the domain of tropical fishes, and crazy of aspect as if abandoned forever by some nomad tribe of fishermen.... To the left a group of barren islets, suggesting ruins of stone walls, towers, and block-houses, had its foundations set in a blue sea that itself looked solid, so still and stable did it lie below my feet.... [W]hen I turned my head ... I saw the straight line of the flat shore joined to the stable sea ... with a perfect and unmarked closeness.... [T]wo small clumps of trees, one on each side of the only fault in the impeccable joint, marked the mouth of the river Meinam.... [T]he tug steaming right into the land became lost to my sight... as though the impassive earth had swallowed her up.... My eye followed the light cloud of her smoke ... till I lost it at last.... And then I was left alone with my ship, anchored at the head of the Gulf of Siam. (648–49)

Something "mysterious" is "submerged," cut off from the captain and inaccessible to his view. Despite his searching gaze, divisions blur; what he is able to perceive is either deceptive ("the sea looked solid"), indistinct ("an unmarked closeness"), or "incomprehensible" to the eye. Like stone ruins whose integrity is lost to the past, the captain appears as if he too may be incomplete, severed from something in the past that has been "swallowed up" or concealed. His relationship with the vessel he commands adds to this impression and brings into relief the extent and nature of his estrangement:

> [W]ith . . . a swarm of stars . . . above the shadowy earth . . . I lingered . . . , my hand resting lightly on my ship's rail as if on the shoulder of a trusted friend. But, with all that multitude of celestial bodies staring down at one, the comfort of quiet communion with her was gone for good. . . . [W]hat I felt most was my being a stranger to the ship; and if all the truth must be told, I was somewhat of a stranger to myself. . . . (649–50)

Estranged from his vessel and himself, the captain seeks to "get on terms with the ship" (652) and share with it a silent "communion." His quest fails. With Leggatt's unexpected arrival, however, the object of this quest shifts. Leggatt becomes someone with whom the captain will be able to commune:

> [Leggatt's] voice was calm and resolute. A good voice. The self-possession of that man had somehow induced a corresponding state in myself. . . . [H]e was young. . . . A mysterious communication was established already between us two. . . . I was young, too. . . . (656)

Leggatt seems to instill in the captain a sense of completeness. Yet the only basis suggested for this sudden feeling of communion and shared self-possession is the proximity of the men's ages. The vague, tenuous nature of their communication is underscored moments later when the captain gives the naked Leggatt one of his sleeping suits to wear:

> In a moment he had concealed his damp body in a sleeping suit of the same gray-stripe pattern as the one I was wearing and followed me like my double on the poop. . . . He rested a hand on the end of the skylight and . . . did not stir a limb. . . .
>
> One of my hands, too, rested on the end of the skylight; neither did I stir a limb. . . . It occurred to me that if [the mate] were to . . . catch sight of us, he would think he was seeing double, . . . the strange captain having a quiet confabulation by the wheel with his own gray ghost. (657–60)

This first reference to Leggatt as the captain's "double" appears grounded in little more than the symmetry of their clothing and body positions. When, after installing Leggatt in his cabin, the captain prefaces his comment that "anybody bold enough to open [the door] would have been treated to the uncanny sight of a double captain busy talking in whispers with his other self" (662) by admitting that "[Leggatt] was not a bit like me, really" (662), the reader begins to wonder whether the captain's claims of doubling and communion are based on any real identity or sharing with Leggatt or are instead products of his imagination.

A response seems to emerge from the captain's reaction to Leggatt's initial account of the murder: "You had better slip down into my stateroom now" (660). With this statement the captain effectively transforms both Leggatt's account and his presence aboard ship into a secret. He creates a situation—as his references to Leggatt as a "double captain" (694), "secret stranger" (697), "secret sharer of my life" (671), and "secret sharer of my cabin" (676, 699) appear to suggest—in which he identifies with Leggatt as a partner or co-conspirator in the secret of his crime and presence. Yet the secret created by the captain's gesture of concealment is not shared. It exists only from the captain's point of view, by virtue of his treating Leggatt's account and existence aboard ship as if asked to keep them a secret, despite the absence of such a request from Leggatt and despite indications of Leggatt's quite opposite intentions. Leggatt makes these intentions explicit once below deck. His original plan, he explains, was to swim to the Java coast as the *Sephora* passed through the Sunda Straits: "I wanted nothing more. I've had a prize for swimming" (663). Kept locked in his cabin and able to jump overboard only when the nearest land was five miles off, he was determined to stay "clear of [the *Sephora* and] not g[o] back. . . . I meant to swim till I sank" (665). He decided to head for the captain's ship because it was "something to swim for" (665). And he asked for the captain because he wanted to talk with someone before swimming on: "[It] was a mere impulse. . . . I don't know—I wanted to be seen, to talk with somebody, before I went on" (667).

From the outset the captain is thus aware of Leggatt's intent to escape judgment by swimming ashore—or to drown trying. "Do you see me before a judge and jury?" (658), Leggatt adds. "For myself I can't see the necessity. . . . I was ready enough to go off wandering on the face of the earth" (664). Leggatt expresses neither the desire nor the intention to conceal his crime (known to everyone aboard the *Sephora* and soon to be made known to our captain's crew by the search party) or to hide himself aboard the captain's ship, risking capture and trial by those unable to understand his conduct. He is therefore not an active participant or sharer in the captain's transformation of his presence and account into a secret. He only passively complies with the captain's order to go below.[7]

To this point in the narrative there is thus no basis for the captain's claim to share a secret with Leggatt. (While he does share his clothing, food, bed, and sympathy with him, these are not secrets.) In fact, all of the captain's gestures and statements of sharing throughout the drama are similarly one-sided, grounded in what appear to be increasingly exaggerated and ultimately hallucinatory flights of imagination. When Leggatt cuts short his agitated description of the miserable character he has killed, for example, and calls upon the captain's maritime experience to fill in the distasteful details, the captain construes this as proof of his own complicity in the act; he imagines himself in Leggatt's place, as having actually participated in the murder:

> "He was one of those creatures that ... wouldn't do his duty and wouldn't let anybody else do theirs. But what's the good of talking! You know well enough the sort of ill-conditioned snarling cur—."
>
> He appealed to me as if our experiences had been as identical as our clothes.... I did not think of asking him for details, and he told me the story roughly in brusque, disconnected sentences. I needed no more. I saw it all going on as though I were myself inside that other sleeping suit. (658)

Later, the captain pretends to be hard of hearing so that Archbold, arrived with the search party from the *Sephora,* will speak loudly enough for Leggatt to hear their conversation below decks. Leggatt, however, never expresses a desire to listen to the exchange or an unwillingness to await the captain's return to hear it recounted. Played out without Leggatt's active participation, the captain's pretense serves to create another artificial scene of secret sharing where in truth no secret is shared.

The captain's fantasy of secret sharing with Leggatt becomes even more intense during his conversation with Archbold. First, he confuses Archbold with Leggatt: "[Unable] to detach my mental vision from the unsuspected sharer of my cabin as though he were my second self...., I looked politely at Captain Archbold ... but it was the other I saw, in a gray sleeping suit" (673–74). Next, the captain imagines that Archbold himself confuses him with Leggatt: "I believe that [Archbold] was not a little disconcerted ... by something in me that reminded him of the man he was seeking—suggested a mysterious similitude to the young fellow" (677). Finally, he fancies himself to be the true subject of Archbold's comment that Leggatt "wasn't exactly the sort for the chief mate of a ship like the *Sephora*" (675):

> I had become so connected in thoughts and impressions with the secret sharer of my cabin that I felt as if I, personally, were being given to understand that I, too, was not the sort that would have done for the chief mate of a ship like the *Sephora*. I had no doubt of it in my mind. (675–76)

One might argue that the threat posed to Leggatt by Archbold's arrival upsets the captain and provokes his erratic behavior. This explanation would lead us to expect the captain to regain a measure of calm with Archbold's departure. Precisely the opposite occurs. When Archbold leaves, the captain's sense of sharing with Leggatt becomes stronger, his behavior more openly aberrant. Standing on deck, he feels that he is "not wholly alone with [his] command" (682), that the stranger in his cabin is also piloting the ship:

> That mental feeling of being in two places at once affected me physically. . . . [H]aving occasion to ask the mate . . . to take a compass bearing . . . I caught myself reaching up to his ear in whispers, [startling] the man. . . . A little later I moved away from the rail . . . with such a stealthy gait that the helmsman noticed it. . . . [I]t's to no commander's advantage to be suspected of ludicrous eccentricities. . . . (682)

Aware that his eccentric behavior is jeopardizing his authority as commander, the captain nevertheless seems impotent to alter it. When Leggatt demands to be marooned after his near discovery by the steward, the way seems open for the captain to act on his sympathy for the sailor and help him fulfill his desire to escape, in the process freeing himself from his perturbing presence. Yet the captain refuses Leggatt's demand. This response, which the captain himself concedes is a "sham," appears even more incongruous in light of his insistence on the "infinitely miserable" (684) days of "horrible maneuvering" (684) he and Leggatt endure, with the latter cramped in the stifling heat of the bathroom, forced to survive on "abominable" (684) tinned food:

> "You must maroon me as soon as ever you can get amongst these islands off the Cambodge shore. . . ."
>
> "Maroon you! We're not living in a boy's adventure tale," I protested. His scornful whispering took me up.
>
> "We aren't indeed! There's nothing of a boy's tale in this. But there's nothing else for it. I want no more. . . ."
>
> "Impossible!" I murmured. "You can't."
>
> "Can't? . . ."
>
> I felt suddenly ashamed of myself. . . . [M]y hesitation in letting that man swim away from my ship's side had been a mere sham sentiment, a sort of cowardice. (688)

Leggatt's scornful dismissal of the captain's refusal as a boy's fantasy hints at the structure of artifice underlying the latter's behavior. Leggatt's departure threatens the fantasized rapport of secret sharing the captain has created. Without this stranger concealed in his cabin, the captain can no longer identify himself, as he does obsessively throughout the narrative, as someone who shares a secret. But why must the captain identify himself as a secret sharer when he is not one? What drives him insistently to create, imagine, or act out scenes of artificial secret sharing when such behavior elicits his crew's derision and jeopardizes not only his career but the life of a man with whom he clearly sympathizes? We can conjecture that repeating through speech, gestures, and hallucinations that he is bound with another in a collective pact of concealment when in fact he is not may be a sign that the captain is haunted by an unspeakable drama, transmitted to him by someone else, and whose content he cannot know. It is possible that his unfounded, irrational insistence on being a secret sharer is symptomatic of the fact that he is unable to share a secret, that he is haunted by a phantom. Confirming this conjecture is contingent upon being able to reconstruct, from traces embedded within the narrative, the content of this unshared, unspoken secret.

2

Certain similarities in the two events framing the captain's story suggest their relevance for such a reconstruction. The captain tells Leggatt to "slip down" (660) into his stateroom and transforms him into an (artificial) secret sharer immediately after hearing his account of murdering a shipmate aboard the *Sephora*. As Leggatt prepares to "slip out" (692) of the stateroom at the end of the tale and the ship heads perilously close to land, the captain violently assaults his own ship's mate in a near murderous rage. The details of this second incident, from which an extended excerpt follows, and their connection to Leggatt's tale are pivotal to determining why the captain decides to hide Leggatt and to identifying the unspoken drama concealed in his narrative.

> [T]o my mate's great surprise [I] put the ship round on the other tack. His terrible whiskers flitted round me in silent criticism. . . .
>
> At noon I gave no orders for a change of course, and the mate's whiskers became much concerned. . . .
>
> . . . It was now a matter of conscience to shave the land as close as possible. . . . I walked over to leeward and my heart flew into my mouth at the nearness of the land on the bow. Under any other circumstances I would not have held on a minute longer. . . .
>
> I had shut my eyes—because the ship must go closer. She must! . . .
>
> Was she close enough? Already she was, I won't say in the shadow of the land, but in the very blackness of it, already swallowed up as it were. . . .
>
> "My God! Where are we?"
>
> It was the mate moaning at my elbow. He was thunderstruck, and as it

were deprived of the moral support of his whiskers. He clapped his hands and absolutely cried out, "Lost!"

"Be quiet," I said sternly. . . .

He made as if to tear his hair, and addressed me recklessly.

"She will never get out. You have done it, sir. I knew it'd end in something like this. She will never weather, and you are too close now to stay. She'll drift ashore before she's round. O my God!"

I caught his arm as he was raising it to batter his poor devoted head, and shook it violently.

"She's ashore already," he wailed, trying to tear himself away. . . .

I hadn't let go the mate's arm and went on shaking it. "Ready about, do you hear? You go forward"—shake "and stop there"—shake—"and hold your noise"—shake—"and see these head sheets properly overhauled"—shake, shake—shake.

. . . I released my grip at last and he ran forward as if fleeing for dear life. (689–97)

In view of Leggatt's well-established prowess as a swimmer, the captain's determination to sail dangerously near to shore in order to "shave the land as close as possible" has to be considered symptomatic. The significance of "shaving the land"—a locution whose overdetermined nature is brought into relief by the captain's repeated personification of his mate's whiskers ("His terrible whiskers flitted round me in silent criticism . . . ; the mate's whiskers became much concerned . . . ; He was . . . as it were deprived of the moral support of his whiskers") and by his horror at "the closeness of the shave" (687) when Leggatt is nearly discovered by the steward—this significance emerges when we recall two earlier passages in the narrative in which Leggatt refers to himself as the biblical figure of Cain, a cultivator, tiller, or "shaver" of the land, who killed his brother Abel and was forced to wander the earth. "Oh, yes!" Leggatt explains to the captain after recounting his tale of murder and slipping down into the stateroom, Captain Archbold's

"wife [was] on board [the *Sephora*]. . . . She would have been only too glad to have me out of the ship in any way. The 'brand of Cain' business, don't you see. That's all right. I was ready enough to go off wandering on the face of the earth—and that was price enough to pay for an Abel of that sort." (664)

Later, Leggatt explains his resolve to be set ashore:

"You must maroon me. . . . What does the Bible say? 'Driven off the face of the earth.' Very well. I am off the face of the earth now. As I came at night so I shall go."[8] (688)

Heard in connection with Leggatt's allusions to Cain, a tiller who plows, cuts the surface or shaves the land, the captain's enigmatic commands to "shave the land as close as possible" and to cut "close enough" so that the ship is "swallowed up" by the earth reveal their ciphered content. Through his orders and maneuvers with the ship the captain (unknowingly) identifies himself as a plower or tiller of the land. Being a tiller or "closely shaving the land" is itself linked in the passage, via the captain's behavior, with the violent, near-murderous shaking of an insubordinate mate, who is "deprived of the moral support of his whiskers" and who flees "as if . . . for dear life." This violent shaking, in turn, echoes Leggatt's account of killing the insubordinate sailor aboard the *Sephora*: "He gave me some of his cursed insolence at the sheet. . . . We closed just as an awful sea made for the ship. . . . I had him by the throat, and went on shaking him like a rat . . . I was holding him by the throat still when they picked us up" (659). The interweaving of these insistent references to shaving, shaking, tilling, and killing enables us to reconstruct, at least partially, the unspoken drama the captain stages in ciphered form while marooning Leggatt. By bringing "the ship closer" to shore in order to "shave the land as close as possible" and by violently shaking and figuratively "shaving" and nearly killing his whiskered mate, the captain draws upon Leggatt's metaphorical allusions to Cain, upon his account of shaking to death his shipmate, and upon his own personification of his mate's whiskers to act out symbolically the drama of a murder. Shaving the land means being a tiller, which means being a killer; it means violently shaking → shaving → (symbolically) killing a mate. The captain's seemingly incongruous behavior with his ship and mate emerges as the encoded and unwitting enactment of a secret killing he can neither state nor share because, we may deduce, it is lodged within him as a nescience, as an unknown knowledge kept secret by someone else and transmitted to him as a phantom.[9]

Precisely who was killed, who committed the murder, and under what circumstances cannot be determined from the elements available in the text. The fact that Leggatt is a chief mate and that the captain attacks his own mate suggests that a "mate"—husband or wife—was involved in the drama. The captain's nightly sequestering of Leggatt in his bunk supports this conjecture. Construed by some critics as evidence of a latent homosexual relationship between the two men, this behavior may be seen instead as a sign that the secret beyond the captain's reach involves two people who shared a bed, that the murder haunting him was a conjugal affair.[10]

Even without specific details of the secret's content and origins, reconstituting from the accessible elements of the narrative an unspeakable murder that perturbs the captain opens the way to explaining Leggatt's function in the text (the question that began this reading) and the reason the captain conceals him in his cabin and hallucinates sharing with him a secret. When Leggatt first arrives, the captain describes him as a "cadaverous, . . . headless corpse" (654), a "mute . . . mystery" (655) seemingly "risen from the bottom of the sea" (655). After hiding him, the captain disregards Leggatt's personal desires and intentions. He ignores his plan to swim off, keeping him in the stateroom despite his visible discomfort and annoyance ("He . . . stood . . . in that little space, his face looking very sunken . . . , the stern, dark line of his eyebrows drawn together by a slight frown [671]; "I pointed to the . . . little campstool. . . . He made a gesture . . . as if of regret" [681–82]), and he refers to him repeatedly as a shadowy or nonexistent figure: "I whispered. 'Now you must vanish into the bathroom.' He did so, as noiseless as a ghost" (671), "[A]n irresistible doubt of his bodily existence flitted through my mind" (686). The captain perceives Leggatt as a ghostly, silent figure without a recognizable identity or past and, hence, as a suitable object or "screen" onto whom he may project an identity or past of his own invention. When Leggatt announces that he has killed a man, the captain does just this, interrupting his account to "fill in" arbitrarily details of his own making:

> "I've killed a man. . . . When I say a man—"
>
> "Fit of temper," I suggested, confidently. . . .
>
> I did not think of asking him for details. . . . I needed no more. I saw it all going on as though I were myself inside that other sleeping suit. (657–58)

This perception of Leggatt as someone to be "filled in," coupled with the fact that the captain tells him to slip down into his stateroom only after Leggatt identifies himself as a mate who has killed a man, suggests the captain's reason for hiding the fugitive. Leggatt's crime must resonate with the secret killing, possibly involving a "mate," that haunts the captain. This resonance (not necessarily any real identity between the killings), together with Leggatt's anonymous, ghostlike appearance, makes him (from the captain's perspective) a suitable figure to incarnate the latter's internal drama. The captain's decision to hide Leggatt, in other words, is not arbitrary; we cannot presume he would behave in the same way with just any fugitive arrived at the ship. By concealing Leggatt in his stateroom and transforming his ghostly presence and specific drama of murder into an artificial secret, the captain creates a situation in which he can symbolically act out sharing the unspeakable killing beyond his ken. A "mute corpse risen from the sea," Leggatt becomes the "ghost" of the secret, buried without a tomb, that haunts the captain. He functions as an unwitting surrogate or "legate" for the person whose unspeakable drama is lodged inaccessibly within the captain as a phantom. The captain's obsessive references to Leggatt as his "double," "other self," "secret self," "secret sharer," and "secret partner," and his feelings of being "dual," "haunted," and "in two places at once" can all be understood as hallucinations through which he tacitly speaks of being cut off from someone whose secret he cannot share. Leggatt, in sum, is not the captain's secret sharer, double, or other self but a catalyst for hallucinations. He is a vehicle for symptom-formation whose concealed presence enables the captain to invent and play out scenarios of fictitious secret sharing that discreetly testify to the perturbing presence within him of an unshareable secret.

The specificity of Conrad's text, its particular interest for psychoanalytic literary interpretation, and what distinguishes it from the other tales discussed in this study and encountered elsewhere by this reader, is the manner in which the phantom's presence is inscribed in the text. The characters in the stories that follow will be seen to act out, virtually from beginning to end of each narrative, the specific contents of the unspeakable secrets haunting them and, in certain instances, the circumstances of the secret's transmission and the reasons for its creation. By contrast, the drama haunting the captain is only partially inscribed and acted out in only one episode of the text. The remainder of the narrative consists of the captain's repeated creation of fictitious scenarios of secret sharing as symptoms or ciphered statements of his estrangement from an unspeakable secret. The narrative's special interest lies in this particular kind of symptom-formation, in the fact that it functions principally as an allegory of the phantom structure. *The Secret Sharer* is a narrative constituted by the captain's unrecognized drive to invent external, imaginary dramas of secret sharing that duplicate and allegorize, by virtue of the lie of sharing at their core, the internal, psychic configuration specific to the phantom. The captain in effect hallucinates and lives out a semblance of a "dual unity," in which he falsely shares a secret with Leggatt, that obliquely points to the "pathological dual unity" or phantom structure in which he is trapped and in which, by definition, a secret cannot be shared. The constellation at the core of psychic distress in all the texts in this study—the inability to share a secret—is thus transformed, in *The Secret Sharer*, into a hallucinatory symptom whose obsessive repetition becomes the fundamental substance of the narrative itself.[11]

Viewing Conrad's text as an allegory of the phantom enables us to address the enigma of its title posed at the outset of the interpretation. Since there is no genuine secret sharer and no secret genuinely shared in the tale, the title itself has to be considered a fiction, as yet another hallucination created by the captain as part of his first-person narrative. The issues of the singular form, grammatical ambiguity, and potentially misleading nature of the title dissolve if we understand "The Secret Sharer" as a symptom of the captain's delusional transformation of Leggatt into someone with whom he imagines sharing a secret.[12] This also explains why the narrative had to be written in the first person. Since there exists no secret sharing and no secret sharer in the tale except from the captain's point of view, the account of this sharing could only have been told from his point of view—as a narrated hallucination.

In light of the foregoing analysis, we can also reconsider the tale's conclusion, perceived by the majority of readers as an uplifting affirmation of the captain's final attainment of self-knowledge.[13] As Leggatt prepares to "slip out" (697), the ship "come[s] to" (697), comes "round" (699), and slips back into the captain's awareness. With surprising ease for a man who seems so attached to his cabin mate and so reluctant to let him go, the captain "forg[ets]" (697) Leggatt and suddenly "remember[s]" (697) that he is a stranger to his vessel and ignorant of how she will respond. Searching for a sign of her speed and direction, he sees floating on the water's surface the hat he has given Leggatt for protection from the sun. Now able to judge the ship's movement, he orders the helm shifted:

> . . . I watched the hat. . . . It had been meant to save his homeless head from the dangers of the sun. And now—behold—it was saving the ship, by serving me for a mark to help out the ignorance of my strangeness. Ha! It was drifting forward, warning me just in time that the ship had gathered sternway.
>
> "Shift the helm," I said in a low voice. . . .
>
> . . . And all was so still in the world that I heard the quiet remark "She's round," passed in a tone of intense relief between two seamen.
>
> "Let go and haul."
>
> . . . Already the ship was drawing ahead. And I was alone with her. Nothing! no one in the world should stand now between us, throwing a shadow on the way of silent knowledge and mute affection, the perfect communion of a seaman with his first command. (698–99)

In the absence of any analysis or recognition on his part of the phantom haunting him, the captain's euphoric claim to have at last emerged from the "ignorance of [his] strangeness" (698) and to share finally "silent knowledge and . . . communion" (699) with his vessel has to be considered illusory. Whereas Leggatt swims off, a "free man . . . striking out for a new destiny" (699), the captain remains a prisoner of the phantom silently transmitted to him. Although he may have acquired some knowledge of how his ship handles, he has not been brought to any consciousness of the secret beyond his reach. His claim to share finally a secret, "silent communion" with his ship has therefore to be construed as yet another hallucination, as still one more symptom of his haunting.

The narrative's final episode is thus marked less by resolution than by a shift in the object with which the captain will henceforth act out sharing a secret. With Leggatt gone, the ship, with which the captain now claims to be joined in a secret partnership or communion, appears to become the new vehicle for symptom-formation, the catalyst through which the captain will presumably continue, in the absence of analysis or understanding, to create scenarios of artificial secret sharing. Precisely why the captain finds the ship a suitable vehicle for symptom-formation and how hallucinating sharing a secret with the vessel is related to the unspeakable drama of murder haunting him are questions the text prompts without enabling us to resolve.[14] We can nonetheless propose that some further light might be shed on the drama or dramas concealed in *The Secret Sharer* by a reading of the story in conjunction with Conrad's other sea adventures explicitly concerned with abandonment, marooning, isolation, and exile, such as *An Outcast of the Islands, Typhoon,* and *The Rescue,* or with those manifestly preoccupied with forms of haunting, including *The Nigger of the "Narcissus,"* in which a ship is haunted, and *The Shadow-line* (paired by Conrad with *The Secret Sharer* as one of his two "Calm-pieces"),[15] in which a captain is haunted by his dead predecessor. One might also look to *Under Western Eyes,* the novel on which Conrad halted work in order to write *The Secret Sharer* and that shares with the latter a preoccupation with concealment, secrets, asylum, murder, conjugal mates, and haunting. There is biographical evidence to suggest that Conrad took time off from his labored efforts to complete *Under Western Eyes* and wrote *The Secret Sharer* to pay for his maid Nellie's ulcer operation.[16] Another, not necessarily contradictory view would consider his finishing the novel not long after writing the short story as a possible sign that the novel in some way "completes" the short story. It is not inconceivable that *Under Western Eyes,* if reconsidered with the reading just elaborated in mind, may be revealed in some sense to "share a secret" with *The Secret Sharer.*[17]

CHAPTER 3

The Interred Sign

L'INTERSIGNE

BY AUGUSTE DE VILLIERS DE L'ISLE-ADAM

Le récit révèle, mais en le révélant, cache un secret:
plus exactement, il le porte.

[Narration reveals, but in revealing hides a secret:
more accurately, it carries it.]
(Maurice Blanchot)

ALTHOUGH he was considered a genius by Mallarmé and other French contemporaries, Jean-Marie-Mathias-Philippe-Auguste de Villiers de l'Isle-Adam (1838–1889) has traditionally lingered on the periphery of literary scholarship, known primarily as a contributor to the French symbolist movement and symbolist theater. The 1986 publication of the Pléiade edition of Villiers's complete works has given momentum to scholars who in recent years have undertaken to reassess Villiers's place in literary history and his role in the evolution of literary genres from the gothic to science fiction. While increased attention has been paid in this endeavor to Villiers's novel, *L'Eve future,* and to several of his short stories, relatively little close analysis has been done of his *Contes cruels.*[1] These works, which continue and expand upon the tradition of German romanticism established by Goethe, Hoffmann, and Tieck, are equally indebted to the French literary current of the fantastic, represented by Nerval, Gautier, and Maupassant, and to the spiritism and occultism of American writers like Hawthorne and Poe. Many of them share these authors' preoccupations with explaining or setting the scene of the enigmatic workings of the mind.

L'intersigne (1867),[2] the earliest of Villiers's *Contes cruels* and probably his best known, is a prime example of such a preoccupation in that it concerns a young man who falls prey to a series of hallucinations, visions, and altered psychic states. The story is particularly rich in implications because these "symptoms" can be interpreted without recourse to classical theories of repression and rhetorical displacement. The protagonist's visions and altered states of mind can instead be understood through the analysis of a secret hidden within the text.

Uncovering this secret hinges on an alternative view of the possible formations of psychic structures and on the availability of different interpretive approaches for detecting them. The result offers an insight into how a phantom can be formed and how a character's own narrative can be read as a symptom or symbol of its haunting presence.

L'intersigne begins when the young baron Xavier de la V***, after suffering one of his frequent attacks of spleen, decides to leave Paris, where he lives with his father, and seek peace of mind during a visit with his longtime friend Maucombe, the priest of Saint-Maur. Upon arriving at the vicarage, however, Xavier finds his sense of well-being erased by two bizarre hallucinations—visions in which both the house and the priest appear before him as hauntingly decrepit images, devoid of life. Xavier's anxiety increases when, in the middle of the night, he perceives a priest standing in the doorway to his room, solemnly holding out a black cloak. When Xavier is unexpectedly called back to Paris the next day, Maucombe offers to accompany him part of the way. As a penetrating rain begins to fall, Xavier persuades his friend to return home lest he fall ill. Agreeing to do so, Maucombe holds out his black cloak, in a gesture identical to that of the priest in Xavier's vision, and insists that the young man wear it for protection. Horrified by this inexplicable coincidence, Xavier flees Saint-Maur, leaving the cloak at a nearby hostel to be returned to Maucombe. Not until he arrives back in Paris does he learn that the priest had caught a chill on the open road and had died, three days later, wrapped in the cloak he had given Xavier—the cloak he had brought back from the Holy Land "and that had touched THE TOMB."

The principal line of inquiry orienting most commentaries on the story has, quite reasonably, been to relate Xavier's hallucinations and visions to the priest's death. The results of these investigations have consistently relied on a particular definition of the word *intersigne* that has a basis in the folklore and superstition of Britanny. "Intersigns," writes Pierre-Georges Castex, quoting from Anatole Le Braz's *La légende de la mort*, a work detailing Breton legends, "Intersigns announce death. But the person who perceives the intersign is rarely the one death threatens. . . . Intersigns are like the shadow, projected ahead, of what must happen."[3] This definition has led Castex and others to interpret the hallucinations and bizarre coincidences recounted in the story as a series of *intersignes* or premonitions warning of the priest's death.[4] While the critics' use of this meaning to interpret the text is understandable, especially in view of Villiers's Breton background, exclusive reliance upon it as the sole key to the text's enigmas leaves unexamined several noteworthy aspects of the tale. In particular, it does not account for the specific ingredients of Xavier's visions and of the descriptions of the cloak and the tomb that distinguish this tale from all other tales of premonition. The following reading aims to address the mysteries posed by these elements from a dual perspective. It proceeds by asking whether an assessment of the title as signifying something other than "premonition" could significantly alter our understanding of Xavier's visions and descriptions. At the same time, it questions whether an alternative interpretation of these textual elements might shed new light on what is meant by an *intersigne*.

1

We first meet Xavier emerging from a spiritualist séance, an experience he describes as "curieuse" (219) ("curious"), as apparently more mystifying than enlightening. Immediately following this session aimed at altering one's consciousness and communicating with the dead or the beyond, he suffers an attack of spleen. The sequential relationship between these two events is the first indication that the renewal of Xavier's anxiety is set off by his unsuccessful séance, by its failure to communicate some knowledge he may wish to obtain. When he describes the trip he is about to take to Saint-Maur in terms of a holy pilgrimage or journey toward some mystical, salutary wisdom beyond common awareness,[5] and when he speaks of his intention to do some "hunting" while there,[6] it gradually becomes clear (without ever being stated explicitly) that his decision to go is motivated by his desire to obtain what he failed to obtain from the séance, by his desire not only to escape his spleen but to seek its origin or cause.

This unstated motive is also evident in Xavier's description of Maucombe. The priest is a "savant . . . et docte recteur" (220–22) ("knowing . . . and learned rector") who can "set things right" (*rectus*) by giving strength and guidance to those with whom he speaks ("conversation fortifiante" [222] ["fortifying conversation"]). He is also an intermediary, a liaison between Xavier and some higher realm of meaning (un "parfait confesseur d[e] Dieu" [222] [a "perfect confessor of God"]). Gifted with an "intelligence mystique" (225) ("mystical intelligence"), Maucombe represents a link with what lies beyond reason and logic, a means of access by which Xavier may reach and ultimately possess a mystical knowledge that eludes him. He is in effect described as a medium, as a person identical to the one in a spiritualist séance through whom contact is made with the other world. When we add to this Xavier's reference to the evenings he and Maucombe will spend together as "veillées" (222), connoting "vigils for the dead," Xavier's purpose in visiting Saint-Maur can be made manifest.[7] He will try to re-create a séance. He will attempt to repeat, with Maucombe as his "medium," the scene through which the unknown may become known and something thus far "dead" to him may be communicated.

Xavier's description of Saint-Maur as a site where altered states of awareness can be achieved sustains this idea: "Ici l'on peut s'asseoir sur la pierre de la mélancolie! —Ici les rêves morts ressuscitent, devançant les moments de la tombe! . . . [I]ci la vue du ciel exalte jusqu'à l'oubli" (223). ("Here one can sit upon the stone of melancholy! —Here dead dreams come back to life, anticipating the moments of the tomb! . . . [H]ere the sight of heaven exalts one into forgetfulness!") Like the séance in Paris, Saint-Maur is a place where something dead ("stone of melancholy" = tombstone) or hidden, as in a dream long defunct ("dead dreams"), can approach while remaining undefinable and obscure ("melancholy" = "dark or black humor"). It is a place where a trancelike state of consciousness ("exalts one into forgetfulness") is associated with recalling something dead ("dead dreams come back to life") and perceiving a beyond ("the sight of heaven").

Yet if Xavier's choice of Saint-Maur as a refuge is motivated by a tacit wish to communicate with the beyond and gain some mysterious knowledge, the series of hallucinations he experiences reveals a conflicting wish, one that obliges the reader to reconsider what is meant in the text by "the beyond" and to recognize that it may instead refer to something "beyond Xavier's field of vision." Xavier's haunting view of Maucombe's house is exemplary in this regard:

> Etait-ce bien la maison que j'avais vue tout à l'heure? Quelle ancienneté me dénonçaient, *maintenant* [Villiers's italics], les longues lézardes, entre les feuilles pâles? —Cette bâtisse avait un air étranger; . . . le portail hospitalier m'invitait avec ses trois marches; mais, en concentrant mon attention sur ces dalles grises, je vis qu'elles venaient d'être polies, que des traces de lettres creusées y restaient encore, et je vis bien qu'elles provenaient du cimetière voisin, —dont les croix noires m'apparaissaient, à présent, de côté, à une centaine de pas. Et la maison me sembla changée à donner le frisson, et les échos du lugubre coup du marteau, que je laissai retomber, dans mon saisissement, retentirent . . . comme les vibrations d'un glas.
>
> . . . Très empressé de voir un visage qui m'aidât . . . à . . . dissiper le souvenir [de cette vue], je poussai le loquet [et] entrai. (223–24)

> [Was this really the house I had seen just a moment earlier? What antiquity was revealed to me, *now* (Villiers's italics), by the long crevices between the pale leaves? —This building had a strange air about it; . . . the hospitable doorway invited me with its three steps; but concentrating my attention upon these gray slabs, I saw that they had just been polished, that traces of engraved letters still remained on them, and I realized that they came from the neighboring graveyard, —whose black crosses now

became visible to me, on one side, about a hundred steps away. And the house seemed to me changed, in a frightening way, and the echoes of the lugubrious stroke of the knocker, which I let drop in my sudden fright, rang out . . . like the reverberation of a death knell.

. . . Eager to see a face that would help me . . . dissipate the memory (of this vision), I lifted the door latch (and) went in.]

The passage functions on two levels simultaneously. The pale, dying leaves, the front steps made from tombstones, the neighboring cemetery with its black crosses, and the ringing of a death knell all suggest the presence or close proximity of the dead. Yet those buried in the cemetery exist only as anonymous crosses; the person for whom the death knell tolls is unknown; and the tombstones, which serve normally to identify the dead, are illegible, their markings almost totally effaced by the passage of time. While the contents of Xavier's vision point to the proximity of the dead, they carefully preserve the secret of their identity. Although Xavier is apparently in the presence of elements beyond his usual awareness, these elements are presented as unavailable to his understanding, as things he cannot and must not see. Xavier's hallucination thus reveals him to be caught in a double structure in which something is both hidden and exposed, in which he is simultaneously shown something frightening and made to remain ignorant of it.

This same contradiction organizes Xavier's second hallucination, his vision of Maucombe:

La figure qui était devant moi n'était pas, ne pouvait pas être celle du souper! Ou, du moins, si je la reconnaissais vaguement, il me semblait que je ne l'avais vue, en réalité, qu'en ce moment-ci. Une seule réflexion me fera comprendre: l'abbé me donnait, humainement, la *seconde* [Villiers's italics] sensation que, *par une obscure correspondance*, sa maison m'avait fait éprouver.

La tête que je contemplais était grave, très pâle, d'une pâleur de mort, et les paupières étaient baissées. . . . —Sa personne s'était revêtue d'une solennité si soudaine que je fermai les yeux. Quand je les rouvris . . . le bon abbé était toujours là, —mais je le reconnaissais maintenant! —A la bonne heure! Son sourire amical dissipait en moi toute inquiétude. L'impression n'avait pas duré le temps d'adresser une question. Ç'avait été un saisissement, —une sorte d'hallucination. (227)

[The face before me was not, could not be the one from supper! or, at least, if I did vaguely recognize it, it seemed to me that I had not really seen it until this moment. A single reflection will make my meaning clear: the abbé gave me, in human form, the *second* (Villiers's italics) sensation that, *by some obscure correspondence*, had been given me by his house.

The head I looked upon was grave, very pale, with the pallor of death, and the eyelids were lowered. . . . —His person had become enveloped in solemnity so abruptly that I closed my eyes. When I opened them again . . . the good abbé was still there, —but I recognized him now! —And none too soon! His friendly smile made all my anxiety disappear. The impression had not lasted long enough to ask him a question. It had been a seizure, —a kind of hallucination.]

Described moments earlier as being in excellent health, Maucombe suddenly acquires an inexplicably deathlike and unearthly appearance that "corresponds," in some "obscure" way, to the house in Xavier's first hallucination. At first glance, this correspondence might seem based on the two visions' mutual resistance to understanding. A closer look reveals that their very modes of resistance are identical. The hallucinations correspond because their obscurity is generated by the same paradoxical system of vision: a system in which the eyes are forced shut ("I closed my eyes") or averted ("Eager to see a face that would help me dissipate [this vision]") at the apparent moment of revelation, a system that hides its significance at the instant it opens it to view.

What then might be the forbidding knowledge whose presence in the form of hallucinations causes Xavier to see things beyond the grasp of his understanding? Xavier's third hallucination offers some hints:

[J]e fus au milieu de la chambre. . . . Comme je m'approchais de la porte, une tache de braise, partie du trou de la serrure, vint errer sur ma main et sur ma manche. . . .

Une chose me paraissait surprenante: la *nature* [Villiers's italics] de la tache qui courait sur ma main. C'était une lueur *glacée, sanglante, n'éclairant pas*. . . . —Mais, en vérité, ce qui sortait ainsi du trou de la serrure me causait l'impression du regard phosphorique d'un hibou!

. . . [L]a porte s'ouvrit. . . . En face de moi, dans le corridor, se tenait, debout, une forme haute et noire, —un prêtre, le tricorne sur la tête. La lune l'éclairait tout entier, à l'exception de la figure. . . .

Le souffle de l'autre monde enveloppait ce visiteur. . . .

Tout à coup, le prêtre éleva le bras, avec lenteur, vers moi. Il me présentait une chose *lourde et vague*. C'était un manteau. Un grand manteau noir, un manteau de voyage. Il me le tendait, comme pour me l'offrir! . . .

Je fermai les yeux pour ne pas voir cela. Oh! je ne voulais pas voir cela! (228–30)

[I was in the middle of the room. . . . As I approached the door, a spot of glowing light, emanating from the keyhole, strayed along my hand and sleeve. . . .

One thing struck me as surprising: the *nature* (Villiers's italics) of the stain that ran along my hand. It was a *frozen* gleam, *blood-red, that gave off no illumination*. . . . —But, in all truth, what emanated from the keyhole gave me the impression of the phosphorescent gaze of an owl!

. . . (T)he door opened. . . . In front of me, in the corridor, stood a tall, black form, —a priest wearing a tricornered clerical hat on his head. The moon lit up his entire figure, except for his face. . . .

The breath of the other world enveloped this visitor. . . .

Suddenly, the priest raised his arm, slowly, toward me. He held out something *heavy and vague*. It was a cloak. A large black cloak, a travelling cloak. He held it out as if offering it to me! . . .

I closed my eyes so as not to see that. Oh! I did not want to see that!]

Projected into an altered and almost trancelike state of consciousness resembling the séance in Paris, Xavier once again perceives what appears to be a message from the beyond. Yet his description of the "blood-red stain" of light wandering on his sleeve suggests that this message or knowledge continues to elude him, that it is preserved in a "frozen" ("glacée") and intact state resistant to understanding ("n'éclairant pas" ["that gave off no illumination"]). No sooner does light ("lueur") and the potential for illumination or enlightenment touch Xavier than this same light is denied. The possibility of further vision is nevertheless maintained by an immediate substitution. An owl, a mythological figure of knowledge associated with Minerva, the goddess of wisdom, takes the place of the knowledge (whatever it may be) removed from view concerning the stain's significance. This same exchange of a figure of revelation for revelation itself is also evident in Xavier's description of the priest's gesture. If the priest's sacrifice of the cloak can be read as the uncovering and transmission of some message from the beyond ("The breath of the other world enveloped this visitor"), the cloak, whose meaning at this point in the text is totally mysterious ("something heavy and vague"), conceals the significance of that message. An object that covers and uncovers, the cloak functions metaphorically by shrouding whatever meaning it conveys.

What then can be made of Xavier's experience on the open road when Maucombe offers him his cloak for protection on his journey back to Paris? There would seem to be something different about this scene, which at first appears essentially identical to Xavier's third vision but which evokes within him the strongest sense of fear and horror he has yet experienced.[8] The difference is Maucombe himself. The identity of the priest in Xavier's nocturnal vision is unknown, his face hidden in shadow. Only on the road to Paris is Maucombe revealed to be at the center of this drama, to be the person who offers the cloak and literally uncovers himself to Xavier. This uncovering, not of an unknown priest but of Maucombe, marks a crucial shift in the text.

Until this point, Xavier's visions could conceivably have been read as messages from the beyond, as signs of some otherworldly knowledge. The dramatic uncloaking of Maucombe on the open road (foreshadowed by the substitution of the priest for the house in Xavier's second hallucination) reveals instead that the tormenting hallucinations Xavier suffers are somehow representative of something that is not (or cannot be) said between the two men. It reveals that these visions in some way link Maucombe with Xavier, that what Xavier is shown is not some otherworldly knowledge but a mystery (or secret, perhaps) associated with Maucombe. It is still unclear what mystery Maucombe withholds from Xavier and whether Xavier suspects that the knowledge he seeks could be related to the priest. The last event of the story provides some help toward solving these puzzles.

When Xavier arrives back home his father gives him a letter, sent by Maucombe's servant Nanon, announcing that the priest died from a chill caught on the open road three days after Xavier's departure. The priest's last words, as transcribed and repeated twice by Nanon, reveal that he died, "heureux d'être enveloppé à son dernier soupir et enseveli dans le manteau qu'il avait rapporté de son pèlerinage en terre sainte, *et qui avait touché* LE TOMBEAU" (238; Villiers's italics and capitals). ("happy to draw his last breath and be wrapped and buried in the cloak he had brought back from his pilgrimage to the Holy Land, *and that had touched* THE TOMB" [Villiers's italics and capitals].) The cloak "touched the tomb." What is concealed within the tomb and whose tomb it is remain unclear. Most readers have assumed it to be Christ's tomb.[9] The assigning of this particular referent to a term linked with several other elements in the text may be somewhat hasty. Nanon's letter, for example, states an immediate connection among the tomb, the cloak, and Maucombe, while both the cloak and Maucombe are already associated with Xavier's two visionary experiences in his room and on the road. The hallucinations, the cloak, Maucombe, and the tomb are all connected in the text. Precisely what constitutes this connection, what these elements have in common, and what they reveal about the contents of the tomb must now be determined.

2

The beginning of a response emerges from Nanon's letter, with its twice-repeated sentence and italicized and capitalized letters. Three different procedures call attention to words and letters in the text, procedures that echo the earlier description of the "traces de lettres creusées" ("traces of engraved letters") in Xavier's first hallucination and Nanon's announcement, the morning after Xavier's arrival, that a letter has just come for him: "—Voici une lettre 'très pressée' que le rural vient d'apporter" (232). (—"Here is a 'very pressing' letter that the postman has just brought.") The text is insistent. It tells the reader that its letters are inscribed, chiseled, and shaped (*creusées*),[10] pushed against each other so that they have become condensed, deformed, disordered (*pressées*).[11] It suggests to the reader that to interpret the text is to reorder the letters of its typographically stressed words and to read these words, and TOMBEAU in particular, as "lettres pressées" ("pressed letters").

What then has been pressed or squeezed into TOMBEAU? If we separate the word we see immediately *tombe eau*: "falls water" or "water falls." A reconfiguring of the letters yields *meau tombe* and its homophone *mots tombent*: "words fall." *Mots tombent*, in turn, evokes *Maucombe*. The initial attempt to iron out the pressing process in the text makes clear that a play of sounds is at stake, that the narrative's typographic insistence upon its letters simultaneously calls attention to the aural quality of its words. A new wrinkle must therefore be added to the task of interpretation. The text has to be heard as well as read. The ability to link *Maucombe* to *tombeau* by aural resonances and thus to "water that falls" leads the reader to surmise that there may be other words in the text, having to do with Xavier's visions perhaps, that also "fall as water." As only a few of the numerous examples to be found in the story reveal, the "obscure correspondence" connecting virtually all the narrative's elements—the hallucinations, Maucombe, and Xavier himself—is in fact the word *eau*.

An apparent incongruity in the text presents the first of these examples. Xavier's story begins, as he says, "—En 1876, au solstice de l'automne" (219) ("—In 1876, on the autumn solstice"), with a reference to the many "precipitous burials" (→ *tombeaux* → *tombe eau*) occurring in Paris at the time. In his critical edition of *L'intersigne*, Emile Drougard notes that there is no solstice in autumn and that Villiers's locution was undoubtedly an inadvertent error.[12] This "error," however, especially when read—and heard—in the context of burials and tombs, may be interpreted not as an error but as a sign that pressed or condensed within the story from its very beginning is the fact that *l'automne* → *l'eau tombe* → "the water falls."

Water can also be found in Xavier's third hallucination and in his reaction to his vision of the priest:

> Je fermai les yeux. . . . Oh! je ne voulais pas voir cela! Mais un oiseau de nuit, avec un cri affreux, . . . me les fit rouvrir. . . . [J]'étais *glacé*; le front *trempé de sueur*. . . . Il me fallut plus d'une minute avant d'*oser* [Villiers's italics] remuer. . . .

> Je résolus de boire un verre *d'eau froide*.... Cependant la fatigue me prit comme *une vague*....
>
> [J]e me réveillai [à] une matinée heureuse....
>
> Complètement ranimé par des *ablutions réitérées d'eau fraîche*, je descendis. (230–31)
>
> [I shut my eyes.... Oh! I did not want to see that! But a night-bird, with a fearful cry, ... made me open them again....
>
> (I) was *cold as ice*; my forehead *drenched in sweat*.... It took me more than a minute before I *dared* (Villiers's italics) to stir....
>
> I resolved to drink a glass of *cold water*.... But fatigue came over me like *a wave*....
>
> (I) awoke (to) a joyous morning....
>
> Completely revived by *repeated splashings of cool water*, I went downstairs.]

The passage mentions water in numerous forms ("cold as ice ... drenched in sweat ... a glass of cold water ... a wave ... repeated splashings of cool water"). It also suggests that opening one's eyes to what is hidden from view in it means hearing fearful sounds and, as Villiers's italics underscore, "*oser* remuer" or "*daring* to stir or shake up" the text. Even before the story begins, the text's Latin epigraph hints that the tale can be re-formed and translated with the sound of water in mind; that to understand what is condensed within it one should read, as the first words of the epigraph command, with the ears: *Attende, homo* (Hear, o man) → "Hear *homo*" → "Hear (in French) *eau mot*" → "Hear the word 'water.' "[13]

The word "water" appears to be woven throughout the text. Indeed it may even be found in the enigmatic *manteau* offered to Xavier. If we obey the commands of the text, implied by the description of the cloak as "très vieux et même rapiécé, recousu, redoublé" (237), and we read this word literally as something "very old, scrambled and pieced or sewn back together, lined or doubled inside," we hear in *manteau* the words *mainte eau*: "a great quantity of water" (*mainte* = the archaic or "very old" form of *beaucoup*). Maucombe himself, at the moment he extends the cloak to Xavier, cryptically conveys that *manteau* may be taken or heard in this way: as "*mainte eau, beaucoup d'eau*": "—Allons! ... *prenez, —prenez ce manteau*! [Villiers's italics] —J'y tiens *beaucoup*! ... *beaucoup*!" (235) ("—Come now ... *take, —take this cloak*! [Villiers's italics] —I am *very much* attached to it! ... *very much*!")

Through a variety of anagrammatic, homophonic, paronomastic, and synonymic procedures involving separating and re-forming what has been pressed together and deformed in the text, the word "water" can be confirmed as a link joining Maucombe, *manteau*, and

Xavier's third and fourth visions. To clarify how Xavier's first and second visions fit into this sequence and how Xavier himself may be connected to "water," a look at the first sentence of the text, the narrator's introduction to the tale Xavier recounts, is helpful: "Un soir d'hiver ... nous prenions le thé ... chez l'un de nos amis, le baron Xavier de la V*** (un pâle jeune homme ...)" (218). ("One winter evening ... we were having tea ... in the home of one of our friends, the baron Xavier de la V*** [a pale young man ...].") Typographic signs (***) once again call attention to words that have somehow been imprinted, pressed, or suppressed within the text, words like the others similarly signaled in the narrative that may be heard as well as seen. Indeed by hearing Xavier's condensed patronymic the reader can discern its link with water. Pronounced aloud, *de la V**** rhymes with the adjective *délavé*: soaked or inundated with water, faded, washed out, pale (*Robert*). Xavier's name is thus connected to all the forms of falling water, rain, drenching, soaking, and washing in the text. At the same time, it reveals how those hallucinations as yet unrelated to these elements may be joined to them. For the word "pale" is found in the text not just in Xavier's name and in the description of him immediately following his name ("a *pale* young man"). It is present in his self-portrayal at the beginning of his story ("je m'aperçus que j'étais mortellement *pâle*!" [220] ["I noticed that I was deathly *pale*"]); in his first hallucination of Maucombe's decrepit house surrounded by "*pale* leaves"; in his second vision of a moribund Maucombe, "very *pale*, with a *pallor* of death"; and in both his third hallucination and its reenactment on the open road in which the light of the moon is twice described as "déserte et *pâle*" (229, 234) ("desolate and *pale*"). If there is an "obscure correspondence" among Xavier's hallucinations, TOMBEAU, Maucombe, *manteau*, and Xavier himself, it is because this correspondence is literally obscured from view, because it cannot be seen but must instead be heard—heard in all its various forms activated within the text: in the synonyms, homophones, rhymes, and anagrams of *délavé*.

Still unexplained is the significance of *délavé*. We can state that "de la V***" is a narrative convention, normally used to indicate the absence or censoring of a name, and that *délavé* fills in this absence. Why it should do so is as yet incomprehensible. If we are to solve this puzzle, it will be useful to recapitulate certain key steps taken to arrive at this point in the interpretation. The word that revealed the importance of *eau* in the text and that led to reading Xavier's name as *délavé* was TOMBEAU. TOMBEAU, as Nanon's letter told us, was touched by Maucombe's *manteau*, itself seen to include the word *eau* and given by Maucombe to Xavier for his return to Paris. When Xavier receives from Maucombe his cloak, therefore, he also receives a cryptic communication from Maucombe, concerning "water," that refers to his own name, *de la V****. The transmission of the garment, in other words, and Maucombe's insistence that Xavier "take this cloak!" ("prenez ce manteau!") may be understood as a message about Xavier's own semantically charged patronymic. It can be read as a cipher one could paraphrase as follows: "Xavier, take this *manteau* as yours. Take this *délavé* as yours. Xavier, your name is not *de la V**** but *délavé*!"

Why such an obscure communication would take place is not readily apparent. One is left to wonder what Xavier's name could possibly hide that would cause Maucombe to transmit this bizarre message. What it hides, a further reading reveals, is the mysterious knowledge from the beyond Xavier has sought to gain, the communication from the "au-delà" whose significance has remained outside his awareness. By listening to Xavier's name as it appears in the text, we can hear in *Xavier de la V**** "Sa vie est délavée" ("His life is soaked, inundated") and its rhyme, "Sa vie est de l'abbé" ("His life is from the abbé"). Xavier, it seems, is "from the abbé." What has soaked, rained down upon, and infiltrated his life, rendering it and him pale and diseased, appears to be the fact that the priest Maucombe is his father. From its very beginning, the text cannily yet emphatically sustains this admittedly surprising conclusion. The epigraph, for example, an excerpt from the *Méditations* by Saint Bernard, describes man as an "inferior" being, born of "fetid sperm," who does not know his origin:

> Attende, homo, quid fuisti ante ortum et quod eris usque ad occasum. Profecto fuit quod non eras. Postea, *de vili materia factus*, in utero matris de sanguine menstruali nutritus, tunica tua fuit *pellis secundina*. Deinde, in vilissimo panno involutus, progressus es ad nos, —sic indutus et ornatus! *Et non memor es quae sit origo tua. Nihil est aliud homo quam sperma foetidum. . . .* (218)

> [Hear, o man, what you were before you were born, and what you will be until your death. Truly, there was a time when you did not exist. Then, *made of vile material*, nourished in your mother's womb from menstrual blood, your garment was *inferior hide*. Next, wrapped in the most vile rag, you came out to us, —in this way clothed and adorned! *And you do not remember what your origin is. Man is nothing but fetid sperm. . . .*]

These allusions to a sordid and inferior birth are followed almost immediately by Xavier's description of the oppressive spleen from which he suffers (and which prompts his visit to Maucombe) as "héréditaire" (219) ("hereditary"), as originating with his parent(s). His hallucinations, in turn, provide evidence of who this (these) parent(s) might be. The fissured and crumbling walls Xavier envisions upon arriving at the presbytery are readable as signs of a loss of integrity not only in the house of Maucombe but in the "house"—family or lineage—of Maucombe. They can be interpreted, as the second hallucination confirms, to reveal that there is something about Maucombe himself that is diseased, disintegrated, no longer intact. Similarly, the "blood-red stain" of light Xavier perceives, while in Maucombe's home, as literally within his grasp (which "strayed [*errer*] along my hand and sleeve") suggests he is touched by some "blood" or familial stain, tainted by something or someone close at hand who has strayed or erred. It is Maucombe, however, who, in response to Xavier's expression of affection, tacitly confesses what he has done and reveals the nature of the familial stain touching Xavier:

> —Mon cher Maucombe ... c'est une chose de toute éternité que l'amitié intellectuelle, et je vois que nous partageons ce sentiment.
>
> —Il est des esprits chrétiens d'une parenté divine très rapprochée, me répondit-il. —Oui. —Le monde a des croyances moins "raisonnables" pour lesquelles des partisans se trouvent qui sacrifient leur sang, leur bonheur, leur devoir. (224–25)

> [—My dear Maucombe . . . a friendship of the mind is eternal, and I see that we share this feeling.
>
> —There are Christian spirits endowed with a divine kinship of the closest kind, he answered me. —Yes. —The world has some beliefs less "reasonable" for which partisans can nonetheless be found to sacrifice their blood, their happiness, their duty.]

Maucombe's words, which Xavier describes as "empreintes de science et ... soutenues par une voix bien timbrée" (225) ("imprinted with knowledge and . . . sustained by a resonant voice"), can be heard to resonate with a knowledge pressed within them. Through his response, Maucombe recasts Xavier's description of their rapport as a "divine *kinship*" and, as a rephrasing of his comment reveals, covertly confesses the source of this kinship while urging Xavier to divine it: "Devine ta parenté. Nous sommes très rapprochés car j'ai perdu la raison et sacrifié le sang, l'intégrité d'une famille." ("Guess your lineage. We are very close because I lost all reason and sacrificed the blood, the integrity of a family.")

The significance of *délavé* is perhaps most cryptically and yet most concretely revealed, however, by Maucombe's reaction to news that Xavier must leave Saint-Maur and by his offer to accompany him part of the way:

> —Positivement, c'est fâcheux! dit l'abbé. . . . La grande affaire, c'est le salut: j'espérais être pour quelque chose dans le vôtre —et voici que vous vous échappez! . . .

—Mon ami, *l'express* part à neuf heures précises.... [J]e vous quitte à l'instant.

—Je vous accompagnerai un peu, dit le prêtre: *cette promenade me sera salutaire.* (232–33; Villiers's italics throughout)

[—How very distressing! said the abbé.... The great question is salvation: I had hoped to play a part in yours —and here you are escaping me! ...

—My friend, the *express* leaves at exactly nine o'clock.... I must leave you immediately.

—I will accompany you a part of the way, said the priest: *The walk will do me good.* (Villiers's italics throughout)]

Maucombe speaks of salvation (*salut*) as an *affaire,* a word frequently used to mean "difficulty, problem, scandal." At the same time, the word *salut* (in its sense of "hail, greetings, salutation") is French for the Latin *ave,* a translation brought to mind by the Latin ecclesiastical epigraph. When we put these two elements together and hear in the typographically stressed word *salutaire* → *salut taire* → "the silencing of *salut*" → "the silencing of the scandal," a cryptic communication emerges from Maucombe's dialogue with Xavier. "The great problem or scandal," the abbé may be understood to say, "is the *salut,* the *ave.* I hoped to reveal that I have some part in your *ave,* in your scandal that has been silenced. I, the abbé, ultimately hoped to state that your *salut* (salvation) is in the *ave,* that your name is Xavier *de l'abbé,* that your life is 'from the abbé,' that you are my illegitimate, *natural* son."[14]

Through his hallucinations, his conversation with Maucombe, his receipt of Maucombe's cloak, and even his reading of the abbé's last words, Xavier is cryptically communicated the identity of his true father. Yet he never grasps this communication, never recognizes that his experiences are a matter for interpretation and contain something that must be understood. When he recounts his story, he adopts the role of a pure reporter of events, of a narrator, as he himself states, with no intention of commenting on what has been communicated to him: "—Voici une histoire ... que je n'accompagnerai d'aucun commentaire. Elle est véridique. Peut-être la trouverez-vous impressionnante" (219). ("—Here is a story that ... I will recount without any commentary. It is a true story. You may find it impressive.") It is up to the reader to recognize that the events Xavier recounts and decides to treat as "insignificant coincidence" (237) do in fact have significance. It lies with the reader to realize that the entire spiritualist and religious frame of the story—the séance, the "pilgrimage to Canaan," the hallucinations of the presbytery and of the priest, the *manteau* from the Holy Land, the *tombeau*—is a way of intimating what can never be explicitly expressed: Xavier carries within himself something that is "beyond him," something to which his eyes have been opened in hallucinations only but that remains beyond his reach—the story of his origin.

When Xavier leaves Saint-Maur and claims to have finally escaped from the realm of nightmares and death ("Je quittais le pays des cauchemars! . . . Je sortais de la Mort" [236] ["I left the land of nightmares! . . . I emerged from Death"]), the reader understands that he has in fact done the opposite—that he has been embraced by the realm of the beyond, by death. In fleeing *Saint-Maur*, Xavier is not just covered by Maucombe's cloak. He is "wrapped" (*ceint*, homophonous with "Saint") in the cloak that enshrouds the *sein-mort* (homophonous with Saint-Maur), that covers at death (*mort*) the father to whose "breast" (*sein*) he once was (or should have been) held. Departing Saint-Maur covered in the cloak, Xavier is wrapped in and weighed down by the secret of his "fetid" origin: "Je m'efforçai de hausser les épaules; un poids secret m'en empêcha" (235). ("I forced myself to shrug my shoulders but a secret weight prevented me.") He is weighed down by the word *manteau*, and thus by *tombeau* → *Maucombe* → *mot* (*in*)*combe*: by a word (*mot*) involving Maucombe that "weighs upon" him (*incombe*), by *délavé* → *de l'ave* → *de l'abbé*.[15]

It is this weight that Xavier transforms into a narrative. While Maucombe was alive, the possibility always existed that he would reveal his identity to Xavier. With Maucombe's death, the possibility of such revelation disappears. Xavier, however, is not left without a legacy. He becomes the unknowing caretaker of his father's secret. By narrating his story, he keeps alive the knowledge buried with Maucombe and preserves intact the secret from "the beyond" that has been silently transmitted to him by the abbé. Xavier is thus far more than the pure, disinterested reporter of events he claims to be. He is a man "living with the dead," with the ghostly presence of his true father encrypted within the words of his tale. He is a man living with a phantom, with an unknown knowledge that has never been and can never be divulged, with the secret of his father that has been cryptically passed on to him and that he unwittingly carries within him, ignorant both of its content and of the fact that it even exists. Xavier's narrative becomes in essence the tomb of Maucombe's secret, the hidden resting place of his unspeakable drama. In this sense it is a true "ghost" story: a story about how a secret kept by the father concerning his child becomes a ghost within that child—a ghost that haunts but is never perceived; a phantom born from the grave or TOMBEAU of the father that survives within the crypt or tomb, that is, within the narrative created by the son.

Xavier is thus a cipher who, through his telling, gives himself to be read. He is an enigma contained within his own story who cannot understand the message it simultaneously conceals and reveals about him. The task of the reader is to decipher this message, to see that *tombeau, manteau, Maucombe, salut, pâle* all hide the key to unscrambling this cipher, hide the key not by any simple metaphoric or metonymic substitution, nor by any readily discernible phonetic, semantic, or rhetorical displacement. Rather they hide the key by a displacement to the second or even third or fourth degree, by a combination of two or more of a variety of lexical relationships including homophony, paronomasia, synonymy, interlinguistic synonymy, and anagrammatization. The reader's charge is to see that these words, which have been pressed, squeezed, inscribed, and deformed, are *cryptonyms,* "words that hide" another seemingly unrelated word through a network of linguistic connections encrypted within them. If homophony transforms *tombeau* into *tombe eau,* synonymy in the text exposes *délavé,* paronomasia *de l'abbé.* Where interlinguistic synonymy uncovers the Latin *ave* in *salut,* rhyming reveals *abbé* in *ave.* To interpret Xavier's tale is therefore to reveal the various (and theoretically infinite) techniques by which meanings are carried or borne from one place, state, or form to another. It means recognizing that the *intersigne* of the text's title, while it may on one level signify an announcement or premonition of death, also refers to "the sign within," to the encrypted signs hidden within and elided from between the words constitutive of the text's substance and its enigma. The "intersign" of the title is an *interred sign,* the sign inscribed and enshrouded within the narrative that reveals Xavier's buried identity, his unspoken yet audible name, the words: *de la V*** → délavé → de l'ave → de l'abbé.*

3

With its hallucinations, visionary experiences, and mystico-religious elements, *L'intersigne* fits well within the generally recognized parameters of fantastic or uncanny literature. Yet what haunts Xavier is not the return of the repressed, a structure psychoanalytic criticism has traditionally associated with works of this genre. Xavier's symptoms testify to his unwitting membership in a pathogenic dual unity, in a "divine kinship" with his secret father, Maucombe, that has prevented him from living life as his own. His visions, spleen, attendance at séances, and desire for mystical intelligence are all symbolic creations by which he cryptically describes himself as driven by an unspeakable drama of illegitimacy beyond his grasp. The death of Maucombe and the loss of the possibility of revelation mark a significant shift in this process of symbolization. Where before Xavier used spiritualist mediums to grope for the unspeakable knowledge beyond his ken, he now transforms himself into a conduit for this knowledge. He becomes the medium of Maucombe's message. Reciting his tale without commentary, Xavier acts as a ventriloquist's dummy, an uncomprehending transmitter of his father's disembodied voice, which speaks through him from the grave to utter enigmatically the secret lying buried with him.

The metaphors of the disembodied voice and the ventriloquist's dummy are not exclusive to *L'intersigne*. My ongoing research on Villiers suggests that they are present in some form in a variety of his texts and can be viewed as evidence of his preoccupation with the haunting effects and incarnations of the phantom. In *Contes cruels* as varied as *Véra, L'inconnue, Le désir d'être un homme, Le traitement du docteur Tristan, Vox populi,* and *Le secret de l'ancienne musique,* in other short works including *Le tueur de cygnes* and *Claire Lenoir,* and in *L'Eve future,* a science fiction novel about the creation of a speaking robot, Villiers systematically links the presence of mental disorder, the ability to "hear" unspoken messages, the possibility of transgenerational communication, and feelings of being possessed or inhabited to figures of ventriloquism and to mechanical devices that function by separating the voice from its source.[16] While it would be overstating the case to extend these preoccupations to all of Villiers's writings, their prevalence in significant numbers of his narratives opens a heretofore unexplored avenue for evaluating his contribution to literature. The current reassessment of the quality, nature, and genres of Villiers's writings and of his role as a precursor of the decadent and science fiction movements emergent in the late nineteenth century could well profit from an analysis of his works pursued with these concerns in mind and with the interpretive possibilities of the phantom and cryptonymy at hand. Such an undertaking might also contribute to interpreting texts traditionally classified as gothic, fantastic, uncanny, mystical, supernatural, symbolist, or science fiction, all categories that have been used to describe Villiers's oeuvre. My reading of *L'intersigne* may be considered a first step in this undertaking.

CHAPTER 4

Legacies of Gold

HONORÉ DE BALZAC'S *FACINO CANE*

L'or et le plaisir. Prenez ces deux mots comme une lumière . . .

[Gold and pleasure. Take these two words as a light . . .]
(Balzac, *La fille aux yeux d'or*)

IT IS a truism that the passion for gold is a dominant theme woven throughout Balzac's works. From *Eugénie Grandet* to *Le cousin Pons*, *Le père Goriot* to *Gobseck*, gold is a much-desired object, fought and schemed for by nobles and peasants, bankers and merchants, lovers and enemies alike. In the vast field of Balzac criticism, *Facino Cane* has more often than not been viewed as a footnote to Balzac's pursuit of this theme, as one more instance of an obsession with gold leading to financial and personal ruin. This exemplary aspect of the tale is beyond dispute.

The story nevertheless raises another question: the origin of the obsession that holds the title character in its grip. When Facino Cane notes that his mother, during her pregnancy, also had a passion for gold, he gives the impression that some special communication occurred between mother and son that precludes accepting this passion at face value in the text. The possibility that Facino Cane's obsession is in some sense "inherited" prompts the conjecture that a phantom may be at work in the narrative. This seems a promising hypothesis given that obsessive behavior is often, although not always, symptomatic of the presence of a phantom, and in light of Cane's incongruous, repetitive, self-destructive manner of life, which includes adulteries, thefts, imprisonment, exile, sudden blindness, and total destitution, and which makes him appear, in the most banal sense of the term, a man possessed. Cane acts as if driven by forces beyond his control. In the context of the preface to his tale, in which an anonymous narrator describes his own uncanny ability to inhabit other people and assume their identities, it does not seem farfetched to wonder whether other characters in the story, and Cane in particular, might be similarly "inhabited" by someone or something else.

This reading aims to respond to this question and to discover a means of making intelligible Facino Cane's perplexing obsession. It happens that various elements and structures in Balzac's tale also lend themselves to Freudian and Lacanian modes of analysis. While my intent is not to offer complete interpretations of the story based on these analytic models, I will take advantage of the inherent richness of the text to sketch out the directions such interpretations could take. This will provide an opportunity to compare these psychoanalytic approaches to literature with my own and to illustrate some of the ways, discussed in chapter 1 of this study, in which the implications for literary analysis of the theory of the phantom and of the workings of cryptonymy differ from the theories and models of Freud and Lacan.

1

First published in the *Chronique de Paris* in March of 1836, *Facino Cane*[1] begins when a struggling young writer, who narrates the tale, describes his remarkable ability to identify with the people he observes and live their lives as his own. He promises to tell the reader all the unusual stories he has accumulated through his observations and begins with the tale of Facino Cane, the blind, impoverished musician he encounters at the wedding of his housekeeper's daughter and with whom he identifies immediately. Excited by this strange character whose dead eyes reflect memories of some bizarre odyssey lived in the past, the narrator questions him, trying to understand how he came to such a miserable end. The young writer gives the narration over to Facino Cane at this point, and the blind man recounts, with virtually no descriptive embellishment, the astonishing series of events that led him to lose his fortune, title, country, and eyesight.

Born a prince of Venetian nobility with an obsession for gold, Facino Cane has spent his life searching for the precious metal. One day in his youth, with his money lost at gambling, he seeks out his lover Bianca. When the two are discovered together by her husband, a wealthy senator, Cane strangles him and flees Venice to escape punishment. He returns in secret to find Bianca and is confronted by a new rival, a Provedittore or state official, who surprises the two lovers in bed. Cane wounds his adversary but is ultimately caught, imprisoned, and condemned to death. He escapes with the aid of the jailer, steals part of the treasure of the ruling Dukes, which he finds buried in a crypt next to the prison, and hides for several years in France, London, Amsterdam, and Madrid, finally settling in Paris under an assumed name. Here, reveling in his enormous fortune of gold, Cane suddenly goes blind.

Forced to reveal his true identity to the woman he now loves (Bianca has died), he is robbed by her of his fortune and committed to the mental hospital at Bicêtre. After the revolution, he enters the Quinze-Vingts, a home for the blind and destitute.

Cane ends his story here. He begs the narrator to accompany him to Venice to recover the riches still remaining there. Moved by the blind man's tale, the narrator agrees to join him, but Facino Cane dies before they can depart.

The two events marking the beginning of Cane's story—his strangling of Bianca's husband and his wounding of the Provedittore—could well suggest an Oedipal structure. Cane's rivals are never identified by name in the text but by their positions of authority: Bianca's husband is a senator or maker of laws; her new lover is a Provedittore or state official who enforces the law. The name of the woman in this repeated triangular structure, "Bianca," is the feminine form of *bianco*, meaning "white,""glittering," "brilliant," and "silvery," and is associated with the image of gold.[2] This is pertinent in view of Cane's comment at the outset of his narrative that his mother, during her pregnancy, had a passion for gold, and that he himself has always had for the metal an obsession whose satisfaction is necessary to his existence. If we follow the Freudian paradigm, a pattern of substitution can be established in which Facino Cane's obsession with gold and his desire for Bianca may be interpreted as the visible symptoms of an unconscious desire for his mother. Bianca's husband and the Provedittore, each figures of the law laying claim to Bianca, can be construed as Oedipal "father figures" who, in manifestly blocking Cane's access to Bianca, symbolically prohibit him from possessing his mother. Facino Cane's sudden blindness at the moment he possesses gold would be interpreted as a symbolic castration resulting from his figurative transgression of the incest prohibition. Possessing gold would signify the satisfaction of the unconscious desire to kill his father and sleep with his mother, crimes that must be punished.

An outline of a Lacanian reading might begin by noting that, in desiring gold, Facino Cane desires the object desired by his mother. In Lacanian theory, the object desired by the mother is the phallus. Cane's story could then be viewed as a lifelong quest to possess the phallus. Based on the meanings of Bianca's name already noted, Bianca would be seen as a substitute for gold and thus, by the process Lacan calls metonymy, a substitute for the phallus. The repeated events in which Bianca and gold slip from Cane's grasp would constitute a signifying chain situating Facino Cane as a subject marked by lack, by the impossibility of possessing the phallus and hence fulfilling his desire: to be the object of his mother's desire. Cane's sudden blindness at the moment he finally seems to possess gold would be construed in terms of his failure to assimilate lack as constitutive of his being. Blindness would be a metaphor of the delusional structure of the Imaginary in which Facino Cane would now be fixed, a structure identifying the subject as blind to the fictive nature of his apparent wholeness and to the impossibility of grasping the phallus. For Freud, the text would be a symbolic account of King Oedipus's plight and of the vicissitudes wrought by the transgression of the incest prohibition. Lacan would consider the story an allegory of the subject's fixation in the Imaginary resulting from his failure to accept the inaccessibility of the object of desire and the incessant slippage of the phallus, both of which define him as a subject in language and as subject to language, as an effect of the signifier.[3]

2

To delineate an alternative to these reading approaches, an as yet unmentioned element of the narrative consonant with the idea of enigmatic transmissions—the proliferation of foreign languages—suggests itself as a point of departure. Although Facino Cane speaks French throughout his tale, his Italian origins surface when he replies in his native tongue to the narrator, who asks him if he is descended from the famous condottiere Facino Cane. "—*E vero*" (1024; Balzac's italics), he says. "—It's true." Besides French and Italian, Arabic, Armenian, and Latin are also mentioned in the tale. While waiting in his prison cell to be decapitated for his attack on the Proveditore, Cane is able to decipher a message etched in Arabic on the stone wall because he is fluent in Arabic, having studied Semitic languages in an Armenian convent.[4] At the end of his narrative, Cane plays on his clarinet a mournful tune described as "quelque chose comme le *Super flumina Babylonis*" (1031; Balzac's italics) ("something like the *Super flumina Babylonis*"). This Latin reference to a biblical psalm recalls the tower of Babel (Babylon was also called Babel), a figure of the multiplicity and confusion of languages.

The variety of forms in which Facino Cane's name appears in the text spells out the profusion of tongues. Although he was born in Italy as *Marco Facino Cane, principe de Varese,* Cane's name undergoes a series of transformations that shorten it—*Facino Cane,* gallicize it—*le père Canet,* deform it—*le père Canard,* and totally eclipse it behind an unspecified Spanish pseudonym.[5] The problem of language raised by the multiplicity of tongues in the story is complemented by the problem of Facino Cane's name, and hence perhaps of his identity.[6]

One wonders whether there might be some connection between the problems of language and proper names in the text and Facino Cane's passion for gold. Cane's comment that the names of his ancestors were inscribed in the *Livre d'or* (Book of gold) implies that this may be the case.[7] "Gold" here is not a metal. It is a word in the title of a book of noble genealogy, of a social register in which the names of nobility were written in letters of gold. Appearing initially as a metal, "gold" is transformed into a medium of writing and is metaphorically related to the history of Facino Cane's family name. Given this association of the word *or* ("gold") with genealogy in the *Livre d'or*, and in view of the adulterations of Facino Cane's name in the text, it can be surmised that Cane's genealogy may itself be problematic. It is unlikely, in other words, that the testimony of the *Livre d'or* can be taken at face value. Where then might we look to find Facino Cane's genealogy? The text's numerous and seemingly incongruous references to Semitic languages, to the Rothschild family, and to the Jews' captivity in Babylon (recounted in the *Super flumina Babylonis*, the 137th Psalm) provide a response.[8] Through their sheer insistence these elements suggest a Jewish context for Facino Cane's origins. They point to a Semitic language never explicitly mentioned in the text: Hebrew. Hebrew, in turn, allows us to hear a new, linguistic form of "gold." For when the French word for gold (*or*) is pronounced, it is aurally indistinguishable from the Hebrew word OR (אור) meaning "light." The original site of the Hebrew word for "light" is a book of origins and genealogy: the Book of Genesis.[9]

The question that began the analysis can be reformulated in terms of this newly uncovered information: what is the significance of Facino Cane's lifelong passion for gold given the apparently Jewish context of his genealogy? If we hear *or* in Hebrew (אור) meaning "light," we can infer that the real object of Cane's passion is light or "enlightenment" about his Jewish origins. This inference is reinforced by the absence of any mention of Cane's father in the text and by Cane's mother who, having had a passion for gold during her pregnancy, appears to have transmitted it to Cane at birth as his "inheritance":

> "Que les fantaisies d'une femme influent ou non sur son enfant pendant qu'elle le porte ou quand elle le conçoit, il est certain que ma mère eut une passion pour l'or pendant sa grossesse. J'ai pour l'or une monomanie dont la satisfaction est si nécessaire à ma vie que dans toutes les situations où je me suis trouvé, je n'ai jamais été sans or sur moi; je manie constamment de l'or; jeune, je portais toujours des bijoux et j'avais toujours sur moi deux ou trois cents ducats." (1026–27)

> ["Whether or not a woman's fancies influence her child while she is carrying him or when she conceives him, it is certain that, during her preg-

nancy, my mother had a passion for gold. I have a mania for gold whose satisfaction is so necessary to my life that, whatever situation I have been in, I have never been without gold in my possession. I handle gold all the time. When I was young I always wore jewelry and I always had two or three hundred ducats on me."]

The bizarre events of Facino Cane's life begin to emerge as parts of a concealed but identifiable drama. A secret has been created concerning Facino Cane's origins, a secret conceived by his mother upon his conception or birth and transmitted to him as a passion for gold. Instead of the identity of his father, Cane receives from her as his patrimony a quest for his origins couched in an obsession with gold (*or*). Cane's sudden blindness at the moment he finally possesses gold can also be explained in terms of this secret patrimony.[10] The loss of sight is a physical expression of the impossibility of his ever seeing his origins and gaining light or enlightenment about his genealogy. The fact that, after going blind, Cane is robbed of his gold and abandoned by his new lover in "Hyde Park" underscores the idea that his origins must remain hidden and never brought to light.[11]

Facino Cane's blindness is thus a tacit acknowledgment that his quest for enlightenment about his origins has to remain unfulfilled, that there is some shame attached to his birth by his mother—presumably because his biological father was a Jew and not a Cane—that is unspeakable and must never be perceived. Cane carries this secret shame within him from the moment of his birth until his death, never knowing either its content or the fact of its existence. Although the code to deciphering the secret is contained within the mother's legacy to her son (the word *or*), the cryptonymic structure of the code effectively conceals the secret's presence and prevents its ever being deciphered by him.[12]

While ostensibly the story of a man possessed by a passion for gold, *Facino Cane* is thus the tale of a man possessed by a phantom, by the secret of his Jewish origins that has been transmitted to him by his mother as his psychic inheritance. Compared to the Freudian and Lacanian interpretations outlined earlier, this analysis of a phantom offers a nondevelopmental, nonphallocentric view of behavior that does not assume as its core a system of substitutions based on either incest and castration or the Imaginary and the Symbolic. It allows us to link influences outside Cane's own lived experience with the creation of a specific symptom that preserves intact an unspeakable secret while cryptically revealing its contents. Cryptonymy permits us to read *or* as the product of a symbolic operation, combining interlinguistic homophony and allosemy (*or* → OR → light → enlightenment), by which the trauma of Cane's unspeakable origins was transcended. The result is that Facino Cane's obsession with gold is explicable not as the symptom of an unconscious desire to possess his mother or the phallus but as a symptom of his "possession" by his father, that is, of his possession by the secret of his father's identity. Carrying gold for Facino Cane is the linguistic means of carrying the sealed contents of his mother's shame.[13]

What then can be the role of Bianca in Facino Cane's story, given the secret drama of his origins just exposed? In his affairs with her, Cane repeatedly intrudes upon a licit or "lawful" couple composed of Bianca and a figure of the law. The significance of this intrusion, in terms of the foregoing analysis, differs markedly from the triangular structures delineated in the Freudian and Lacanian readings of the tale. Facino Cane's behavior as an "intruder" does not identify him as the Oedipal son but rather as his own biological father. In each scene with Bianca, Facino Cane reenacts the behavior of his real father, who disrupted the licit marriage between his mother and (nominal) father and engaged in adultery. Cane's resigned assumption of the seemingly playful adulterations of his name—*le père Canet* and *le père Canard*—point to his assumption of this second identity as "father" (*père*) while in the presence of Bianca.[14] Bianca, whose name can mean "blank" or "empty,"[15] is in turn revealed as playing, from Cane's point of view, someone else's role in this drama. Rather than a substitute for gold and hence for the mother or the phallus, however, Bianca (unknowingly) plays the part of the adulterous wife, engaged in a lawful union, who committed an illicit act with the intruder.

Bianca and *or* thus do not function as interchangeable signifiers in a signifying chain leading to the mother or the phallus; they are two distinct symbols created in response to two separate aspects of the drama of Cane's conception. When in quest of *or* Facino Cane is the son in search of his origins. In seeking Bianca he transforms her into the adulterous wife and assumes the role of his own father, the illicit intruder who begat an illegitimate son. This explains why Cane describes his passion for Bianca as greater than for any other woman in his life. Her conjugal circumstances and her name suit her perfectly for the role of adulteress in Cane's psychic drama.[16]

The manner in which Cane reenacts the drama of his origins with Bianca also makes intelligible the extraordinary series of dangerous and unlawful adventures that constitute his life and repeatedly land him in prison or exile. In each of these episodes, Cane plays the role of his father. He is not the father as adulterer, however, but the father as Jew. The *Super flumina Babylonis*, the lament of the Jews held captive in exile in Babylon which Cane plays on the clarinet, is the crucial symbol fragment that permits reconstruction of this scenario. By repeatedly exposing himself to imprisonment and exile, Facino Cane tacitly identifies himself with the captives in exile in Babylon; he acts out his father's—and hence his own—unspeakable identity as Jewish. The seemingly fantastical, impulsive, self-destructive behavior constituting his existence can thus be understood as a function of the symbolic re-creation of the secret drama of his origins, which he alternately reenacts and seeks to know.

3

The role of the narrator in the text can be explained in light of Cane's psychic drama. In introducing himself and Cane's tale, the narrator speaks of the series of bizarre stories he has collected while living in Paris:

> Je ne sais comment j'ai si longtemps gardé sans la dire l'histoire que je vais vous raconter, elle fait partie de ces récits curieux restés dans le sac d'où la mémoire les tire capricieusement comme des numéros de loterie: j'en ai bien d'autres, aussi singuliers que celui-ci, également enfouis; mais ils auront leur tour, croyez-le. (1020–21)
>
> [I don't know how I have been able to keep untold for so long the story I am about to tell you; it is one of those strange tales stored in the bag from which memory draws them out at random like numbers in a lottery. I know many more, as odd as this one and buried as deeply. But their turn will come, you may be sure.]

The narrator never tells any of these other stories. At the end of Cane's account, he replaces his promise to the reader with a different promise—to Facino Cane. He will accompany Cane to Venice and help the blind man find the gold he believes still hidden there:

> ". . . malgré ma cécité [dit Cane], allons à Venise! . . . je verrai l'or à travers les murailles, . . . nous rachèterons mes biens, et vous serez mon héritier, vous serez prince de Varese. . . ." "—Nous irons à Venise, m'écriai-je. . . ." (1030–31)
>
> [". . . in spite of my blindness (said Cane), let us go to Venice! . . . I shall see the gold through the walls, . . . we shall buy back my property, and you will be my heir, you will be Prince of Varese. . . ." "—We shall go to Venice, I exclaimed. . . ."]

The legacy of stories the narrator bequeaths to the reader at the outset of the text is annulled by the legacy he inherits from Facino Cane:

his quest for gold. This quest we now know to be a quest for Cane's origins. In adopting Cane's search for *or*, the narrator thus adopts as his own Cane's search for his identity. He receives or "inherits" the phantom transmitted to Cane by his mother. Why the narrator should be disposed to such a strange inheritance is not readily comprehensible. If we are to resolve this enigma, it will help to determine why Facino Cane's story, above all the others the narrator keeps in his sack of memories, holds a particular attraction for him.

At the beginning of the tale, the narrator describes the "sole passion" (1019) in his life as wandering in the neighborhood and taking over the bodies and souls of strangers:

> [J]e pouvais épouser leur vie . . . , leurs désirs, leurs besoins, tout passait dans mon âme, ou mon âme passait dans la leur. . . . Quitter ses habitudes, devenir un autre que soi . . . , telle était ma distraction. (1020)

> [I was able to live their lives; . . . their desires, their needs, all passed into my soul, or perhaps it was my soul that passed into theirs. . . . To discard my own habits, to become someone other than myself . . . , such was my amusement.]

Given to assuming many identities instead of a single, stable one, the anonymous narrator renders problematic the possibility of establishing precisely who he is. This problem gains significance when juxtaposed with the randomness of his decision to recount Cane's tale:

> [L]'histoire que je vais vous raconter . . . fait partie de ces récits curieux restés dans le sac d'où la mémoire les tire *capricieusement comme des numéros de loterie*. . . . (1020–21)

> [(T)he story I am about to tell you . . . is one of those strange tales stored in the bag from which memory draws them out *at random like numbers in a lottery*. . . .]

The stories the narrator recounts are born through chance. They are also *borne by* chance:

> L'imagination n'atteindra jamais au vrai qui s'y cache [dans le faubourg] et que personne ne peut aller découvrir; il faut descendre trop bas pour trouver ces admirables scènes ou tragiques ou comiques, chefs-d'oeuvre *enfantés par le hasard*. (1020)

> [It is impossible to imagine the truth that is concealed in (the neighborhood) and that no one is able to reveal; one would have to dig too deeply to discover these wonderful scenes of tragedy and comedy, these masterpieces *borne by chance*.]

These two statements establish a critical link. The fragmented, uncertain identity of the narrator, who assumes others' identities (and recounts their stories), becomes interchangeable with the stories themselves, progeny (*enfanter*) of undefined origins whose identities cannot be determined. Like the "illegitimate" stories he recounts, the narrator's identity itself appears *enfantée par le hasard*. This conclusion allows us to suggest the hidden motivation behind his "love of science"(1019) and his willing submission to a "monastic life" (1019) dedicated to research and study. The narrator is (unknowingly) in search of the *hasard* or "chance" that bore him; he seeks knowledge ("science") of his own identity, the truth of his origins. He is in search of his parents.

This unspoken search explains his assumption of Facino Cane's identity and his willingness to carry on Cane's legacy.[17] By becoming heir to Cane's quest for *or*, the narrator inherits Cane's search for his origins as his own search. He relinquishes his identity as a "child of chance" (as well as his desire, symptomatic of this identity, to recount others' stories as his own) to become a child of *or*. *Or* will now be the narrator's paternity while (we can assume) Cane's mother will become his own adoptive mother. The secret of the two men's origins is thereby joined, and the narrator's unconscious search for his parents is forever put to rest, replaced instead by the search for *or* in its concrete (and conscious) form: the quest for the metal gold.

With the narrator's decision to accompany him to Venice, Facino Cane's need to remain alive and guard intact the secret he holds is also put to rest. After years spent trying to engage consuls and emperors as associates (and, we may surmise, potential heirs) in his quest for gold,[18] he has at last found a suitable and willing prospect to whom he can bequeath his secret legacy:

> "Venez, partons pour Venise . . . et vous serez mon héritier. . . ." "—Nous irons à Venise, m'écriai-je. . . . —*J'ai donc trouvé un homme,*" s'écria-t-il, le visage en feu. . . . (1031)

> ["Come, let us leave for Venice . . . and you will be my heir. . . ." "—We will go to Venice, I exclaimed. . . . —*At last I have found a man,*" he cried, his face flushed with excitement.]

Facino Cane has at last found a man worthy of the name, an able guardian who, in agreeing to carry on Cane's search for gold, will preserve whole and untouched his mother's secret. The filial responsibility Cane has borne his entire life can now be passed on to the narrator. The secret is no longer threatened with extinction, and Cane is at last free to die:

"Partirons-nous demain? dit le vieillard.
—Aussitôt que nous aurons quelque argent.
—Mais nous pouvons aller à pied, je demanderai l'aumône. . . . Je suis robuste, et l'on est jeune quand on voit de l'or devant soi."
Facino Cane mourut pendant l'hiver après avoir langui deux mois. Le pauvre homme avait *un catarrhe.* (1032)

["Shall we leave tomorrow? asked the old man.
—As soon as we have some money.
—But we can go on foot, I will ask for alms. . . . I am sturdy, and when a man sees gold before him he is young."
Facino Cane died during the winter, having lingered for two months. The poor man had *a catarrh.*]

The text ends with this last sentence but its haunting effect lingers. The invisible ghost born in one generation has survived to haunt the two generations that follow. One man's unknowing search for his origins has ended so that another's unwitting quest for *or* may begin. If the narrator recounts no more stories to the reader, it is because he is on the verge of living a new one. His activities no longer directly determined by his mute search for his parents, he will presumably spend the rest of his life in quest of gold—and haunted by the invisible phantom he has unknowingly been bequeathed.[19]

Facino Cane is thus a tale that blurs the distinctions between living an adventure and telling a story, between a character's life and a poetic artifact. It depicts the existences of two men in terms of the perpetual re-creation or living out of others' unspoken stories. Cane creates his life as the cryptic narrative of the tale his mother could not utter. The narrator abandons storytelling in order to live the unspeakable account of both his and Cane's origins. The two men become in essence living poems, each one an "Odyssey" (1023), as the narrator calls Cane, whose contents and peregrinations are inspired by forces beyond their control and comprehension.

For this reason, the commentaries on *Facino Cane* that have concentrated primarily on its autobiographical elements, interpreting the narrator's ability to identify with others and penetrate their souls as a reflection of Balzac's imaginative and creative powers, may have resonated with the more general issue of narrative production inscribed within the tale.[20] It may be that Balzac used the figure of the narrator to contemplate the mysteries of the origin of poetic creation and the possibility that obsession, possession, and haunting play a role in textual genesis. Certainly no conclusions about Balzac's immense oeuvre can be drawn based on this one text. A work that does come to mind as an apt site for pursuing this hypothesis and that might well benefit from the methodological approach used here is *La fille aux yeux d'or*. Better known and more frequently the subject of critical investigation than *Facino Cane*, this tale is replete with foreign languages and proper names, questions of illegitimacy, bought paternities, ambiguities of sexual identity, emotional possession and slavery, uncontrolled passions for gold, and a character's singular obsession with someone whose name—"The Girl with the Eyes of Gold"—contains both the word *or* and a reference to sight.[21] Although astute commentaries on some of these textual elements exist,[22] the possibility that *La fille aux yeux d'or* might shed light on the presence of phantoms in other Balzac texts remains to be explored. Such an inquiry might also illuminate the significations of the theme of the passion for gold found throughout Balzac's works. Finally, it could help explain the presence of the many characters of Jewish origin explicitly identified in Balzac's writing, as well as the motivation behind Balzac's creation of a text—*Facino Cane*—about concealed, shameful Jewish origins.

CHAPTER 5

In the Mind's I

THE JOLLY CORNER OF HENRY JAMES

A mote it is to trouble the mind's eye.
(*Hamlet* 1.1.112)

1

The Jolly Corner (1908),[1] one of Henry James's last completed works, is not nearly as well-known or as fervidly debated as *The Turn of the Screw*, the James text to which it is most frequently compared. It has nonetheless been host to numerous and often conflicting commentaries from biographical, sociohistorical, psychoanalytic, and structuralist perspectives that are noteworthy for both the variety of their concerns and the textual enigmas they leave unaddressed.

Biographical approaches to the story have viewed it as a reflection of James's ambivalent feelings toward the United States. In 1904 James made one of three voyages to America during his almost forty-year expatriation in France and England in order to prepare *The American Scene*, a collection of impressions of the country, and to supervise the New York Edition of selected novels and stories. James's mixture of regret at having to leave the United States to earn a living as a writer and dismay upon seeing his native land become an impersonal country, driven by commercial interests, is often cited as the emotional source for Spencer Brydon, the protagonist of *The Jolly Corner*, who returns to New York after years of exile in Europe to find out what he might have been had he not left. Spencer's warm reunion with his old friend, Alice Staverton, is said to represent the nostalgia James felt for America, while the specter of Spencer's *alter ego* (James's italics), richly attired with a horrifying face and mutilated hand, is seen as embodying the crass business world America had become and the loss of moral and aesthetic sensitivity James is thought to have felt would have maimed his writing had he remained.[2]

Shifting the emphasis away from James's personal experience, sociohistorical approaches to the tale perceive Spencer Brydon as a figure of the nascent capitalist, torn between traditional, European values of artistic beauty and production and the new, American, commercial values of a burgeoning country, living and blossoming from construction and the accumulation of rents. In these readings Spencer's mutilated alter ego becomes a figure of the corrupting influence of the builders and destroyers doing battle against a romantic, old-world past.[3]

Like so many of James's works, *The Jolly Corner* has also provided fertile ground for psychoanalytic interpretations. The relationship between the author's psyche and his literary production is discussed in an often-cited essay by Saul Rosensweig, who sees in the alter ego's mutilated hand a symbol of the psychic wound left on James's life and writing by his father, whose leg was mutilated in a boyhood accident.[4] While Rosensweig's dependence on Freudian theories of castration anxiety and the return of the repressed will not convince readers unallied with these analytic models, the correspondences he notes between the specter in *The Jolly Corner* and mutilated figures in other works by James are quite suggestive. They would doubtless prove useful for studying the possible links between James's psychic life and his poetic creations.[5]

Although concerned with the author-text relationship, Rosensweig's approach is exemplary of the vast majority of intratextual interpretations of James's tale in that they too use Freudian theory, explicitly or implicitly, to explain the identity or function of Spencer's alter ego. Their differences in specific content and terminology notwithstanding, these interpretations invariably take their cue from the "duplication of consciousness" (214) Spencer is said to experience upon encountering his alter ego and from his denial that the mutilated figure in any way resembles him. They conclude that Spencer's mind is divided into two distinct parts, that each part represents a separate aspect of his being or self, and that one of these parts is embodied by the alter ego he seeks and finds in the corridors of his childhood home. Disagreements among the readings lie essentially in whether these two parts of Spencer represent his actual and potential self, true and false self, good and bad self, conscious and unconscious self, ego and superego, or id and ego.[6]

The biographical, sociohistorical, and psychoanalytic concerns just outlined are all valid areas of inquiry. Although one might object to the particular methodologies employed or the results achieved, it is hard to disagree that the image of the mutilated alter ego invites these kinds of considerations, especially coming as it does at the end of James's career, when retrospection toward the influences on his life's course and introspection about the nature and genesis of his literary creations may be expected.

It is therefore interesting that, despite virtually unanimous agreement on the importance (if not the specific signification) of this alter ego, almost no critical attention has been paid to the form of its mutilation, a precision the text takes pains to point out: "a special verity . . . surpassed every other, the fact that one of the [alter ego's] hands had lost two fingers, which were reduced to stumps, as if accidentally shot away" (225). In the analysis that follows, the indisputably central questions of the signification of the alter ego and of Spencer's "duality of consciousness" will be reconsidered in conjunction with the enigma of the alter ego's two missing fingers. This interpretive tack will lead to an examination of the text's ungraspable syntax and pronominal confusion, which frequently render the identity of the speaker, the addressee, and the subject of discussion highly problematic. A small sample of the dialogue between Spencer Brydon and Alice Staverton, after Spencer's encounter with his alter ego, offers eloquent testimony to this effect:

> ". . . in the cold dim dawn of this morning I too saw you."
> "Saw *me*—?"
> "Saw *him*," said Alice Staverton. . . . "He came back to me. Then I knew. . . . He had come to you." . . .
> "*He* didn't come to me."
> "You came to yourself". . . .
> "But. . . . He's none of *me*. . . ." (230–31; James's italics, ellipses mine)

Tzvetan Todorov has noted this play of pronouns in the text and assessed it from a structuralist perspective. In two chapters of *The Poetics of Prose* entitled "The Secret of Narrative" and "The Ghosts of Henry James,"[7] he proposes that the motivating force of *The Jolly Corner* is Spencer's quest for the secret of his "authentic identity" or essential "I."[8] When Spencer encounters his alter ego and finds a total stranger, this quest is exposed as vain. Spencer instead discovers the love of his companion Alice Staverton, the "you" across from his "I": "Having set out in search of a profound *I*, Brydon ends by discovering a *you*. . . . [E]ssence is an illusion. . . . *I* [is supplanted] by *you*."[9] For Todorov, the text's pronominal confusion points to the impossibility of situating or grasping the real or true "I" and to the subject's ghostly, illusory state of being as an effect of a bipolar relationship with another.

Although Todorov's use of the terms "secret" and "ghost" are quite different from my own and his concern with the organizing function of structural oppositions has little in common with my analytic approach, his remarks on the slippery nature of the text's pronouns, on their tendency to supplant one another, and on the presence in the narrative of something concealed beyond reach resonate with the ideas of unspeakable secrets and possession by phantoms central to this study. If we consider alongside the text's grammatical and pronominal elusiveness the fact that it is riddled with typographical marks (italics and quotation marks) and with words in foreign languages, it becomes increasingly apparent that certain narrative elements have meanings that must not be taken exclusively at face value or that belong to another context from which they have been repeated or quoted. The text, in short, identifies itself grammatically, typographically, and interlinguistically as a story about intersections, crisscrossings, conflations, and superimpositions. It thereby encourages the conjecture that it may have to do with something other than the kinds of secrets and ghosts Todorov has in mind; it may be a phantom-text.

The goal of my interpretation is to pursue this possibility by locating the angle or corner at which these intersections, conflations, pronominal confusions, and slipping subjects meet the enigma of Spencer's mutilated alter ego. The initial result, which may be stated here without fear of ruining the surprises held in store by this astonishing tale,[10] is that an unspeakable secret will be found hidden within the text. Unlike the secrets in *The Secret Sharer*, *L'intersigne*, and *Facino Cane*, however, the secret in *The Jolly Corner* can and will be identified relatively early in the interpretation and will, through the manner of its unraveling, reveal the text to be a progression or cascade of secrets, encrypted words, and encrypted narratives. The eventual uncovering and reading of these embedded texts will show that Spencer Brydon is not a divided or dual consciousness who alternately embodies two distinct aspects of himself, as virtually all previous psychoanalytic interpretations have maintained in one form or another. Rather he is one single seat of consciousness within which reside, mingle, and intertwine several ghostly incarnations, having nothing to do with him per se, that have returned from a buried part of his family history to haunt him. Before I begin to sort out the ghosts inhabiting *The Jolly Corner*, it will be helpful to recall in some detail the specific events of the tale.

Spencer Brydon, an unnamed narrator tells us, has just returned to New York after a thirty-three-year self-imposed exile in Europe. Now fifty-six years old, he has come back to look at the two houses he has recently inherited. He begins to renovate one as an apartment house. The other, the house in which he was born, in which several generations of his family have lived, and which is located on what he calls "the jolly corner" (194) of the street, he decides to keep intact. He visits the construction site of the first house with Alice Staverton, a longtime friend who has remained in New York all these years and with whom he spends many moments sharing memories of their past, and discovers in himself a certain capacity for business dealings. Afterward, they walk to the other end of the street, to the jolly corner, empty and uninhabited, but "lived in . . . [and] furnished" (203), as Spencer explains, by his family's ineffaceable presence. A few days after this visit, Spencer confesses to Miss Staverton his curiosity to find out "what he personally might have been, how he might have led his life and 'turned out' " (203), had he stayed in America. Following this admission, the second part of the story begins, the lengthy narrative of Spencer's unobserved, nightly visits to the jolly corner to encounter what he calls his "*alter ego*" (204; James's italics).

Prowling silently through the house, room to room and corridor to corridor, Spencer gradually becomes convinced that his "other self" (225) is present, lurking hidden behind some door. Sure that he has finally cornered him, Spencer is suddenly overwhelmed by terror. The situation has somehow "turned" (218), and he decides his only recourse is "Discretion" (218). He abandons the hunt and begins to descend the stairs toward the bottom of the house. As he approaches the last flight, he again senses the presence of a figure hiding behind a door. Then, suddenly, it appears. A dark, ominous-looking man in evening clothes, with a double eyeglass piece and a strangely mutilated hand, stands erect before Spencer's eyes. This cannot possibly be the figure he has sought for so long, Spencer thinks. He is too awful, too hideous. His identity fits Spencer's at no point. As Spencer laments the time he has wasted seeking this grotesque figure, it begins to advance toward him, nearer and nearer until, finally overwhelmed by a mixture of horror and denial, Spencer falls back and drops to the floor in a dead faint.

On waking, he finds Alice Staverton cradling his head in her lap. She had come to the house to find him when he did not return to his hotel. He tells her he has seen the figure but that it in no way resembles him. Miss Staverton reminds him reassuringly that he would have been very different had he stayed in New York. Spencer protests but, as he draws her to his breast, admits that, whoever this figure was or whatever power he had, he did not have her.

One of the most puzzling moments in the story, evident even from this brief summary, is Spencer's decision, after finally cornering his "other self," to abandon the hunt in the name of "Discretion." A turning point in the narrative, it is also the moment in which the ideas of nonrevelation and secreting are implicitly, "discreetly" announced as pivotal to the text. To determine the possible reasons for Spencer's discretion, and to understand what might be kept secret or discreet within the text, it is necessary to return to the beginning of Spencer's quest for his alter ego.

First described as fearlessly stalking a wild beast and as enjoying the pleasure of the "chase" (210), Spencer loses his self-assurance after a three-night absence from the jolly corner. Although he resumes the hunt, he now has the sensation of being himself "tracked at a distance . . . , kept in sight while remaining himself . . . sightless" (212):

> "I've hunted him till he has 'turned' . . . he's the fanged or the antlered animal brought at last to bay . . . now, worked up to anger, he'll fight!" [Then Spencer] closed his eyes . . . with that instinct of dismay and that terror of vision. (213–15)

Something has been revealed to Spencer during his stalking of the beast that he cannot or dares not see. Yet little is offered to suggest what this might be, apart from the more precise description of his prey as a "fanged or antlered animal" who "has 'turned.' " The moment just prior to his abandonment of the hunt provides a few clues to the enigma of this revelation. When Spencer notes that a door he had left open moments earlier is now closed, he concludes that there is in fact someone present with him in the house:

> [W]hat else was clear but that there had been another agent? *Another agent*? . . . he felt his eyes almost leave their sockets. Ah this time at last they *were* [James's italics], the two, *the opposed projections of him* . . . and this time . . . the question of danger loomed. With it rose, as not before, *the question of courage*. . . . Oh to have this consciousness was . . . to feel the thing in another, in a new and terrible way. (217–18)

It is not just a "fanged or antlered animal" Spencer dares not see but "another agent" who, while raising in a new way the idea of "courage" and bringing into focus the presence of "two opposed projections of him," so threatens Spencer that his eyes nearly leave their sockets, leaving him sightless. "Another agent," "the rising of courage," and "two opposed projections" must thus be added to fangs and antlers as elements so menacing that they make it virtually impossible for Spencer to see what he hunts and also to pursue it:

> [T]he situation itself had turned . . . to a . . . supreme hint . . . of the value of Discretion! . . . it saved the situation. . . . [W]ith his eyes bent . . . [h]e listened . . . but this attitude . . . was his own communication. ". . . I spare you and I give up . . . you convince me that *for reasons rigid and sublime*—what do I know?—we both of us should have suffered. I respect them . . . and . . . I retire, I renounce. . . . So rest for ever—and let *me* [James's italics]!" (218–20)

With this unspoken reflection Spencer cryptically explains why he abandons the hunt in the name of Discretion and provides the link joining the elements causing him fear: "for reasons rigid and sublime," for reasons stiff or unbending and elevated or raised high. The threat posed by fangs and antlers has apparently less to do with their potential for bodily harm than with their stiff and erect form. The menace of two opposed projections does not come from projections in the sense of visual images or representations but in the sense of rigid and raised protrusions, of two physical projections. And the danger that rises from the question of courage emanates not from the possibility of combat but from the physical image of courage, an image conveyed earlier by Spencer's decision to remain in the house despite his growing fear:

> He would wait. . . . It would prove his courage. . . . What he . . . felt . . . was that, since he hadn't originally scuttled, he had his *dignities* . . . all to preserve and to carry aloft. This was before him in truth *as a physical image*, an image almost worthy of an age of greater romance. . . . The only difference would have been that, *brandishing his dignities over his head as in a parchment scroll*, he might then . . . in the heroic time—have proceeded . . . with a drawn sword in his other grasp. (215–16)

Courage, in the passage, is represented by scrolled "dignities" or titles of honor held aloft. If the "raising" of the question of courage frightens Spencer, therefore, and if courage is equated with a physical image of something curved or spiraled that rises above the head, it must be because Spencer perceives courage as a form that literally rises, that coincides with "antlers" and "two opposed projections" and, not insignificantly, with the traditional representation of courage and power in both mythology and militarism: as two rigid and erect horns.[11]

Horns appear to be the reasons "rigid and sublime" for Spencer's terror and his abandonment of the hunt. Why horns should so horrify him, and how they may be linked to the as yet unexplained element of "another agent" remain problems. Pursuing their solution entails exploring another corner of the text where horns or physical projections appear—the "jolly corner" itself.

Described as "superlatively extended" (195) with a "large 'extension' . . . abound[ing] in nooks and corners" (212), the jolly corner is a place of prolongations and projections, a place of horns. But if the house contains physical projections and extensions, it also contains extensions of the "house" or family that has inhabited it. The jolly corner is the place in which Spencer "had first seen the light, in which various members of his family had lived and had died, . . . and which . . . had, through the successive deaths of his two brothers and the termination of old arrangements, *come wholly into his hands*" (194–95). It is a place filled with "the annals of nearly three generations, counting his grandfather's, the one that had ended there" (201), a place in which "his parents and his favourite sister, to say nothing of other kin, in numbers, had run their course and met their end" (203). To the list of physical protrusions and extensions in the text must thus be added familial projections and genealogical prolongations. The significance of horns, in turn, has to be reconsidered within the context of these additions. If horns are physically present within the house on the jolly corner and can be found linguistically embedded within the name of the house, the "jolly *corner*" ("corner" comes from the Latin *cornu* meaning "horn"), we can expect that they will also be embedded within the "house," annals, or history of Spencer's family with its extensions or generations of births and deaths.[12] What comes into Spencer's hands, in other words, can no longer be construed as merely a piece of " 'property' " (194). As the text's quotation marks suggest, this " 'property' " must belong to another context that, in light of the foregoing, is somehow linked to horns.

What then "comes wholly into [Spencer's] hands" and involves horns? A partial answer emerges from the question itself. What is handed down is precisely "hands":

> [Spencer] spoke of the value of all he read into [the jolly corner], into the mere sight of the walls, mere shapes of the rooms, mere *sound* of the floors, mere *feel*, in his *hand*, of the old silver-plated *knobs* of the several mahogany doors, which suggested *the pressure of the palms of the dead*; the seventy years of the past in fine that these things represented, the annals of nearly three generations. . . . (201)

To read what is "represented" in the jolly corner is to read not just with the eyes but with the ears and the hands. It is to listen to the sounds of the house and to "read its palms," to feel, with the hands as a guide, a story left by hands, imprinted in knobs, protuberances, horns. A joining of hands, sounds, reading, and projections is also discernible in the description of Spencer's social encounters:

> [P]eople . . . had truly not an idea of him. It was all mere surface sound, this murmur of their welcome, this popping of their corks—just as his gestures of response were the extravagant shadows, emphatic in proportion as they meant little, of some game of *ombres chinoises*. (208; James's italics)

A game of reading illusory images projected by the play of light upon the hands or upon objects manipulated by the hands, *ombres chinoises* (Chinese shadows) represents only one of a long list of terms in the text alluding to hand games. The worth of the two houses that "come into [Spencer's] hands," for example, is expressed by the locution, "the value of the pair" (195), not noteworthy in itself until one observes other locutions, many of them in quotation marks, that underscore its particular significance and provide a new way of interpreting Spencer's hunt for his alter ego. When Spencer refuses "to agree to a 'deal' " (202), takes pleasure in " 'standing-up' to" (197) a contractor despite his limited knowledge of construction, decides to "really 'go into' figures" (196), becomes "flushed" (198) by the thrill "created by big game" (210), feels tricked by the adversary he hunts as "Pantaloon [is] by . . . Harlequin" (213), determines " 'to stay' " (213) after the antlered animal has " 'turned' " (213), and, sensing that the door separating him from the animal dares him to " 'show us how much you have!' " (218), announces to himself, " 'I retire, I renounce . . . ' " (219), what we read is the cryptic narrative of a high-stakes poker game. Spencer is engaged in "dealing" cards, bluffing (" 'standing-up' "), and anteing up or " 'going in' " to the pot. He has a "flush" but senses he may be tricked or beaten by two jokers (Pantaloon and Harlequin), decides to call his adversary's bet without raising the stakes (" 'to stay' "), and then, seeing what his adversary has "turned" over and obliged to "show what he has" in his own hand, realizes he does not have the cards ("renounce": failure to follow suit in a card game [*OED*]), throws in his hand, and "retires" from the game: "the situation itself had turned . . . to a supreme hint . . . of the value of Discretion! This slowly dawned [on him] for . . . so perfectly . . . *had he been stayed*" (218).

Hands, in the text, are connected with games of illusion and deception. This connection provides the key to reading the mysterious palms of the dead that touched horns and that come into Spencer's hands. It informs us that "palms" are to be understood in the story in the context of illusions created by hands, of card playing, and of being "tricked from behind by . . . Harlequin" (213) or a joker. It signals that "palms" be heard in the sense of "to palm"—"to conceal a playing card in the hand with the intent to deceive"—and in the sense of "to palm" or "impose a thing upon someone by trickery or fraud" (*OED*). By grasping the key to reading "palms" cryptically offered by "hands," the reader is able to move a crucial step closer to determining the nature of Spencer's inheritance and of the alter ego he seeks to encounter. We can surmise that what comes into Spencer's hands as the jolly corner has something to do with the concealment of a fraud, perpetrated upon (or by) the dead, that is somehow readable in "horns." We can similarly deduce that the horned beast Spencer hunts and then attempts to flee is not merely an animal but also in some way represents or embodies this fraud. With the description of Spencer's sighting of his "other self" these deductions are confirmed:

> *Rigid* and conscious, *spectral* yet human, a man of his own substance and stature waited there to measure himself with his *power* to dismay. . . . [W]hat made the face dim was the pair of *raised hands that covered it* and in which, so far from being offered in defiance, it was buried as for dark deprecation. So Brydon . . . took him in . . . in the *higher light, hard and acute*—his planted stillness, his vivid truth, his . . . white masking hands, his queer actuality of evening-dress, of dangling double eye-glass, of *gleaming silk lappet* and *white* linen, of *pearl* button and *gold* watch-guard and *polished* shoe. (224–25)

With his "rigid" stature and "power" to dismay, recalling "stiff" antlers and "courage," the figure Spencer perceives can be linked to horns. At the same time, the "raised pair of hands that cover" his face evokes the sequence hands → palm → concealment/imposter. But if horns and a deception can be read in the description, the significance of "hard and acute light," "gleaming white" cloth and "polished" shoes, the luster of "pearl," and the sparkle of "gold" remains opaque for the reader as well as for the now frightened and mystified Spencer. A clue to explaining this insistence on radiant light is provided by another context in the narrative in which light impresses by its hard brilliance:

> [Spencer] closed the door [to the jolly corner] and . . . took in the comparatively harsh actuality of the Avenue, which reminded him of the assault of the outer light of the Desert on the traveller emerging from an Egyptian tomb. (202–3)

This seemingly inconsequential reference to ancient Egypt alerts the reader to a prior reference to the ancient past, to the "memories and histories" (197) shared by Spencer and Miss Staverton of their common, "quite far-away, *antediluvian* social period and order" (196). "Light" thus leads from ancient Egypt to the period before the flood described in the Bible. When we couple these findings with the earlier description of dignities as a "parchment scroll" (216), with Spencer's confession that he "followed strange paths and worshipped strange gods" (205) during his "exile" (205) from home, with his fascination for the "vulgar" (195) aspect of the things he sees around him, and with the repeated presence of Latin in the story (highlighted by the grammatically unnecessary italicizing of *alter ego*, an expression totally assimilated into English), the existence of another encrypted narrative in the text is confirmed. Hidden within *The Jolly Corner* is a series of allusions to the Bible, to the Latin *Vulgate* and the Book of Exodus, in particular. This book recounts the Jews' exile in the Egyptian desert and their momentary worshiping of strange gods and idols. It also names the "rays of light" emanating from the head of their leader Moses in a form of the Vulgar Latin, *cornua*: "horns."[13]

Just as an encrypted narrative about "hands" revealed that "palms" can be read in the text as "deception or fraud," an encrypted narrative about the Bible signals that "light" in the story may be understood in a Vulgar Latin form of "horns." The decrypting of this biblical narrative does more than confirm the link between the figure standing before Spencer and horns, however. It suggests that horns themselves may have to be understood in the story in a Vulgar Latin or Romance context. It hints that uncovering the deception guarded by the "black-vizored sentinel" (224) Spencer perceives, exposing the fraud he conceals with his hands, and finally grasping the dilemma of these horns means hearing the remaining words and images depicting the alter ego in the context of a "vulgar" Romance language:

> No portrait by a great modern master could have presented him with more intensity, *thrust him out of his frame* with more art, as if there had been "treatment," of the *consummate* sort, in his every shade and salience. The revulsion, for our friend, had become, before he knew it, immense—this drop, in the act of apprehension, to the sense of his adversary's *inscrutable manœuvre*. That meaning at least, while he gaped, it offered him; for he could but gape at his other self in this other anguish, gape as a proof that *he* [James's italics], standing there for the achieved, the enjoyed, the triumphant life, couldn't be faced in his triumph. Wasn't the proof in the splendid covering hands, strong and completely spread?—so spread and so intentional that, in spite of a special verity that surpassed every other, the fact that *one of these hands had lost two fingers, which were reduced to stumps*, as if accidentally shot away, the face was effectually guarded and saved. (225)

What is the "proof" offered by these hands and by the mutilated hand in particular, whose significance initially stumped this reader if not others? How is it possible to read or translate such a hand in a "vulgar" Romance context? The passage provides an encrypted dictionary with which to perform such a translation. If the image before Spencer is described as "thrust out of its frame" or projecting outward beyond clearly marked limits, if its "manœuvre" or literally "handwork" (from the French *main* + *oeuvre*) cannot be readily seen ("inscrutable") but is a source of revulsion and apprehension, if there is " 'treatment' " or handling involving a "consummation" of some kind, and if the "special verity" revealed by an intentionally spread hand consisting of two fingers and two stumps "surpasses" or extends outward, then the "meaning" offered by this hand, one that resonates with or is readable as "horns" in a vulgar Romance context, must be the story of a vulgar romance, of an "inscrutable manœuvre" involving deception, a concealed "consummation," and an imposter (handwork + handling → palming). It is the drama signaled by the intentional spreading of the fingers of the hand and the bending of the two middle fingers to resemble stumps; the drama articulated by the vulgar gesture of a two-fingered hand "thrust out" at someone in mockery of "his adversary's inscrutable manœuvre"; the drama whose meaning is figured by and readable in horns and whose verbal equivalent in a "vulgar" Romance language is the French *cornard*! cuckold![14]

The rigid, erect, brilliantly adorned figure standing before Spencer in the jolly corner with his poor, mutilated hand is the embodiment or incarnation of a cuckolding. He is the spectral mise-en-scène of the story of a husband who has been outmaneuvered, deceived, and "given horns" by his wife. Although the identities of this figure and of the other player(s) in the scene remain for the moment unknown, the text's last lines provide a telling clue as to who might have done what to whom.

"He has been unhappy, he has been ravaged," Miss Staverton reassures Spencer as he recovers from his encounter with the awesome figure and learns that she herself has seen him in a dream. "His great convex pince-nez," she continues, "—I saw it, I recognized the kind—is for his poor ruined sight. And his poor right hand—!" (232) The figure before Spencer cannot see clearly, the sine qua non for a cuckolding. This adds to the drama just unveiled a second act. For the man's ruined sight is signaled by a "pince-nez," an instrument used to read something otherwise out of focus or illegible. "Pince-nez" is also a foreign word belonging to a Romance language which, like *ombres chinoises* and *alter ego*, demands to be heard "in translation" or in some other context in the tale. If we take our cue from this and use "pince-nez" to bring into focus something within the word itself that must be read and heard differently, we learn that the man before Spencer is not only blind to his wife's infidelity but to the fact that there was someone "born" (in French *nez*: "nose" is homophonous with *né*: "born") from the "hand" (*pince*, in popular, "vulgar" French), from the palm → palming → deception → fraud. The figure before Spencer does not see that he has been, as Miss Staverton says, "ravaged," robbed of his honor and also his paternity, tricked into bearing or accepting as his own a fraudulent heir issued from his wife's concealed consummation.[15]

2

The drama before us is still far from unraveled. Although we can now state that a cuckolding has taken place somewhere in the Brydon "house" and that an illegitimate heir issued from it, we still do not know who was cuckolded and who was palmed off as the heir. On the one hand, it seems reasonable to cast Spencer in the role of the fraudulent offspring, given the repeated references to the horned animal he pursues as his alter ego and his "other self." On the other hand, such a conclusion is immediately contradicted by Spencer's unequivocal reaction upon finally perceiving the "beast":

> The face, *that* face, Spencer Brydon's? . . . It was unknown, inconceivable, awful, disconnected from any possibility—! He had been "sold," he inwardly moaned. . . . Such an identity fitted his at *no* point . . . —the face was the face of a stranger. (225–26; James's italics)

There is no "point," no *horn*, we hear, connecting this figure to Spencer, no "point" or place in Spencer's lineage where this figure might "fit" him. The text seems to have maneuvered us into a corner, placed us before a seemingly irreconcilable paradox in which the image before Spencer both is and is not related to him—unless what is at stake here is an altogether different conception of the notions of "other self" and alter ego. It may be that what the text calls for, and what would permit us to resolve this dilemma, is a new way of reading or translating these expressions, a way that would not assume as its base the conventional idea of a double as a divided, separate self. The analysis that follows aims to investigate this possibility.

Spencer returns from Europe, it will be recalled, because he inherits two houses, the house on the jolly corner and another, "not quite so 'good' " (195), which stands at the westward, "dishonored and disfigured" (198) end of the street. Spencer has lived off the "rents" (195) of both houses during his years abroad and now, with a newly discovered "sense for construction" (195), oversees the conversion of the less attractive " 'property' " (194) into an " 'apartment-house' " (197), "not in the least 'minding' that the whole proposition, as they said, was vulgar and sordid, and ready to . . . really 'go into' figures" (195–96). Knowing, as we do, that the word "house" in the text is polysemic and that words in quotation marks demand a second (or third or fourth) reading, we can translate these seemingly innocuous elements at the story's beginning to reveal still another encrypted narrative. The legacy of "rent 'property' " Spencer inherits consists not merely of two income-producing houses but of two "houses" (families) marked by a rent, tear or splitting apart involving a "vulgar and sordid proposition" that "dishonored and disfigured." Spencer's conversion of the "not so 'good' " property into an apartment house represents a reconstruction of this split, a literal re-creation of the "house" or family line set apart by the tacit insertion of a false heir into its frame.

The continued decrypting of the narrative opens to view still more information. If Spencer's surprising talent for construction represents the "stir[ring of] a compartment of his mind never yet penetrated" (195), and if he does not "min[d] 'going into' figures," it must be because this re-creation of his "rent" line is not merely played out in an arena of steel and concrete but in the arena of his mind. Moreover, if Spencer describes the beloved house of his childhood as a "great gaunt shell" (199) where "vacancy reigned" (199) and as a place with values "other than the beastly rent-values . . . in short, in short—" (200), it can only be because this reenactment of the division in his line occurs in the place whose name (as the reference to Spencer's neighborhood as a "vast ledger-page . . . of ruled and criss-crossed lines and figures" [196] underscores) means "the place where lines (of houses/'houses') intersect and criss-cross." In short, it must be in the jolly *corner* that Spencer will imagine the crisscrossing of lines, that he will re-create in his mind the generating of a "vacancy," the truncating or shortening of a lineage.

How such a re-creation might take place and what it means to imagine or one could say "mind" a rent in the line is articulated in the enigmatic narrative of Spencer's hunt for the antlered beast. From the first words of Part II of the text, the jolly corner is described as a "scene" (207) where Spencer "really felt life to begin" (207), where he "let himself go" (207) and "watched . . . [for] the . . . show, . . . the revelation he pretended to invite" (207). The jolly corner is a place where Spencer only pretends to await a show, where he will not just perceive a drama or "vision . . . [whose] essence . . . was all rank folly" (209) but will "project himself" (208) into that vision, into the drama of a deception or folly in the ranks. This role playing, as we will shortly see, is far more subtle and complex than any innocent child's game of make-believe. When Spencer "surrender[s] to his obsession" (207) for the "hunt" and lets himself go, it is not to act out any single role or figure but literally to " '*go into*' figures":

> The terms, . . . the very practices of the chase . . . came . . . into play. . . . *He found himself* at moments . . . *effacing himself* behind a door or in an embrasure . . . ; *he found himself* . . . living in the . . . supreme *suspense* created by big game alone. (210)

Spencer "effaces himself," lets himself go to "find himself" as an other self, as a hunter. His own name resonates in the passage to suggest it; Spencer is held in "suspense," temporarily made to disappear and cede his place to someone else. What might at first be construed as a simple division or doubling of identity, however, is quickly revealed to be a far more complicated process:

> He wasn't afraid . . . because of the impression . . . that he himself produced . . . a dread [and] alarm . . . , leaving him always to remark . . . on his probably having formed a *relation,* . . . a *consciousness unique* in the experience of man. People . . . had been in terror of apparitions, but who had ever before so turned the tables and *become himself, in the apparitional world,* an incalculable terror? . . . It made him feel, *this acquired faculty,* like some monstrous stealthy cat. . . . (210–11)

Spencer is now a monstrous cat. No longer just a hunter, he has "acquired a new faculty" and "turned" into a hunter's prey as well, a prey that itself intimidates and causes fear. An apparently simple doubling has thus grown into what may indeed be called a special "relation," a "unique"—and puzzling—"consciousness." But before we can get a clear picture of the precise nature of this "consciousness," we must add several more pieces to its puzzle:

> He had . . . [the impression]—absolutely unmistakeable, and *by a turn* dating from . . . his resumption of his campaign after a *diplomatic drop, a calculated absence* of three nights—of his being definitely followed. . . . It worried, it finally *quite broke him up*. . . . He was kept in sight while remaining himself—as regards the essence of his position—sightless, and his only recourse then was in *abrupt turns. . . . He wheeled about . . . as if he might so catch* . . . some other quick *revolution*. . . . [H]is *fully dislocalised thought* of these manœuvres recalled to him Pantaloon, at the Christmas farce, buffeted and tricked from behind by ubiquitous Harlequin. . . .
>
> On his *return* . . . he . . . looked up the staircase with . . . certainty. . . . "He's *there* [James's italics], *at the top,* and waiting—not . . . falling back for disappearance. He's holding his ground . . . which is proof, isn't it? that something has happened for him." So Brydon argued. . . . "*Harder pressed?*—yes, *he takes it in,* . . . [it is] clear to him that I've come, as they say, 'to stay!' . . . I've hunted him till he has 'turned' . . . he's the fanged or the antlered animal brought at last to bay." There came to him . . . the next moment . . . a thrill that represented . . . the strangest, the most joyous, possibly the next minute almost the proudest, *duplication of consciousness.* (212–14)

Spencer's hunt is a series of turns and re-turns, revolutions and wheelings about, drops and absences, all of which "break him up," "dislocalise," and fragment his thought. This breaking up and fragmenting of his mind explains how he can be described as a hunter, a hunter's prey, and a hunter's prey that hunts; how he can be both Pantaloon outmaneuvered by Harlequin and someone who outmaneuvers and "brings to bay" his adversary. Where else but in a broken-up or "rent" mind might all these identities coexist? Where else but within the "thought" of someone who has "diplomatically" or tacitly "dropped," "absented," or "effaced" himself could these other identities have "their turn"? If Spencer wheels about in order to "catch" some other presence, it is because underlying the entire narrative of his hunt for the antlered beast is the fact that he holds caught in his fragmented mind the fragments of several different minds. It is because the "essence of his position" is to be continually out of position, to be "revolving," "turning," "wheeling," and "suspending" a series of identities that inhabit him.

Who then are these identities? What are the specific fragments literally occupying Spencer's mind? A first clue is offered by Spencer's impression of himself as a "terror . . . in the apparitional world" (211) and by his only half-joking response to Miss Staverton that, as for "ghosts—of course [the jolly corner] must swarm with them!" (202). Spencer sees himself as belonging to the world of apparitions. At least one of his identities must therefore be a ghost, a figure that profits from Spencer's nightly returns to the house in order to return from the dead. A second clue is contained in Spencer's identification with Pantaloon at the Christmas farce. Spencer is linked with the dupe in a scene performed on the anniversary of a birth conceived under what may respectfully be called "unnatural" circumstances. The most telling clue, however, can be found in Spencer's awareness, as he leans over a staircase in the "extension" of the house, "that he might, for a spectator, have figured some solemn simpleton playing at hide-and-seek. Outside in fact he might himself make that ironic *rapprochement*" (212; James's italics). The text furtively suggests the *rapprochement* or connection to be made here. It is the French connection between a simpleton or dupe and the game of hide-and-seek or *cache-cache*. It is the word cried out by the francophone child while hiding so as to draw everyone's attention. It is *coucou,* the name of a bird given to laying its eggs in the nests of other birds, which hatch them and rear the offspring, and whose variant form, *cocu,* is the vulgar French for "cuckold." The fooled, cuckolded husband in the Brydon family line is thus not just a ghostly, mutilated figure Spencer encounters at the end of his hunt. It is one of the identities lodged within his fractured mind. Spencer is not only "Spencer," the hunter of the antlered prey we know to be a cuckold. He is the prey as well; he is the cuckold.[16]

A brief word about the analytic and didactic problems posed by the fracturing just discussed may be fruitful at this point. A major obstacle in interpreting James's text is the variety of identities within Spencer, all of them expressed in the narrative by the indiscriminate pronouns "he," "his," or "him." On numerous occasions, readers may themselves feel brought close to delirium by the difficulty, if not the impossibility, of determining the content of these continually shifting pronouns. For this reason, when I say "he," it may at times be as difficult to isolate precisely to whom I am referring as it is to determine to whom the text is referring. Only in the course of the analysis will this enigmatic situation be somewhat clarified, or at least its generating principle explained.

To return to the analysis, the question that opened the second part of the interpretation—Who is the cuckold Spencer perceives?—may now be re-posed with an additional modifier: Who is the cuckold Spencer perceives and, by turns, embodies? The answer can be read in two places in the text, in "the rear of the house" (212) and "*there*, at the top" (213; James's italics) of the staircase. The cuckold perceived and embodied by Spencer inhabits the "rear" or anterior part of the "house." He resides *there* at the "top," at the highest, most remote point in the genealogical line of the Brydon family that lived there. Knowing as we do that the jolly corner contains inscribed within it "the annals of nearly three generations, counting [Spencer's] grandfather's, the one that had ended there," we can deduce that the cuckold at the "rear" or "top" of this "house" must have belonged to the first and oldest of these generations, that the ancestor present both before and within Spencer is his grandfather.

The allusions in the text to Spencer's alter ego and "other self" are thus not references to some symmetrical other half or reflection from which Spencer has been divided or split. The alter ego is not his "other I" but other "I's," other identities lodged within a corner of Spencer's mind. Similarly, the strange "duplication of consciousness" Spencer experiences while occupied by these identities does not mean he himself is doubled. What is duplicated or double in Part II of the text is not any single character but the entire drama of the hunt. While "Spencer" hunts the antlered prey we now know to be his cuckolded grandfather, the prey itself—as the text has already told us—hunts and intimidates *its* prey. The grandfather who (along with "Spencer" the hunter) inhabits Spencer's mind is himself in search of an adversary. He is himself a hunter of a fanged, antlered, or horned beast, of an adversary whose appearance says to him: "Cuckold!" In short, he seeks the adulterer haunting the Brydon "house" and who, in addition to the grandfather and "Spencer," must now be seen as still another "I" inhabiting Spencer's mind.

The identities lodged within Spencer are thus not a simple cast of discrete characters taking their respective turns on stage. They are conflated and coalesced within each other, "harder pressed," as the text has told us, squeezed and condensed together, each one harbored, absorbed, and "take[n] in" by the other. The "rare shift" that occurs as Spencer/"Spencer" senses the antlered beast turn to fight can be understood in these terms:

> [I]t would have shamed him that a character so associated with his own should triumphantly succeed in just skulking, should to the end not risk the open; so that the *drop* of this danger was, on the spot, a *great lift* of the whole situation. Yet with another *rare shift* of the same subtlety he was already trying to measure by how much more he himself might now be in peril of fear; so rejoicing that he could, in another form, actively inspire that fear, and simultaneously quaking for the form in which he might passively know it. (214)

The "rare shift" announced by the passage involves a "drop" and a "great lift," a shedding of one identity and a rising up in the line to the level of another. Spencer, the host to all this pressing, squeezing, and admixing, is at this moment totally absorbed, dropped, and evacuated as an identity. As the sentence immediately following the passage tells us, he suddenly feels the

> need to hold on to something, even after the manner of a man slipping and slipping on some awful incline. . . . The state of "holding-on" was . . . the state to which he was reduced; if there had been anything in the great vacancy, to seize, he would . . . have . . . clutched it. . . . (214–15)

Spencer "slips" out going up an "incline." His place is "vacated," emptied of his presence, ready to be occupied by someone higher up. The text itself declares not only the fact of this evacuation but the identity of the occupier. For "he" in the story is no longer explicitly attached to the name Spencer Brydon, as is the case throughout Part I. In Part II, it is *Brydon* (213) who argues, "He's *there,* at the top"; it is "*Brydon* [who] taste[s] of a sensation more complex than had ever before found itself consistent with sanity" (214). Spencer is no more. He has become totally absorbed by the so-called alter ego he began by hunting. His own identity has been evacuated, replaced by the person at the top of the incline whose patronymic he shares. Spencer has *become* Brydon; he has become his paternal grandfather.

The turns, returns, drops, and shifts of the text continue to multiply. From Spencer, a character by turns occupied by fragments of several identities, the narrative shifts to Brydon, the ghost of the grandfather, who invades and wholly possesses the void we know to be called Spencer.[17] This shift, in turn, means that henceforth "he" in the text has to be read as the grandfather and that the hunt for the "beast," the lengthy descriptions of the stealthy tracking through the house from "room to room and from storey to storey" (209), must be read as the story of the grandfather's search for the adulterer. The text, however, as we might by now expect, subtly shifts once again. "He" (the grandfather) is described as suddenly certain of the presence of his adversary because he finds a door he himself had left open to have been closed since "his former visitation" (216) moments earlier:

> [T]his exactly was what he never did; it was against his whole policy ... the essence of which was to keep vistas clear. He had them ... *quite on the brain*: the *strange apparition* ... of his baffled "prey" ... was the form of success his *imagination* had most cherished, *projecting into* it always a refinement of beauty. He had known fifty times the *start of perception that had afterwards dropped*; had fifty times gasped to himself "There!" under some fond brief *hallucination*. (217)

The presence the grandfather seeks is an effect of "visitations" or "apparitions" in the brain, of "projected perceptions" and "hallucinations" in "his imagination." What haunts Spencer, invades and occupies his mind, and constitutes the drama we are about to witness are not the actual events of the grandfather's hunt but the internal imaginings and fantasies of this pursuit that preoccupied *his* (the grandfather's) mind. Haunting Spencer is the tale of a passage, from "storey to storey," of apparitions and visions, of the grandfather's internal psychic drama that "slips" down from its "incline" and is pressed into Spencer's mind:

> [I]f he hadn't [closed the door] ... what else was clear but that there had been *another agent*? ... It was so logical, ... this time at last they *were* [James's italics] the *two, the opposed projections of him* ...; and this time ... the question of danger loomed. With it rose ... the question of courage—for what he knew the blank face of the door to say to him was "Show us how much you have!" ... Oh to have this consciousness was to *think* [James italics]—and to think, Brydon knew, ... was ... not to have acted! ... —that was the misery and the pang.... [H]e pause[d] ... for his *vibration* had already changed.... Shut up there ... with the *prodigy of the thing palpably* proveably *done* [James's italics], ... the situation itself had turned; and Brydon at last ... *made up his mind* on what it had turned to.
>
> It had turned ... to a supreme hint ... of the value of Discretion! ... Discretion—he jumped at that ... because ... *it saved the situation*.... [W]ith his eyes bent ... [h]e listened [at the door] ..., but this attitude ... was *his own communication*. "If you won't then—good: I spare you and I give up. You affect me as by the appeal positively for pity: you convince

> me that for reasons rigid and sublime—what do I know?—we both of us should have suffered. I respect them then, and, though moved and privileged as, I believe, it has never been given to man, I retire, I renounce—never, on my honour, to try again. So rest for ever—and let *me* [James's italics]!"
>
> That, for Brydon was the deep sense of this last demonstration. . . . (217–19)

What in fact is the "deep sense" of this demonstration? With the keys already provided by the text we can unlock its mystery and look behind the door the grandfather dares not open, a door behind which he imagines or "projects" two adversaries who have *done* or produced some "prodigy" that can be "palpably" proven. What he perceives, we translate, is the "doing" or creating of "an exceptional child," of a prodigy associated with a palpating → touching → handling → palming → fraud.[18] No sooner is this projection realized, however, than Brydon's "vibration" or imagination takes another turn whose sense is cryptically revealed by "his own communication": "If you won't reveal yourself," we may hear him say to the other agent or "other gent," "fine, I won't reveal you either. What I know is that all this has to do with reasons rigid and sublime, it all has to do with a cuckolding. And although I have every right as the husband to denounce you, I won't, and I won't ever try again. I retire, I close my eyes to this; I must not see it or know it. So let it rest in peace forever and let me bury it. Let me be discreet and shut up forever about what is shut up behind that door."

With this, Brydon (the grandfather) retreats and begins to make his way out of the house, concluding that the closing of the door had been for him "an act of mercy" (221): "There was the whole of the rest of the house to traverse, and . . . [t]his *conception* held together, it worked; but what it meant for him depended now clearly on the amount of *forbearance* his recent action, or rather his recent inaction, had *engendered*" (221). What is at stake here, as the reader may already have guessed, is not Brydon's physical descent through the house. It is his projection of the passage or "traversing," down through the "house," of the "forebear" or future ancestor who may have been "engendered" by the adulterous "conception" he has imagined. The detailed account that follows of Brydon's climb down through the mansion, from room to room and story to story, is in fact the tacit description of his projection, through the family line, of the repercussions of the adulterous scene preoccupying him.

With this in mind we can reread the description of the rigid figure of a man in evening clothes and pince-nez whom Brydon finally encounters, a man who, "as for dark deprecation," hides his face with his hands, one of which is missing two fingers. This figure can no longer be understood solely as the image of the cuckolded grandfather who "visits" Spencer. If, upon reaching the last flight of stairs in the house, Brydon gazes down and suddenly senses the presence of some "inconceivable occult activity" (224), "all unnatural and dreadful" (224), that appears to him as the "prodigy of a personal presence" (224), it is because he—the grandfather—finally "sees" the figure that would mark the bottom or end of the "house." He, the grandfather, projects before him the offspring issued from an unseen or "occult" activity, the offspring blind to his ancestry and hidden from disapproval, whose mutilated hand says, "Cuckold!"—not in the accusatory context seen earlier of "you are a . . ." but in the declarative sense of "I am the product of someone who was a. . . ." Occupying Spencer's mind at this moment is the grandfather's projected vision of the bastard, of the monstrous prodigy palmed off as a true heir, and of the line-ending rent this imposter would install in the house. The sight, however, is unbearable for the grandfather. He makes a crucial decision and another dramatic shift in the text occurs:

> The hands . . . dropped from the face and left it uncovered and presented. Horror, with the sight, had leaped into Brydon's throat, gasping there in a sound he couldn't utter; for the bared identity was too hideous as *his*, and his glare was the passion of his protest. The face, *that* face, Spencer Brydon's? —he searched it still, but looking away from it in dismay and denial, falling straight from his height of sublimity. It was unknown, inconceivable, awful, disconnected from any possibility—! . . . Such an identity fitted his at *no* point, . . . the face was the face of a stranger. . . . Then . . . sick with the force of his shock . . . he felt the whole vision turn to darkness and his very feet give way. His head went round; he was going; he had gone. (225–26; James's italics)

Projected before us is the moment of the grandfather's decision to keep a secret and hide the adultery forever. The sight of this offspring is literally too horrible for words. Brydon must not, cannot utter a sound. The adultery must be kept silent; it is awful, unsightly, unspeakable. The creation of this secret coincides with yet another major shift in the text. With nothing left he can possibly say, the grandfather exits the scene. The instant he does so, in the middle of a sentence and in the space of a semicolon, of an unuttered half-stop or suspension, *Spencer* Brydon returns to take his place. James's italics are cryptically eloquent: "Horror, with the sight, had leaped into Brydon's throat, gasping there in a sound he couldn't utter; for the bared identity was too hideous as *his* . . . *that* face, Spencer Brydon's?"

Spencer's return by no means marks the denouement or resolution of the drama. Once back on stage Spencer takes *his* turn at not seeing. Although haunted from the beginning of the story by an obsession to perceive something invisible and catch sight of his elusive, ghost-like alter ego, Spencer denies vision; he remains unable to see what is before him. The secret that has never been uttered and which now haunts him remains "unknown" and unknowable, "inconceivable," "disconnected," unsightly, unseeable. Spencer's return is thus really only the continuation of his absence. The "occult activity" embodied before him stays occulted. The scene is blacked out, as Spencer himself blacks out.

3

If for no other reasons than its relative brevity and terminal position in the text, the six-page-long Part III of the story suggests itself as a coda or epilogue to the drama just played out. On encountering it, however, readers who have successfully wended their way through the pronominal confusions and syntactic convolutions of the text's first two parts, and who hope that at least some if not all the loose ends still dangling will now be neatly tied together, are destined to be somewhat dismayed. This coda does not at all seem to tie ends together; it has the quite opposite effect of cutting loose what few supports or stays one may have clung to in following the text to this point. A veritable cascade of shifts and italicized turns inundates the reader, rendering the task of comprehension more daunting than ever. While the text describes "him" as returning to consciousness from a "prodigious journey" (227) that has "brought him to knowledge" (227), it is not at all clear what state of awareness he has returned to, what he really "knows," or who "he" really is. A fairly extended excerpt from Part III of the tale, beginning with "his" return to consciousness as he lies prone at the bottom of the stairs, his realization that Alice Staverton is holding his head in her lap and that for a moment she believed him to be dead, and ending with the final words of the text, will permit a more precise articulation of these and related enigmas. (All italics are James's.)

> "It must have been that I *was*. . . . Yes—I can only have died. You brought me literally to life. Only . . . how?"
>
> It took her but an instant to bend her face and kiss him, and something in . . . the way her hands clasped and locked his head . . . answered everything. "And now I keep you," she said.
>
> "Oh keep me, keep me!" he pleaded. . . . It was the seal of their situation. . . .

". . . I've known, all along," she said "that you've been coming. . . . I knew you *would*," she declared.

"That I'd persist, you mean?"

"That you'd see him."

"Ah but I didn't!" cried Brydon. . . . "There's somebody—an awful beast; whom I brought, too horribly, to bay. But it's not me."

. . . "No . . . it's not you! Of course it wasn't to have been."

"Ah but it *was*," he gently insisted. . . . "I was to have known myself."

"You couldn't!" she returned consolingly. And then, ". . . in the cold dim dawn of this morning I too saw you."

"Saw *me*—?"

"Saw *him*," said Alice Staverton. ". . . —in my dream . . . I knew it for a sign. He had come to you."

At this Brydon raised himself. . . . "*He* didn't come to me."

"You came to yourself," she beautifully smiled.

"Ah I've come to myself now—thanks to you, dearest. But . . . this brute's a black stranger. He's none of *me*, even as I *might* have been," Brydon sturdily declared.

. . . "Isn't the whole point that you'd have been different? . . . when this morning I . . . saw [him] I knew it would be because you had—and also . . . because you somehow wanted me. *He* seemed to tell me of that. So why," she strangely smiled, "shouldn't I like him?"

It brought Spencer Brydon to his feet. "You 'like' that horror—?"

"I *could* have liked him. And to me," she said, "he was no horror. I had accepted him."

" 'Accepted'—?" Brydon oddly sounded.

". . . yes. And as *I* didn't disown him, as *I* knew him—which you . . . so cruelly didn't, my dear—well, he must have been . . . less dreadful to me. And it may have pleased him that I pitied him."

She was beside him on her feet, but still holding his hand—still with her arm supporting him. . . . "You 'pitied' him?" he grudgingly, resentfully asked. . . .

"Ah I don't say I like him *better*," she granted. . . . "But he's grim, he's worn—and things have happened to him. He doesn't make shift, for sight, with your charming monocle."

"No"—it struck Brydon: "I couldn't have sported mine 'downtown.' They'd have guyed me there."

"His great convex pince-nez—I saw it, I recognized the kind—is for his poor ruined sight. And his poor right hand—!"

"Ah!" Brydon winced—whether for his proved identity or for his lost fingers. Then, "He has a million a year," he lucidly added. "But he hasn't you."

"And he isn't—no, he isn't—*you*!" she murmured as he drew her to his breast. (228–32)

An aspect of the text not yet addressed, the function of Alice Staverton, can now be examined and used to help piece together the puzzle of the story's last pages.[19] From the beginning of the narrative, Miss Staverton tactfully encourages and even pushes Spencer toward a confrontation with his alter ego. She discreetly suggests, for example, that Spencer "may still, after all, want to live" (201) in the jolly corner. She acknowledges sharing his curiosity about the alter ego, which Spencer likens to a "full-blown flower . . . blighted" (204) in its bud, by saying, "you wonder about the flower, . . . [s]o do I. . . . I feel it would have been quite splendid, quite huge and monstrous" (204–5). Finally, she admits to having seen his "other self" twice in a dream—"I saw him as I see you now" (206)—but, refraining from giving any details, responds to Spencer's query, "What's the wretch like?" (207), with the provocative, "I'll tell you some other time!" (207). It is no coincidence that Part I of the story ends with this remark and that Part II finds Spencer prowling the jolly corner in search of his "other self."

From the beginning, then, Alice Staverton is a conciliator of sorts. She seems eager to bring Spencer and his "ghost" together. In the text's last section this role is continued and expanded. The encounter having taken place, Alice effects a tacit resonance with the ghost. Without ever indicating whether or not she knows what this resonance consists in, she draws Spencer and his "other" together through her speech: " '. . . this morning I too saw you.' 'Saw *me*—?' 'Saw *him*,' said Alice Staverton [James's italics]." The distinction between Spencer and the ghost is linguistically confused, lost in an intertwining of pronouns. "He had come to you," she says. "*He* didn't come to me," Spencer replies. "You came to yourself," she smiles. Without in any way unraveling the situation or explaining its mystery, and without going beyond the limits of Spencer's own speech and ability—or rather inability—to articulate what has transpired, Alice Staverton, through a meshing of pronouns, performs a reconciliation between Spencer and the ghost. At the same time, she explicitly urges an accommodation between them. "He is not so terrible," we may hear her say if we expand upon her disjointed responses. "He is to be pitied, accepted. Whoever or whatever he is, accept him, live with him. I will help you to do this. I will hold your hand, support you, help you keep the other at bay. I will hold your head locked together, seal him up within you, and thereby lay the ghost to rest."

In the end, this is precisely what Alice Staverton accomplishes. If she has "brought Spencer back to life," it is not because the presence in him of the dead has been totally evacuated. On the contrary, as the constant shifting not only of pronouns but of the two proper names attached to "he" in Part III declares, Brydon, the ghost of the grandfather, is still very much on the scene:

"Ah but I didn't [see him]!" cried *Brydon*. . . .
It brought *Spencer Brydon* to his feet. "You 'like' that horror—?"
". . . I had accepted him" said Alice.
" 'Accepted'—?" *Brydon* oddly sounded. (My italics)

If Part I of the text describes Spencer Brydon's return to America and his desire to know his alter ego, and if Part II is the drama of the invasion of Spencer by *Brydon*, the ghost of his grandfather, Part III recounts the joining of Spencer and Brydon through the mediation of a third element. It stages the reconciling of two adversaries via the intervention of someone who holds at bay a secret that cannot be uttered. In the process, it reveals Alice Staverton's function in the tale as an unanalytic mediator, an unquestioning source of support and comfort with whom Spencer/Brydon can tacitly speak about the ghost and silently commune in the lie of his being "brought to knowledge." For ultimately there is no knowledge, no understanding, no real coming to consciousness in this text. The story ends steeped in the same grammatical ambiguity that has permeated it from its beginning, in the same cryptic silence in which it has buried and mutely articulated its secret. It ends with the italicized and triply silent "*—you*!": a pronoun signifying either Spencer, Brydon, or both Spencer and Brydon, whose ambiguity remains forever unquestioned, suspended between Alice Staverton and *him*.

4

A horned dilemma posed by the narrative remains unaddressed: the identity of the fraudulent imposter palmed off as a legitimate heir. The final task of this interpretation will be to determine who this offspring was or was imagined to be, an offspring who fits Spencer at no point but resides in and haunts the Brydon "house."

A key to the mystery is contained in the continuation of the passage cited earlier describing Spencer's reading, in the palms of the dead, of "the annals of nearly three generations, counting his grandfather's, the one that had ended there, and the impalpable ashes of his long-extinct youth, afloat in the very air like microscopic motes" (201). Syntactic and pronominal ambiguity are once again eloquent. The impalpable ashes of whose long-extinct youth are in question here? Spencer's? Very possibly. But an equally grammatical reading says it is the grandfather's "youth," the cuckold's "impalpable" → palm → fraud → fraudulent offspring, responsible for the "extinction" of a long line, whose ashes are afloat in the air like "microscopic motes." Motes? The word stops us by its archaic if not extinct resonance. Motes are specks.

Microscopic specks. Specks that function like a microscope. We hear: "microscopic spectacles." The grandfather's illegitimate offspring is floating suspended in spectacles. This is less startling than it may first appear. We have already read in other spectacles—the alter ego's pince-nez—a fraudulent birth. But "motes" floats elsewhere as well, namely, in the encrypted narrative of the Bible partially exposed earlier, in the annals of Matt. 7:2, where we hear its most ancient context: "And why beholdest thou the mote that is in thy brother's eye, but considerest not the beam that is in thine own eye?" The cryptonym "motes"[20] does more than tell us that the grandfather's fraudulent offspring is suspended in spectacles. It reveals that "motes" must also be read as the singular "mote" ("the mote . . . in thy brother's eye"), that this offspring is suspended not just in spectacles but in one spectacle, for one eye, and that this spectacle is in some way related to a brother.

Where might we look to find this single spectacle? The final dialogue between Spencer/Brydon and Miss Staverton catches the eye. "But he's grim, he's worn," Miss Staverton explains, speaking of the mutilated man they have seen. "He doesn't make shift, for sight, with your charming monocle." To which Brydon responds, "No . . . I couldn't have sported mine 'downtown.' They'd have guyed me there." If seen by others Spencer's monocle would be guyed, mocked, ridiculed. His monocle is the place where a mockery (giving horns), a fraudulent heir (from motes → specks → spectacles → pince-nez), and a brother are joined. Miss Staverton's curious turn of phrase tells us precisely how these elements must be connected to identify the grandfather's "youth." If the monocle "makes no shift," as far as sight is concerned, with the figure's pince-nez, and if pince-nez, unlike *rapprochement, ombres chinoises,* and *pour deux sous* (204), is a French word that is not "shifted" or printed in slanted, *italicized* letters in the text, it must mean that monocle is like pince-nez in that it is also an unitalicized French word in the tale. When we pronounce in French this word (whose meaning and spelling are identical in French and English), we hear suspended in this spectacle the name of the man issued from the concealed cuckolding, the identity of the offspring born (or imagined to be born) from an adulterous union and palmed off as a legitimate heir. We hear in *monocle: mon oncle,* "my uncle," the brother of Spencer's father.

This is why the figure before Spencer fits him at no point. This is why, in speaking to Miss Staverton of his decision to exile himself in Europe, he looks through "his single eye-glass" (204) and explains, it was "almost in the teeth of my father's curse, as I may say" (204). The "curse" haunting Spencer almost has to do with his father but not quite. It almost means he is the son of a bastard but not exactly. The rent in the Brydon house does not directly touch Spencer because it is in "the other side of the house" (219) (which is exactly where the grandfather sees the mutilated figure). It is in the uncle's house.[21]

"I's" in the text, as the narrator cannily tells us, are thus indeed monstrous: " 'You may still . . . want to live [in the jolly corner, Alice Staverton said to Spencer] . . . *with* such a home—!' But she . . . had too much tact to dot so monstrous an *i*" (201; James's italics). It is *I's*—and *eyes*—that haunt Spencer and bear witness to the phantom infiltrating the rent line of his forebears. *The Jolly Corner* may in fact be described as the story of the transmission of a drama from the "mind's eye" of the grandfather into the mind's *I's* or alter egos of Spencer Brydon; as the narrative of a secret or "occult" scene that is passed down and worn as an unseeing *oculus,* as an eye blind to the spectacle before it.

5

If *The Jolly Corner* can be read through Spencer's spectacle, it is because the tale *is* a spectacle, a drama played out before us. A fundamental distinction between James's phantom-text and those of Villiers and Balzac lies precisely in this fact.

In *L'intersigne,* an attempt and a failure at communication take place between Maucombe and Xavier. The reader cannot be sure whether Maucombe actually wants to reveal the secret of his paternity to Xavier, or whether his conversation only reflects the emergence of an unwitting desire to do so. It is certain, however, that, had Maucombe's communication succeeded and been heard by Xavier, the story as a haunting would not exist. The failure of communication during Maucombe's life, therefore, and the impossibility of communication installed by Maucombe's death generate the formation of the phantom and the creation of Xavier's narration as the symptom or symbol of its haunting presence.

In *Facino Cane,* no communication or attempt to communicate a secret occurs. The story is about the vicissitudes of a phantom already installed within Facino Cane, the effects its haunting has on him, and the circumstances of its transmission to the narrator. Whereas *L'intersigne* is the tale of what might be called the "inception" of the phantom as it grows out of an identifiable and present source of concealment (Maucombe), *Facino Cane* begins further along in the phantom's "existence." The secret motivating Cane's behavior can only be conjectured through its symptoms, manifested as Cane's obsession with *or,* his intrusions upon lawful couples, and his episodes of captivity and exile. These last two symptoms add an element to Balzac's text not present in *L'intersigne*. Through them Cane acts out the specific circumstances of his illegitimate birth, by turns dramatizing his father's identity as an adulterer and as a Jew.

The Jolly Corner, as it has just been interpreted, adds still another degree of complexity to the manner in which a phantom can determine a character's behavior. In James's tale, as in Balzac's, there is no attempt made to communicate the secret. We encounter the phantom at a late stage of its existence—two generations removed from its inception—and must, as in *Facino Cane*, reconstitute the secret from its effects of haunting. The novelty of *The Jolly Corner* lies in the fact that, once the secret is uncovered, the entire text emerges as the drama or spectacle of the events that preceded its creation. Unlike *L'intersigne*, the narrative is not concerned with the attempt and failure of a direct communication, since the grandfather is long dead. Unlike *Facino Cane*, the circumstances of the secret's transmission (as between Cane and the narrator) are not depicted in the story. James's text is constituted almost entirely by the performance of the drama of adultery and conception haunting the Brydon family. This performance, moreover, is far more complex than that of Facino Cane, whose life is defined by the quest for his origins and who only episodically assumes the role of his father as adulterer or as Jewish. In *The Jolly Corner* Spencer Brydon plays all the roles in his family drama simultaneously. In the guise of Spencer who seeks to know what he would have been had he stayed in New York, he is at once "Spencer" who hunts the grandfather, the grandfather in search of the adulterer, and the grandfather who envisions the bastard born of the cuckolding. The grandfather's secret is not merely the motivating force of Spencer's behavior, driving him to seek knowledge beyond his grasp; the mise-en-scène of its drama is the very substance and content of his behavior and, ultimately, of the text itself.

The following chapter on Poe's *The Fall of the House of Usher* will add still another degree of complexity to the ways in which the behavior of fictional characters can be traced to the invisible presence of a phantom. It will allow us to reconstitute not just the drama that is transformed into a secret but the internal psychic conflict that led to the secret's creation. It will also elaborate new directions a phantom may take in its path of haunting. In *L'intersigne* this path was delineated as the unspoken transmission of a secret from a parent to a child. *Facino Cane* expanded upon this by showing how a phantom can be transmitted to someone outside a family (the narrator) who is nonetheless susceptible to its haunting effect. The idea that phantoms are not restricted to family lines but may peregrinate in other directions will be explored further in *The Fall of the House of Usher*. So too will the possibility that a phantom may affect those in close proximity to it without entirely possessing them, and that it may haunt more than one person in the same generation.

In *The Jolly Corner*, the destiny of Spencer's phantom—to whom, if anyone, it will be transmitted—cannot be discerned from the text.[22] It is apparent that Alice Staverton is not possessed by Spencer's ghost. Rather she neutralizes its haunting effect by admitting the ghost's reality. In reading the text, I have not performed the same function as Alice Staverton. Although I have created a resonance with the ghost, this resonance has not been tacit. I have not kept the ghost at bay but have defined it as a phantom and explained its presence in terms of a haunting. Where Alice Staverton helps Spencer to keep his "I's" sealed up and intact, my project has been to sift out these I's, determine their roles within an encrypted drama of illegitimacy, and delineate the analytic process by which the phantom-effect created by their presence can be understood and, theoretically, removed or "exorcised." In her role as friend and unanalytic listener, Alice Staverton thus tacitly points to the void of interpretation circumscribed by the text and implicitly calls upon the reader to fill that void and perform the work of analysis. In a literary context this analysis does not involve effecting a cure of the fictive character. It means identifying the specific mechanisms by which the character's behavior and language thwart comprehension and teasing out their hidden principles of coherence. The achievement of the reader/analyst is not therapeutic but hermeneutic.

To the extent that *The Jolly Corner* can be shown to encrypt within itself traces of a secret drama that has been elided from it, it differs from many of the short stories by James with which it is usually associated. The so-called secrets or "essential truths" in texts like *The Beast in the Jungle, The Figure in the Carpet, The Real Right Thing,* and *The Aspern Papers* are objects of conscious quests that fail because the special verity of these truths lies in their deceptive nature. These and similar tales of James may be considered allegories of reading in which something seems constantly to escape knowledge, either because it is too apparent or because it is nonexistent, and in which the search to possess it invariably leaves the seeker (or reader) duped, blind, or lost. *The Jolly Corner* and the other tales in this book are fundamentally different in that they concern knowledge that is unspeakable and quests that are unrecognized. They are not allegories of reading but dramas of haunting that oblige the reader to render intelligible what must remain opaque for the characters. The reader is not implied by the text as potential dupe or misreader but is called upon to hear that to which the characters and the text itself are deaf.

One of James's ghost stories that does, I think, bear some similarity to *The Jolly Corner* and that would benefit from a reconsideration in terms of the phantom is *The Turn of the Screw*. Although recent interpretations have tended to view the tale as an example of the Freudian notion of the uncanny or as an allegory of reading, it may be proposed hypothetically that there is an unspeakable secret encrypted in the narrative that has to do with the death of a child.[23] The scene of Miles's "dispossession" and death at the end of the tale may be part of a reenactment of this concealed drama that could, upon analysis, potentially expose other elements of the text, ranging from the appearance of the ghosts to the embedding of narratives and narrators, as symbol fragments broken off from the haunting secret generative of the characters' speech and behavior. It may also be that *The Jolly Corner*, written ten years after *The Turn of the Screw*, in some manner complements the earlier text. While this conjecture will have to be pursued at a future date, the manner in which texts may function as complements or co-symbols of each other will be explored presently in Poe's *The Fall of the House of Usher*.

CHAPTER 6

A Meeting of the Minds

EDGAR ALLAN POE'S *THE FALL OF THE HOUSE OF USHER*

That motley drama—oh, be sure
  It shall not be forgot!
With its Phantom chased for evermore
  By a crowd that seize it not . . .
    (Poe, "The Conqueror Worm")

THIS READING of Edgar Allan Poe's *The Fall of the House of Usher*[1] is intended as both an expansion and a commentary on the preceding texts and interpretations in this study. It treats in a way not previously seen the questions of how a secret can be shared, how a phantom may be transmitted, and what forms a phantom's haunting may take. It also responds to an issue not yet addressed: what makes a drama traumatic? that is, what causes a drama to be made into a secret? Poe's tale contains encrypted within it the decision-making process, "lived" by a character, that led to the concealment of an affair and illegitimate birth. Unlike *The Jolly Corner,* in which the moment of decision to keep a secret is reenacted by one of several identities inhabiting Spencer Brydon, *The Fall of the House of Usher* presents one identity, divided between two characters, who together embody and play out the specific ingredients of someone else's internal psychic conflict whose "resolution" resulted in a secret's creation. The implications of this highly complex structure, both for the formation of narrative and for the process of interpretation, will be explored at length.

Coextensive with these areas of inquiry is the reflection offered by Poe's tale on the notion of "text." A poem entitled "The Haunted Palace," which sits apart from the action of the narrative, will be seen to function as a co-symbol of the text without which the secret concealed within it could not be uncovered. What it means to read a text within a text that both interprets and is interpreted by its enclosure, and what a work of fiction constituted in this way might reveal about the relationship between analyzing literature and the symbolic process will be of central interest in this chapter.

The concerns of past readers of *The Fall of the House of Usher* would at first glance seem to be at odds with the subjects of investigation just outlined. A substantial number have concentrated on the rapport between Roderick Usher and his sister Madeline, concluding, based on either psychoanalytic or sociological models of behavior, that the siblings' relationship is an incestuous one.[2] Others have viewed the story as a psychological allegory in which the forces of life and death or reason and madness do battle for possession of Roderick, who is ultimately consumed by the decay and madness of his race.[3] Still others have focused on the texts within the tale, either interpreting "The Haunted Palace" as an allegorical description of the head of Roderick Usher, whose eyes, blond hair, teeth, and lips are deemed to correspond to the palace's windows, yellow banners, and pearl and ruby door,[4] or dismissing the poem as a banal and ludicrous exaggeration.[5] The "Mad Trist," a second fiction contained in the narrative, has been similarly treated by some who have condemned it as nonfunctional trumpery.[6]

The questions of incest, degeneracy, madness, allegory, and the correspondence among inserted texts are most assuredly evoked by the tale and cannot be ignored. One of the aims of this analysis is to determine in what form the narrative demands these questions be posed and in what context their response may be heard. It can then be decided whether these are fundamentally self-contained problems, each responsive to a particular critical approach, or whether they may somehow be understood as elements or effects of a secret drama silently rehearsed by the tale. A result of this inquiry will be to demonstrate that "The Haunted Palace" and the "Mad Trist" are integral parts of the narrative and that their deciphering provides keys to the text's interpretation.

Aside from Johnson and Garber's essay on *The Secret Sharer*,[7] the texts in this study have received relatively little attention from poststructuralist critics and almost none from practitioners of deconstruction. *The Fall of the House of Usher* is the exception. Joseph Riddel's "The 'Crypt' of Edgar Poe" is, I think, quite representative of deconstructive approaches to reading, of the textual problems they confront and of the insights they can provide.[8] Before pursuing my own interpretation, I would like to summarize very briefly Riddel's argument. This is not an arbitrary point of emphasis but speaks to an issue raised in chapter 1: what are the points of convergence and divergence between deconstructive and anasemic approaches to reading? Riddel's analysis, which is as strong a reading of Poe's text as I have encountered, will permit an initial but pertinent articulation of some of these points. It will also help situate my approach to literary analysis more specifically with respect to this particular current of contemporary theory and criticism.[9]

Riddel views the story in terms of a tension between two opposing tendencies. Attempts to sustain difference, maintain the integrity of a "deficient" genealogical line, and thereby forestall the collapse of the Usher family and the narrative itself are in conflict with an underlying tendency toward unification, the erasure of difference, and the end of both family and narrative. The effect of this tension or conflict is Usher's "neurosis" (128). Its terms are articulated in various forms: in the " 'specious totality' " (125) of the Usher mansion, with its zigzag fissure bearing "no scrutable beginning or end" (125); in the " 'deficiency' "(126) of the Usher family line, which has produced no collateral issue and whose end is near; and in the peasantry's use of the appellation "House of Usher" to refer to both the residence and the family, obliterating distinctions between residence and family, outside and inside, literal and metaphorical. Proper signification itself tends toward collapse as the Usher line heads toward extinction. "It is the idea of the 'direct' unbroken 'line' of a teleological (and hence a narrational) order that is broken in this incompatible 'house' " (126). Usher's improvisation of "The Haunted Palace" is seen as representing an attempt to restore structure and signification; but the ordered, harmonious monarchy he describes degenerates into exhaustion and discord, figuring the inevitable decay of the Usher family. Usher's library of books, "each in one way or another devoted to the idea of 'the sentience of all vegetable things' " (128), seems to convey centered unity and secure order. Yet the "exclusiveness of the library" (128) and absence of " 'collateral issue' or ideas" (128) reproduces the deficiency of the family line. Usher's attempt to defy death by burying his sister alive is similarly futile, since the crypt only points to the absence of life in the house, to the "death or nothingness" (129) at its center. The house, family, and story can only collapse upon themselves as "an infinitely refracted series of fictions without origin or end, without the sustaining center of the crypt" (130), which encloses as it itself is enclosed.

Riddel provides other examples of his thesis, expanding on the "fictional labyrinth" of metaphor that structures the tale. "Everything in 'The Fall of the House of Usher' is a metaphorical detour, a delay in the course of a narrative which pushes toward its own tautological conclusion" (129–30). What Riddel does not address, presumably because he does not believe it can be resolved from within the text, is the origin or nature of the "deficiency" in the Usher family and the reason the family is doomed to destruction. In the following analysis, I will try to respond to these issues and to determine whether they may be linked to the elements of tension, disorder, incoherence, inversion, and discord Riddel points out in the narrative. My thesis is that these elements of discontinuity and the degeneration of the Usher race can in fact be explained by an underlying principle of coherence, linked to the concealment of a secret, that is not readily apparent but is nevertheless inscribed within the text.

1

The story begins when the narrator, having been summoned to the Usher mansion by his boyhood friend Roderick Usher, finds both Usher and his sister Madeline suffering from a vague but insidious malady. While Madeline, reclusive and prone to frequent attacks of catalepsy, silently wastes away, Roderick is oppressed by "a morbid acuteness of the senses" (280) and spends much of his time improvising excited rhapsodies on his guitar, one of which—"The Haunted Palace"—the narrator recounts. When Madeline finally succumbs, Usher buries her in a vault beneath the mansion, prior to her final interment, alluding to the deceptive, deathlike symptoms of her disease.

Following several days of bitter grief, Usher grows more and more agitated and filled with a vague sense of terror that gradually infects the narrator as well. One night, when both men are awakened by a violent storm and overcome by strange feelings of foreboding, the narrator reads a story to Usher, the "Mad Trist" by Sir Launcelot Canning (in fact written by Poe), hoping to calm him. The effect is precisely the opposite. As the narrator reads the passage describing the battle between the knight Ethelred and the dragon, both he and Roderick hear grating, ripping sounds emanating from the depths of the house. As the sounds grow louder, Usher, convinced it is Madeline he hears tearing herself free from the vault, cries out in horror that he has buried his sister alive and that she has now returned from the crypt to take revenge upon him. Suddenly, the door to the room opens revealing a bloodstained Madeline, her emaciated frame giving evidence of some bitter struggle, who totters for a moment upon the threshold and then, uttering a low, mournful cry, falls inward upon her brother, bearing him to the floor a corpse.

The narrator, upon witnessing this scene, flees the house in terror. As a wild light shoots across his path, he turns back in time to see the zigzag fissure in the wall of the mansion—the barely perceptible fissure he had noted upon his arrival—rapidly grow wider until the walls of the mansion are rent apart and the entire house of Usher crumbles in fragments into the tarn below.

One of the central enigmas of the text is the nature of the malady infecting Roderick Usher. He describes his condition to the narrator in strikingly paradoxical terms, first in his letter summoning his friend and later while in his company. "The writer spoke," the narrator tells us, "of acute bodily illness—of a mental disorder which oppressed him" (274). "[Upon my arrival] he said [it was] a constitutional and a family evil, and one for which he despaired to find a remedy—a mere nervous affection, he immediately added, which would undoubtedly soon pass off" (280). The one specific source Usher suggests for his affliction, "the severe and long-continued illness—[and] evidently approaching dissolution—of a tenderly beloved sister—his sole companion for long years—his last and only relative on earth [whose] 'decease . . . would leave him . . . the last of the ancient race of the Ushers' " (281), he admits only "with hesitation" (281).

Usher's contradictory descriptions of a malady both mental and physical, chronic and temporary appear to offer little clarification of the nature or origin of his illness. One can nevertheless cull from his words several key elements that correspond to other enigmas in the text. When Usher speaks of the acute bodily aspect of his malady, it recalls the strange physical symptoms from which he suffers: "the most insipid food was alone endurable; he could wear only garments of certain texture; the odours of all flowers were oppressive; his eyes were tortured by even a faint light; and there were but peculiar sounds, and these from stringed instruments, which did not inspire him with horror" (280). Usher's references to a mental disorder involving a family or constitutional evil, the death of a loved one, and an ancient race correspond to his unexplained penchant for singing bizarre, improvised dirges, one of which, "The Haunted Palace," is explicitly concerned with evil, disorder, and death in an ancient family. The description of Usher's illness may thus be less of a paradox than a sign of interpretation, a signal to analyze his physical and mental symptoms in tandem, to read his sensorial acuity and his wild poetic rhapsody as two "texts" in dialogue, responding to and informing one another mutually. To explore the possibility of such a joint reading, let us look at "The Haunted Palace" as it appears in its entirety in the middle of the story.

I

In the greenest of our valleys,
By good angels tenanted,
Once a fair and stately palace—
Radiant palace—reared its head.
In the monarch Thought's dominion—
It stood there!
Never seraph spread a pinion
Over fabric half so fair.

II

Banners yellow, glorious, golden,
  On its roof did float and flow;
(This—all this—was in the olden
  Time long ago)
And every gentle air that dallied,
  In that sweet day,
Along the ramparts plumed and pallid,
  A winged odour went away.

III

Wanderers in that happy valley
  Through two luminous windows saw
Spirits moving musically
  To a lute's well-tunèd law,
Round about a throne, where sitting
  (Porphyrogene!)
In state his glory well befitting,
  The ruler of the realm was seen.

IV

And all with pearl and ruby glowing
  Was the fair palace door,
Through which came flowing, flowing, flowing
  And sparkling evermore,
A troop of Echoes whose sweet duty
  Was but to sing,
In voices of surpassing beauty,
  The wit and wisdom of their king.

V

But evil things, in robes of sorrow,
  Assailed the monarch's high estate;
(Ah, let us mourn, for never morrow
  Shall dawn upon him, desolate!)
And, round about his home, the glory
  That blushed and bloomed
Is but a dim-remembered story
  Of the old time entombed.

VI

And travellers now within that valley,
  Through the red-litten windows, see
Vast forms that move fantastically

To a discordant melody;
While, like a rapid ghastly river,
Through the pale door,
A hideous throng rush out forever,
And laugh—but smile no more.

Within the idyllic description of a glorious ruler in a stately, majestic palace, Usher's sensorial symptoms are evoked—in an inverse or oppositional mode. The "radiant palace" with its "fair fabric" in the first stanza resonates with Usher's sensitivity to bright light and fabric while identifying the qualities he is unable to tolerate. The "gentle air," "sweet day," and "winged odour" of the following stanza suggest the idea of pungent and savory odors and tastes, a contradiction of his obsessive preference for insipid food and vapid smells. Finally, the third and fourth stanzas' references to the melodious music of "a lute's well-tunèd law" and to the "sweet" singing of Echoes mark a counterpoint to Usher's ability to bear only odd, peculiar sounding musical notes.

With the last two stanzas of the poem a reversal occurs. Usher's abhorrence of bright light and fabric, savory odors and food, and melodic music matches the description of the now-transformed dominion of the monarch where all that was radiant, sweet, gentle, and well-tuned has become "pale," "dim," bitter and "sorrow"-filled, "hideous," and "discordant." An understanding of Usher's physical symptoms would therefore seem contingent on explaining the mysterious shift that occurs in the poem. A clue to this mystery lies enclosed within the parentheses of the third stanza identifying the ruling king as a "porphyrogene," a word past readers of the text have curiously tended either to misdefine or completely overlook.[10]

The word comes from the Greek *porphurogenêtos* meaning "born in the purple" (*OED*). It was used in antiquity to refer to a male heir of the imperial family at Constantinople born during the reign of his father, and it issues from the word *porphyra* (purple), the name of the palace where the empress would lie in and whose birthing chamber had walls lined with porphyry. The poem is thus about the reign and fall of a so-called porphyrogenite monarch. "So-called" because, if this king is assailed in his claim to his "high estate," and if, as a result of this attack on his legitimacy, he suddenly dies ("Ah, let us mourn, for never morrow / Shall dawn upon him desolate"), the glowing purplish colors of the palace ("all with . . . ruby glowing / Was the fair palace door") grow pale ("Through the pale door") and dim ("the glory / That blushed and bloomed / Is but a dim-remembered story"), and those who henceforth issue from its door are a "discordant," disordered throng, it must mean that this "porphyrogenite" was falsely born in purple, that he was not the son of the king, and that those who descend hereafter from him ("A hideous throng rush out forever") are doomed to perpetuate his illegitimacy.

"The Haunted Palace" thus tells the story—buried or kept secret for generations ("a dim-remembered story / Of the old time *entombed*")—of the infiltration of a family line by an illicit heir and of the line's ensuing fall. The story of this fall is echoed by the description of Roderick Usher's symptoms. Usher's sensorial acuity, when read in terms of his poetic rhapsody, suggests a correspondence between the "constitutional and family evil" affecting him and the fall of the monarch's line in "The Haunted Palace." It hints that his vague, ill-defined malady may be related to the entombed or concealed infiltration of an imposter within his own line. To pursue this hypothesis, let us turn to another element of the text that creates a resonance with the poem, the other "palace" in the tale: the house of Usher.

The principal feature of the mansion is its "excessive antiquity" (276). Despite being overspread with fungi and crumbling in parts, the masonry still gives the impression of overall stability:

> No portion of the masonry had fallen; and there appeared to be a wild inconsistency between its still perfect adaptation of parts, and the crumbling condition of the individual stones. . . . Beyond this indication of extensive decay, however, the fabric gave little token of instability. Perhaps the eye of a scrutinising observer might have discovered a barely perceptible fissure, which, extending from the roof of the building in front, made its way down the wall in a zigzag direction, until it became lost in the sullen waters of the tarn. (276–77)

Presenting an outwardly solid appearance which draws the eye away from its inner decay, the fabric of the Usher house has an architectural structure identical to the familial structure of the house of the monarch in "The Haunted Palace," whose majestic facade camouflages the fissured integrity of its diseased genealogical line. But more than the external appearance of the Usher mansion links it with the house of the assailed king, as the narrator reveals at the beginning of the story:

> I had learned . . . the very remarkable fact, that the stem of the Usher race . . . had put forth, at no period, any enduring branch; in other words, that the entire family lay in the direct line of descent, and had always, with very trifling and very temporary variation, so lain. It was this deficiency, I considered, while running over in thought the perfect keeping of the character of the premises with the accredited character of the people, and while speculating upon the possible influence which the one, in the long lapse of centuries, might have exercised upon the other—it was this defi-

> ciency, perhaps, of collateral issue, and the consequent undeviating transmission, from sire to son, of the patrimony with the name, which had, at length, so identified the two as to merge the original title of the estate in the quaint and equivocal appellation of the "House of Usher"—an appellation which seemed to include, in the minds of the peasantry who used it, both the family and the family mansion. (275)

The age-old meshing of the name of the estate with the family, and the narrator's insistence on the substitutability of the latter for the former, leads us to read what is said about the Usher house as reflective of the Usher race. This, in turn, when joined with the previously established identity between the physical structure of the house and the ruptured genealogy of the king in "The Haunted Palace," sustains the hypothesis that the race of the Ushers is itself analogous or equivalent to the race of the fallen monarch; that the Usher family is split by some internal and barely visible fissure in its lineage.

There is some hint of this in the descriptions of Roderick's disposition as "incoheren[t]" (279), "inconsisten[t]" (279), and "alternately vivacious and sullen" (279). Usher's allusion to the particular nature of the influence exerted upon him by his family mansion, however, most succinctly confirms the genealogical identity between the House of Usher and the bifurcated origins of the assailed monarch in "The Haunted Palace":

> [Usher] was enchained by certain superstitious impressions in regard to the dwelling which he tenanted, and whence, for many years, he had never ventured forth—in regard to an influence whose *supposititious force* was conveyed in terms too shadowy here to be re-stated—an influence which some peculiarities in the mere form and substance of his family mansion, had, by dint of long sufferance, he said, obtained over his spirit. . . . (280–81)

The word "supposititious," which has been overlooked by past readers of the text along with "porphyrogene," is heavy with meaning; it signifies: "fraudulently substituted for the genuine thing or person, spurious, counterfeit, false" and, when referring to a child, "set up to displace the real heir or successor, illegitimate" (*OED*). The malady of Roderick and of the entire Usher family, the inner decay and fissured structure of the Usher mansion, and the consanguineous corruption of "The Haunted Palace" emerge as adjoining facets of the same drama. The House of Usher is infected by the "shadowy," unseen intrusion into the family line of a fraudulently substituted heir, of an illegitimate son whose father was not an Usher. Like the race of kings in Roderick's poetic rhapsody, the Usher race (just like the Usher mansion) is split by an invisible cleavage in its path of ascendancy, by a concealed, *zigzag* fissure or deviation in its supposedly "undeviating transmission, from sire to son," of the Usher name and patrimony. The House of Usher, in sum, is "The Haunted Palace." It is a House haunted by a phantom, infiltrated by and bearing suspended within it an unspoken and unspeakable birth, an entombed secret whose oppressive, supposititious force has weighed down upon and been transmitted through successive generations of Ushers, falling inexorably upon its ultimate victims: Roderick and his sister Madeline.

2

Call me what instrument you will, though you can fret me,
you cannot play upon me.
(*Hamlet* 3.2.388)

The uncovering of this secret in no sense means the text's significance has been unveiled or its complexities exhausted. If the entire line of Ushers has suffered a "constitutional and family evil," it is still unclear why Madeline's symptoms of transient catalepsy and wasting away are so different from Roderick's. Also unexplained is her violent reemergence from the burial vault, the crumbling into fragments of the house of Usher at the end of the tale, and the role played by the narrator in the story. These problems can be connected through an as yet unexplored component of the narrative: its cryptic elaboration of the circumstances—not just the event—that led to the fraudulent infiltration of the Usher line. These circumstances may be reconstituted with the help of a previously overlooked aspect of "The Haunted Palace": its explicitly poetic, rhyming nature and the fact that Usher accompanies himself on the guitar, a stringed instrument ("[Usher played] upon the guitar [and] not unfrequently accompanied himself with rhymed verbal improvisations . . . one of [which was] entitled 'The Haunted Palace' " [284]). A sung poem and a guitar both recall the epigraph of the text, the last two lines of "Le refus" (The refusal), a rhyming song about a lute by the French poet Pierre-Jean de Béranger:

Son coeur est un luth suspendu;
Sitôt qu'on le touche il résonne.

[His/her heart is a suspended lute;
No sooner is it touched than it resounds.][11]

The epigraph brings attention to verbal rhyme and resonating sound in the tale. It also tells us to read the text in another language, not necessarily French, but one that resonates or resounds in some way with English. We have already seen that a secret affair—an affair of the heart, if we listen to the epigraph—is suspended in the Usher line. In the epigraph, *coeur* and *luth* are linked by suspension. If we do as the epigraph says and touch or make vibrate this suspended *coeur*, the nature of its link with *luth*, and of what it actually suspends, begins to emerge. To touch *coeur* is to make *luth* vibrate; it is to make *luth* resonate or "rhyme" with *lutte*, the French word for "struggle." The epigraph thereby permits us to connect a suspended affair of the heart and a struggle. These elements also meet in the "Mad Trist," a story whose title signifies "an agreement between lovers to meet in secret," and whose plot concerns Ethelred's struggle with a hermit and a dragon. A passage from this fiction, invented by Poe and read aloud to Usher by the narrator, will allow us to investigate this coincidence. Ethelred, the hero of the "Trist," is unable to gain peaceable admission to the hermit's dwelling and proceeds to enter by force:

> "And Ethelred, who was by nature of a doughty heart, . . . waited no longer to hold parley with the hermit . . . but . . . uplifted his mace outright, and, with blows . . . cracked [the door], and ripped, and tore all asunder . . . [so] that the noise of the dry and hollow-sounding wood alarumed and reverberated throughout the forest." . . .
>
> "But . . . Ethelred, now entering within the door, was . . . amazed to perceive no signal of the maliceful hermit; but, in the stead thereof, a dragon of a scaly and prodigious demeanour . . . which sate in guard before a palace of gold . . .; and upon the wall there hung a shield of shining brass with this legend enwritten—
>
> Who entereth herein, a conqueror hath bin;
> Who slayeth the dragon, the shield he shall win;
>
> And Ethelred uplifted his mace, and struck upon the head of the dragon, which fell before him, and gave up his pesty breath, with a shriek so horrid and harsh, and withal so piercing, that Ethelred had fain to close his ears with his hands against the dreadful noise of it, the like whereof was never before heard." (292–94)

If we read the "Mad Trist" with the epigraph in mind, Ethelred is engaged in a struggle → *lutte* → *luth* → *coeur* → (of the) heart. What is not immediately discernible is who Ethelred is and who else's heart, besides his own, is involved in this struggle. A first, cryptic clue is offered by the image of the dragon sitting in guard before a palace of gold wherein hangs a shining brass shield. The meaning of this shield is never explained in the "Trist." The fact that it is suspended within a golden palace suggests that the key to its signification might be found hanging within the other golden palace of the text, within the "radiant" dwelling of "The Haunted Palace," with its "banners yellow, glorious, golden." Indeed, when we look through the windows of this palace we see—and hear—this suspended key. We see and hear "spirits moving musically / To a *lute's* well-tunèd law." What the dragon guards suspended within the golden palace of the "Mad Trist," the text cryptonymically reveals, are the resonant, rhyming sounds of a lute → *luth* → *lutte*, of a struggle of the heart performed by spirits floating suspended in the air. Whose spirits are these? Half of the response emerges from the process of cryptonymic analysis that has led us to this point.

It is now clear that to read the "Mad Trist" is simultaneously to read, translated into the "foreign language" of the epigraph, "The Haunted Palace." It is to recognize that the fiction of the "Trist" harmonizes with and echoes the two other musical fictions embedded within Poe's tale, explicating and being explicated by them. For this reason, what Ethelred rips into, cracks open, and tears asunder can no longer be understood simply as the dwelling of the hermit. What is broken into and rent apart must also be interpreted as the integrity of "The Haunted Palace," itself already seen to be synonymous with the (fissured) integrity of the House of Usher. Ethelred, in other words, is a figure of the person who, generations past, struggled violently to break into the Usher line. He is the allegory or spirit of the secret intruder who, long ago, forced his way into the *ethel*, "the ancestral estate or patrimony" (*OED*) of the House of Usher.[12]

The identity of the other spirit, of the "heroine" who plays opposite Ethelred's hero in this affair of the heart, remains to be brought out of the text, as does the reason the story of this violent breaking-in is called a "*Mad* Trist." The circumstances surrounding the reciting of the fiction within Poe's tale offer some clues to these riddles.

As the narrator concludes the first portion of the "Trist" describing Ethelred's cracking open of the door to the hermit's home, he hears resonate with his own words ripping and tearing sounds emanating from deep within the house:

> At the termination of this sentence I started . . . for it appeared to me . . . that, from some very remote portion of the mansion, there came . . . to my ears, what might have been, in its exact similarity of character, the echo . . . of the very cracking and ripping sound which Sir Launcelot had so particularly described. (293)

With the next passage recounting Ethelred's slaying of the dragon, it becomes apparent that the sounds the narrator hears are identical to the "unusually sharp grating sound" (288) of the iron door of

Madeline's vault as it moved upon its hinges earlier during her entombment:

> Here again I paused abruptly . . . for there could be no doubt whatever that . . . I did actually hear . . . a low and apparently distant, but harsh, protracted, and most unusual screaming or grating sound—the counterpart of what my fancy had already conjured up for the dragon's natural shriek as described by the romancer. (294)

With the passage describing the death of the dragon and the "great and terrible ringing sound" (295) of the enchanted shield falling at Ethelred's feet, it becomes clear that the sounds accompanying the narrator's reading of the "Trist" emanate from Madeline's crypt at the center of the Usher mansion.

> No sooner had these syllables passed my lips, than—as if a shield of brass had indeed . . . fallen heavily upon a floor of silver—I became aware of a distinct, hollow, metallic, and clangorous, yet apparently muffled reverberation. . . . [T]he huge antique panels [of the door] threw slowly back, . . . and there DID stand the lofty and enshrouded figure of the lady Madeline of Usher. There was blood upon her white robes, and the evidence of some bitter struggle upon every portion of her emaciated frame. (295–96)

While the struggle in the "Mad Trist" is ostensibly between Ethelred and the dragon, its signs are clearly perceivable upon the body and robes of Madeline. Madeline must therefore be the heroine struggling with Ethelred in the "Trist." She must be the other "spirit moving musically" through the "haunted palace," just as she moves, ghostlike, through the rooms of the Usher mansion after the narrator's arrival: "While [Usher] spoke, the lady Madeline (for so was she called) passed slowly through a remote portion of the apartment, and . . . disappeared" (281). Indeed who but a spirit could arise from a crypt buried deep beneath the house and return among the living?

Yet if Madeline is a spirit, it is not yet apparent whose spirit she is and whose struggle she has fought. Once again we may look to the "Trist" for a response. If Ethelred, the hero of this secret meeting between two lovers, is a figure of the man who broke into the Usher race, the heroine of the story, Madeline, can be none other than the woman, already in the Usher family, who engaged in the affair and bore the illegitimate heir. Madeline must be the spirit of the forebear who inaugurated the supposititious line. Indeed her name, which is preceded throughout the text by the prefix "the lady," a prefix to which the narrative explicitly draws attention—"the lady Madeline (for so was she called)"—this name, when heard together with the full and even more insistent form by which she is identified upon her return from the vault—*the lady Madeline of Usher*—tacitly yet eloquently reveals this to be her identity. It names Madeline as *the lady* (who) *Made* (the) *line of Usher*, as the incarnation or spirit of the woman who installed the fissure in the Usher House and replaced the lord Usher as the maker or progenitor of the Usher line.[13]

This explains (at least in part) why the "Trist" is called "*Mad.*" Its story not only recounts that the lady of Usher made the line but that *Made*line is the embodiment of this lady and her struggle. The precise nature of this struggle has still to be identified. We know that it involves a violent ripping, tearing, and "breaking up of the enchantment" upon a shield: " 'And now [Ethelred], . . . bethinking himself of the brazen shield, and of the breaking up of the enchantment which was upon it, removed the [dragon's] carcass . . . and approached . . . the shield . . . upon the wall; which . . . fell down at his feet . . .' " (295). We can also deduce, since the "Mad Trist" and "The Haunted Palace" are co-symbols, each complementing or "filling-in" the enigmatic traces of the other, that this struggle is somehow elaborated in Usher's rhyming, impromptu rhapsody. But it is only by joining this information with the narrator's comments that Roderick's abhorrence of all but certain effects of "stringed instruments . . . perhaps . . . *gave birth*" (284) to the fantastic character of his impromptus, and that the "words of one of these rhapsodies . . . [had] *forcibly impressed*" (284) themselves upon him, that the pieces of this puzzle resonate with each other and articulate in a clear voice how the sounds of Madeline's (of the lady-who-made-the-line's) struggle are to be interpreted. What Roderick Usher sings in "The Haunted Palace," we may now hear, is not just a rhapsody but a *rhyming rhapsody* marked by *force*. It is a *rape's ode*, a song about a "fervid *impromptu*" (284), an unexpected passion that, as Poe's italicizing of *impromptu* marking it as a foreign word emphasizes, also resounds in French. It is an ode to a rape → to a *viol* (in French) → homonym of the English *viol*, a sixteenth-century stringed instrument whose "peculiar sound," shared by the *viol*in, *viol*a, *viol*incello, *viol*a da braccio (arm viol), *viol*a da gamba (leg viol), and, perhaps above all, *viol*a d'amore (viol of love), can now be identified as the mysterious sound "emanating" from stringed instruments that haunts Roderick, the sound that is never—and can never be—pronounced because it "says" the secret possessing the line.[14]

The creation entitled "The Haunted Palace" to which Usher "gives birth" on a stringed instrument, the creation that "forcibly impresses" the narrator and resonates with a brutal ripping and tearing of the "enchantment" on a "shield," is thus the tale of a violently imposed birth.

It is the story, as the poem from which the epigraph (another co-symbol of the rhapsody) is drawn implicitly states, of "The Refusal" of an amorous advance by the woman in the Usher line and of the child born from her violation. It is the story, as Usher unwittingly conveys, of a "supposititious force," of the infiltration into the race of a fraudulent heir—conceived by force.

3

By "The Haunted Palace" I mean to imply a mind haunted by phantoms—a disordered brain. . . .
(Poe, Letter to Griswold)

From the beginning of the story, the family malady and Roderick's suffering from it are explicitly discussed. This marks a significant departure from the phantom-texts previously studied in which there is no serious avowal or recognition by the haunted protagonists of their suffering any mental disorder or disturbance. The captain in *The Secret Sharer* admits that his behavior may appear eccentric to his crew and wonders on one occasion whether he might be imagining Leggatt's presence, but he never seriously doubts his sanity. In *L'intersigne,* Xavier blames his visions of the house and Maucombe on "intellectual lapses" and "fatigue." Despite transient moments of fear, he dismisses each incident as a "mere hallucination," "nightmare," or inconsequential episode of "sleepwalking." Facino Cane is similarly unaffected by thoughts of malady or disorder, vaguely attributing his obsession with gold to his mother's passion. Finally, neither Spencer Brydon nor Alice Staverton in *The Jolly Corner* ever questions the mental state of someone who prowls through a house hoping to meet his alter ego.

This distinctive feature in Poe's text will be the concern of the remainder of this reading. One possible explanation for the explicit articulation of the theme of mental disorder and derangement in the tale might be found in Poe's personality and the fact that psychic unrest was so much a part of his own life. Given the diabolical playfulness of many of Poe's works, it could be proposed alternatively that the thematization of madness is a ploy to lure unwary readers into accepting ready-made solutions to the text's mysteries, thereby making them as much dupes of the story's events as some of Poe's characters. A third hypothesis, which in no way discounts the potential validity of either the first or the second, concerns the secret the text elaborates.

It is possible that the references to mental illness, disorganization, and madness in *The Fall of the House of Usher* are not solely allusions to Roderick's and Madeline's state of mind but are readable as lexical entities, like Usher's physical symptoms and the elements of the rhapsody and the "Trist" already analyzed, that carry encrypted within them fragments of the secret inhabiting the line. It may be surmised that the "Trist" is called "*Mad*" not only because it involves *Mad*eline as the spirit of the lady-who-made-the-line but because "madness" or "going mad" is somehow part of the secret drama buried within the Usher House and allegorized by the "Trist."

Support for this conjecture appears in the text immediately following "The Haunted Palace." The narrator explains that this ballad led him and Roderick into a particular "train of thought" (286), shared by others before them, but that took on a special insistence for Usher:

> [Usher's] opinion, in its general form, was that of the sentience of all vegetable things. But, in his *disordered fancy,* the idea had assumed a more daring character, and trespassed . . . upon the *kingdom of inorganization.* I lack words to express . . . the earnest *abandon* [Poe's italics] of his persuasion. The belief . . . was connected . . . with the gray stones of the home of his *forefathers.* The conditions of the sentience had been here, he imagined, fulfilled in the method of collocation of these stones—*in the order of their arrangement,* as well as in that of the many *fungi* [Poe's italics] which *overspread* them, and of the *decayed trees* which stood around. . . . Its evidence . . . was to be seen . . . in the . . . *condensation* of an atmosphere of their own about the waters and the walls. The result was discoverable, he added, in that *silent, yet importunate and terrible influence* which for centuries had *moulded the destinies of his family,* and which made *him* [Poe's italics] what I now saw him—what he was. (286–87)

In light of the analysis done to this point, it is not difficult to hear in the references to forefathers, ordered stones of the Usher house, decayed trees, condensation, overspreading fungi, and a silent, terrible, molding influence upon the family a condensed description of the decaying effect spread by the importunate, forceful forefather who shaped and molded the Usher family tree.[15] The interest of the passage, however, lies not merely in the way Usher's behavior and beliefs reflect the acting presence of the phantom. It lies in the fact that this phantom is associated with a "disordered fancy" or disruption involving an affair of the heart (or "fancy") and something present in the mind or imagination (a "fancy"). The secret struggle waged by the lady-who-made-the-line, which haunts the race and is inscribed in Roderick's behavior, appears to be mental as well as physical. The paragraph, following the one just cited, in which the narrator describes the books he and Roderick read together to pass the time confirms this suspicion and indicates what elements might constitute such a psychic conflict:

> Our books—the books which, for years, had formed no small portion of the mental existence of the invalid—were, as might be supposed, in strict keeping with this character of phantasm. We pored together over such works as the Ververt et Chartreuse of Gresset; the Belphegor of Machiavelli; the Heaven and Hell of Swedenborg; the Subterranean Voyage of Nicholas Klimm by Holberg; the Chiromancy of Robert Flud, of Jean d'Indaginé, and of De la Chambre; the Journey into the Blue Distance of Tieck; and the City of the Sun of Campanella. One favourite volume was . . . the *Directorium Inquisitorum*, by Dominican Eymeric de Gironne; and there were passages in Pomponius Mela, about the old African Satyrs and Ægipans, over which Usher would sit dreaming for hours. His chief delight, however, was found in the perusal of an exceedingly rare and curious book in quarto Gothic—the manual of a forgotten church—the *Vigilæ Mortuorum secundum Chorum Ecclesiæ Maguntinæ*. (287; Poe's italics throughout)

This time it is not stringed instruments but an entire choir that resounds in a foreign language to reveal a struggle: the *Vigilæ Mortuorum secundum Chorum Ecclesiæ Maguntinæ* → the *Vigils for the Dead according to the* Choir → (in French) *choeur* → (homophone of) *coeur* → *luth* → *lutte* → "struggle" *of the Church of* (the German city) Mainz → (by paranomasia) "minds." While alluding to Usher's fate as the unwitting guardian of the family phantom, the title of Usher's "chief delight" specifies what he guards: the "dead's struggle of the minds." The long deceased lady-who-made-the-line over whose secret Roderick unknowingly stands vigil, the decrypting of this forgotten manual's name reveals, was apparently of two minds about something. The nature of her conflict can be heard voiced by the other texts cited in the passage.[16]

While the references to satyrs and the *Belphegor*, also known by the title *The Demon Who Took a Wife*, evoke images of lust and forced carnal possession that correspond to the rape, the unseen or occult transmission of this event and its offspring through a genealogical line is suggested by the *Subterranean Voyage of Holberg* (Tieck's tale of a young knight's journey into a realm beyond), by the otherworldly states depicted in the *City of the Sun* and the spiritualist works of Swedenborg, and by the pamphlets on chiromancy, concerned with the crossing or intertwining of lines and, as *De la Chambre's* name suggests, something issued from a bed chamber.

The remaining references to the *Ververt et Chartreuse* of Gresset, two satirical, anticlerical poems, and to the *Directorium Inquisitorum*, an instruction manual written by the inquisitor-general of Castille for priests eliciting confessions from heretics and exorcising witches, combine to disclose at least in part the content of the "two minds" struggling within the lady. When we hear the twice-repeated French word for "green" in Gresset's *Ververt* repeated a third time by *Chartreuse*, a synonym of (yellowish) green, and when this repetition echoes with the *Ververt's* plot concerning the adventures of a parrot, the idea of a discourse marked by redundant, parroted, essentially empty sounds emerges—in direct contrast to the full, weighty speech of confessions and exorcisms described by the *Directorium*. The conflict or struggle in the lady's mind, these texts suggest, may have been between saying and not saying, between confessing the truth and uttering hollow, empty sounds. Whether this is the case, and how such a conflict might be linked lexically to mental disorder and the "*Mad* Trist," is still not evident. Three elements in the passage—the *Ververt*, *Chartreuse*, and the comment that Usher's disordered fancy trespassed upon the "kingdom of inorganization"—indicate where such a link might be found, in the only other place in the text one finds a kingdom, the "*greenest* of . . . valleys," and "*yellow* banners": in "The Haunted Palace."

> In the greenest of our valleys,
> By good angels tenanted,
> Once a fair and stately palace—
> Radiant palace—*reared its head*.
> In the monarch *Thought's* dominion—
> It stood there!

We are, the poem relates, in the realm of Thought. Juxtaposed with the description of the "radiant palace" that "reared its head" and the twice-repeated image of the "vacant *eye-like* windows" (273, 274) of the house of Usher (synonymous with the haunted palace), this fact argues for a third reading of the rhapsody in which the palace is understood as a figure of a human head and the goings-on within it as thoughts. The head and thoughts of whom? The narrator's remark that he was forcibly impressed with "The Haunted Palace" because, "in the under or mystic current of its meaning, I fancied that I perceived . . . [Usher's consciousness] of the tottering of his lofty reason upon her throne" (284) suggests a response. Usher's reason totters not on *its* but on *her* throne, on a female throne. The monarch "at the head" of the dominion of Thought and occupying its throne, the narrator implies, is a woman. Which woman? It can only be the woman (pre)occupied "in the olden time long ago" by the harmonies of a "lute's well-tunèd law," by the rhyming resonances of a *lutte* → a struggle. It can only be the lady-who-made-the-line. With the last three stanzas of the poem, the precise content of this lady's thoughts is revealed.[17]

The realm of Thought, we read, is inhabited by Echoes—women deprived of speech except to repeat meaninglessly the words of others—who parrot "the wit and wisdom of the king" and leave unquestioned the integrity of the line. It is also tenanted by vaguely described "evil things in robes of sorrow" whose mourning "dresses" (*robes* in French) suggest they too are female and who speak out to assail this integrity. A conflict between two women's voices—or two voices of a woman—can thus be heard echoing within the lady's mind, a conflict between saying nothing and thereby keeping the head of the line, and proclaiming the fraudulent ascendancy, thereby losing the head of the line.

With the poem's final stanza, the manner in which the lady resolved this conflict is unveiled and, with it, the lexical connection between her struggle and the "Mad Trist." The lady, the rhapsody reveals, kept the secret. The Usher line, although now a "hideous throng," rushing "like a rapid ghastly river through the pale door," continues to issue from the house.[18] The continuation of the line, however, is accompanied by a disturbed, deranged, "discordant melody" (and malady) within the lady's mind ("Through the red-litten windows . . . / Vast forms . . . move[d] fantastically / To a discordant melody"). In the process of hiding the truth and preserving the integrity of the race, the lady suffered a mental discordance or derangement. She went mad, lost her head. Through this loss or lapse into madness the psychic struggle tormenting her found its solution. By keeping the secret and going mad, the lady both kept the head (of the line) *and* lost the (her) head. She both said nothing and cryptically voiced the secret's content: "(As a result of the rape) *I lost the head* (of the race)."[19]

It is a moot question whether this is what Poe intended when he wrote to Rufus Griswold in 1841, "By 'The Haunted Palace' I mean to imply a mind haunted by phantoms—a disordered brain. . . ." On the one hand, it is most unlikely that Poe's notion of phantom corresponds to its elaboration here. His reference to a "disordered brain," on the other hand, poses a new and potentially fertile perspective from which to view the text. This expression can be understood, like its synonyms "madness," "mental discord," and "mental inorganization," as another cryptonym of the secret haunting the Usher race (madness, disorder → "lose one's head" → "lose the head [of the family]"). It is thus not just the fictions embedded in *The Fall of the House of Usher*—"The Haunted Palace," the "Mad Trist," and "Le refus"—that function as its co-symbols but a "nonfictional" piece of correspondence, ostensibly outside the text, that may be read as a symbol fragment complementing, interpreting, and being interpreted by the text. The implications of this dialogue between a text that is present and one that is absent will be explored shortly. Before this can be done, another kind of dialogue, exchange, or correspondence in the tale must be considered: the relationship between Roderick and Madeline Usher.

4

Les absents viennent moins par évocation que par convocation. Pour qu'il frappent, pour qu'ils veuillent bien frapper, il faut qu'ils comprennent que leur absence fut toujours déjà présence sous la forme d'une *nescience.*

[Spirits return less by evocation than by convocation. For them to knock, and be willing to knock, they must understand that their absence was always already a presence in the form of a *nescience.*]
(Maria Torok, *Théorêtra* [Torok's italics])

Uncovering the lady's mental conflict, while proferring a new perspective from which to consider the "theme" of madness in this and other works of literature, also opens a path for solving another riddle posed by the tale: the strange dissimilitude between the symptoms of Madeline and Roderick, both of whom suffer the same, age-old malady pervading the Usher race. It should now be apparent that the lady Madeline's symptoms—a "settled apathy, a gradual wasting away of the person, and frequent although transient affections of a partially cataleptical character" (282)—correspond exactly to the lady-who-made-the-line's struggle not to speak about the loss of the head. Like the figure of Echo who pined away to nothing but a hollow, dispossessed voice and who has already been linked to "not saying" by "The Haunted Palace," Madeline gradually and silently fades away, literally dissolving under the weight of keeping the secret ("[Usher dreaded her] approaching dissolution" [281]).

Given this correlation, the earlier conclusion that Madeline embodies the struggling mother of the fissured race must be modified. It would be more accurate to say that Madeline is the embodiment of *half* of the mother, the half wanting to keep intact the head of the line. This correspondence is all the more striking for the fact that Roderick's behavior parallels exactly the other half of the lady's struggle: her battle to voice the secret and expose the fraudulent heir. This is first evident the moment the narrator arrives at the mansion:

> I was at once struck with . . . an inconsistency [in Usher arising] from a series of feeble and futile struggles to overcome an habitual trepidancy. . . . His voice varied rapidly from a tremulous indecision . . . to that species of energetic concision— . . . that leaden, self-balanced and perfectly modulated guttural utterance. . . . (279)

Roderick's struggling efforts to articulate something are also apparent in the wild improvisations (including "The Haunted Palace") he plays "on his speaking guitar" (282), in the "utter simplicity [by which he] painted an idea" (283) on canvas, and, most explicitly, in his "unceasingly agitated mind [which seemed at times to be] labouring with some *oppressive secret, to divulge which he struggled for the necessary courage*" (289).[20]

A further modification of the conclusions drawn to this point is in order. If Roderick's behavior complements the part of the lady embodied by Madeline, it must be because he too is the dwelling place of a portion of the lady's "ghost" or "spirit." Roderick, whose "cadaverousness of complexion [and] ghastly pallor of the skin" (278–79) are so deathlike that the narrator "doubted to whom [he] spoke" (279), is, like Madeline, inhabited by the dead. He is the living incarnation of the deceased person who created an oppressive secret and fought to divulge it. He is the half of the lady-who-made-the-line and struggled to speak.

It may be asked why this halving of the lady and of her struggle occurs. Such a structure has not been seen in the phantom-texts previously studied, nor does it seem to fit with the notion, revealed in this reading as central to Poe's text, of the silent and integral transmission of a secret through successive generations of a family. The narrator's account of Madeline's burial within the family vault furnishes an explanation for these unusual circumstances. At the same time, it brings into focus another path a phantom may take in its peregrinations:

> Having deposited our mournful burden upon tressels within this region of horror, we partially turned aside the yet unscrewed lid of the coffin, and looked upon the face of the tenant. A striking similitude between brother and sister now first arrested my attention; and Usher, divining, perhaps, my thoughts, murmured out some few words from which I learned that the deceased and himself had been twins, and that sympathies of a scarcely intelligible nature had always existed between them. (288–89)

Madeline, a twin to Roderick, is positioned to inherit half of the Usher "patrimony," to become a psychic collaborator or partner in the hidden legacy of rape and illegitimate birth passed down through the family. By virtue of their simultaneous births, Roderick and Madeline have become genuine "secret sharers" of the Usher phantom, unwitting co-beneficiaries of the family inheritance. Until now transmitted in its totality to each successive heir in the line, the Usher secret is now split between the two siblings who, together, carry it as one.

Whereas *The Jolly Corner* could be called a false double story in which various identities in a hidden drama of adultery take up residence in the mind of one person (Spencer) who only appears to be double or split in two, *The Fall of the House of Usher* is a true double story. It is the tale of how a haunting can be shared between two siblings; how one secret and the agent encrypting it (the lady) can be split between two characters who, together, embody it. Like the co-symbolic relationship between the "Mad Trist" and "The Haunted Palace," brother and sister bear complementary fragments of the secret whose content becomes readable only through their joining. Neither sibling can be bypassed if we are to reconstruct the drama buried by the mother of the fissured race. Neither can be understood except as the embodiment of a portion or share of that drama. Roderick and Madeline are, together, a unity that is dual. They are, as their patronymic may be heard to say, *Us-her*: "*Us*, we are *her*. We are, together, the lady-who-made-the-line."[21]

(The critical commentaries on the story having incest at their center may be reappraised in terms of this structural dual unity. While I would maintain that there is no concrete textual evidence to support an interpretation of incest in the tale, it can legitimately be proposed that the interlocking relationship, born of an illicit affair of the heart, that is shared by brother and sister is conducive to an incestuous rapport and could well be the catalyst for such a hypothetical tryst. It is perhaps with the [textually undeveloped] possibility of such a secret sharing that the critics opting for this interpretation of the tale have, unbeknownst to themselves, resonated.)

A secret, then, may be transmitted not just successively from one person to another inside a family line (as in *The Jolly Corner*) or outside it (as in Facino Cane's legacy to the narrator). It may undergo a bifurcation in its path of migration and be split between two identities in a complementary, asymmetrical relationship. The asymmetry in Poe's text is entirely different from that observed in *The Secret Sharer*, where the captain creates a semblance of a dual unity with Leggatt as a symptom of the pathogenic dual unity or phantom haunting him. In Poe's tale, a secret is genuinely if unknowingly shared between Roderick and Madeline in a structure analogous to the symbolic operation. Brother and sister function as two disparate fragments bearing traces of the whole from which they have been broken. By reading these traces together, we can reconstitute the unspeakable drama they collectively conceal.

Understanding the rapport of dual unity between Roderick and Madeline opens to interpretation several as yet unaddressed enigmas presented by Poe's story. Specifically, it provides a way of explaining the role of the narrator, Madeline's reemergence from the crypt, and the violent crumbling and fall of the house of Usher. It will be recalled that the narrator travels to the Usher mansion in response to his boyhood friend Roderick's letter, which resembles less an invitation than a summons: "[Usher's] letter, . . . in its wildly importunate nature, . . . admitted of no other than a personal reply . . . and I accordingly obeyed forthwith what I still considered a very singular summons" (274–75). The narrator reveals that Usher's insistence derives from his illness:

> The writer spoke . . . of an earnest desire to see me, as his best, and indeed his only personal friend, with a view of attempting, by the cheerfulness of my society, some alleviation of his malady. It was the manner in which all this . . . was said—it was the apparent *heart* [Poe's italics] that went with his request—which allowed me no room for hesitation. . . . (274–75)

Roderick's convocation of the narrator comes from the heart and is aimed at alleviating a malady. It is a summons, we can now hear, to help bear the heart → *luth* → *lutte* → struggle of a *malady* → of my lady, to help share the lady's secret.[22] With the narrator's arrival and peculiar vision of the Usher domain, it becomes apparent that the forceful, importunate nature of Roderick's summons has already had an effect:

> I know not how it was—but, with the first glimpse of the building, a sense of insufferable gloom pervaded my spirit. . . . I looked upon the scene before me—upon the mere house . . . upon a few rank sedges—and upon a few white trunks of decayed trees—with an utter depression of soul which I can compare to no earthly sensation more properly than to . . . the hideous dropping off of the veil. There was an iciness . . . a sickening of the heart. . . . What was it—I paused to think— . . . that so unnerved me in the contemplation of the House of Usher? It was a mystery all insoluble; nor could I grapple with the shadowy fancies that crowded upon me as I pondered. (273–74)

Without any awareness of his doing so, the narrator "glimpses" the "hideous . . . scene" that brought "decay" within the Usher family "tree." His "fancy" or imagination appears to have been forcibly infected and "crowded upon" by the "grappling" struggle of the lady inhabiting Roderick's mind, a struggle that has passed down through the Usher "ranks."[23] The narrator himself unknowingly alludes to the source of his altered state of awareness when he describes the valet who "ushered me into the presence of his master" (277), and when he speaks of the activities he shared with Roderick: "I listened, as if in a dream, to the wild improvisations of his speaking guitar . . . as a closer and still closer intimacy admitted me more unreservedly into *the recesses of his spirit*" (282).

If the narrator is gradually "ushered" or made a participant in the Usher family haunting, it is not until the death of Madeline that the extent and terms of his participation can be clearly perceived. After helping Roderick bear Madeline to rest in a "donjon-keep" (288) lying "immediately beneath that portion of the building in which was [his] own sleeping apartment" (288), the narrator retires with his friend to the rooms of the "upper portion of the house" (289). There Usher's mental disorder worsens as he sits for hours, "as if listening to some imaginary sound. It was no wonder," the narrator recounts, "that his condition terrified—that it *infected me*. I felt creeping upon me, by slow yet certain degrees, the *wild influence* of his own fantastic yet impressive superstitions" (289–90). Several nights later, the nature of this infecting influence is (cryptically) unveiled:

> It was . . . the night of the seventh or eighth day after the placing of the lady Madeline within the donjon, that I experienced the full power of such feelings. Sleep came not near my couch. . . . *I struggled to reason off* the nervousness which had dominion over me. . . . An irrepressible tremour gradually pervaded my frame; and, at length, *there sat upon my very heart an incubus of utterly causeless alarm. Shaking this off with a gasp and a struggle,* I . . . hearkened—I know not why, except that *an instinctive spirit prompted me*—to certain low and indefinite sounds which came . . . I knew not whence. Overpowered by an intense sentiment of horror, unaccountable yet unendurable, I . . . endeavoured to arouse myself from the pitiable condition into which I had fallen, by pacing rapidly to and fro through the apartment. (290)

An "incubus," an evil spirit that has sexual intercourse with women in their sleep, sits upon the narrator's heart while he struggles to "reason off" or quiet the "spirit" pervading his frame. Whose spirit? It can only be the spirit of the lady far up in the line, in the "upper portion of the house," who battled against an "overpowering" incubus or sexual attacker and fought to "reason off" a conflict and "keep the head." It is the spirit of the lady-who-made-the-line-and-tried-to-keep-it-a-secret. With the death of Madeline, the narrator becomes infected by the half of the Usher phantom embodied by Roderick's sister. The vicissitudes wrought by this infection, however, involve more than vague feelings of unease or even terror. As the continuation of the passage just cited testifies, without any recognition of his doing so, the narrator actually plays out the role left vacant by Madeline's demise. He carries on the struggle Madeline herself waged before being buried beneath his bedroom in the donjon-keep:[24]

> I had taken but *few turns* in this manner, when . . . Usher . . . rapped . . . at my door. . . . His countenance was, as usual, *cadaverously* wan—but . . . there was a *species of mad hilarity* in his eyes—an evidently restrained *hysteria* [Poe's italics] in his whole demeanour. . . .
>
> "And you have not seen it?" he said abruptly . . . "you have not then seen it?—but, stay! you shall." Thus speaking . . . he hurried to one of the casements, and threw it freely open to the storm.
>
> . . . A whirlwind had apparently collected its force in our vicinity; for there were . . . violent alterations in the direction of the wind; and the exceeding density of the clouds (which hung so low as to press upon the turrets of the house) did not prevent our perceiving the life-like velocity with which they flew *careering from all points against each other*. . . . [T]he . . . agitated vapour . . . w[as] glowing in the unnatural light of a . . . gaseous exhalation which hung about and enshrouded the mansion.
>
> "You must not—you shall not behold this!" said I . . . to Usher, as I led him, with a gentle violence . . . to a seat. "These appearances, which bewilder you, are merely electrical phenomena . . . or . . . they [may] have their ghastly origin in the rank miasma of the tarn. Let us close this casement;—the air is . . . dangerous to your frame. Here is one of your favourite romances. I will read, and you shall listen;—and so we will pass away this terrible night together." (290–92)

This passage marks a dramatic shift in the text. With the abrupt, disjointed nature of Roderick's intervention, suggesting his utterance is part of another context and his words those of someone else, and with the narrator's pacing "to and fro" for a "few turns" and insistence that his friend not behold the violent storm, it becomes evident that the exchange between Roderick and the narrator is a dialogue between two other identities, that each of the two men takes a turn at articulating the discourse of someone absent. Of whom? Usher's cadaverously ghostlike appearance and the "species of mad hilarity" and "restrained *hysteria*" throughout his demeanor provide half the answer. They identify him as the ghost of a "mad species," as the spirit of the mad *woman* (*hysteria* = woman's madness ascribed to "disturbances in the womb") or lady, "restrained" or confined within him, who wanted to let escape the agitated and "unnatural . . . exhalation" "pressing upon" the House of Usher and give expression to the "violent and life-like alteration" in the air → heir. Roderick, in urging the narrator to behold the storm, speaks as the lady-who-made-the-line-and-sought-to-expose-the-secret. And it is as the opposing half of this lady that the narrator insists this sight not be seen, that no one get wind of the unnatural heir threatening the "frame" or structural integrity of the Usher house. It is as the voice of the lady-who-made-the-line-and-struggled-to-keep-the-secret that the narrator responds to Usher and tries to silence the discourse emanating from him.

Upon the death of Madeline, the narrator thus assumes her role in the drama haunting the Usher race and (unwittingly) reenacts with Roderick the lady-who-made-the-line's unspoken psychic conflict between hiding and revealing the fraudulent heir. With the narrator's reciting aloud of the "Mad Trist" in an effort to calm Usher, a second shift occurs. The narrator takes a turn in still another role and becomes the unknowing catalyst of the catastrophic events of the story's end.

As he begins the passage describing Ethelred's slaying of the dragon, the narrator notices "a strange alteration . . . in [Usher's] demeanour" (294). "[H]is lips trembled as if he were murmuring inaudibly, . . . [h]is head had dropped upon his breast . . . [and] he rocked from side to side" (294–95), his eyes wide open and fixed by the "stony rigidity" (295) permeating his whole countenance. With the narrator's reading of the paragraph detailing the fall of the shield at Ethelred's feet, Usher's trancelike state grows even more acute. Disturbed by this odd behavior and wondering whether Usher has heard, as he has, the sounds of the dragon's death and the shield's fall reverberating through the house, the narrator approaches his friend:

> [As] I placed my hand upon his shoulder, there came a strong shudder over his whole person . . . and . . . he spoke in a low, hurried, and gibbering murmur, as if unconscious of my presence. . . .
>
> "Not hear it?—yes, I hear it, and *have* heard it. Long—long—long—many minutes, many hours, many days, have I heard it—yet I dared not—oh, pity me, miserable wretch that I am!—I dared not—I *dared* not speak! *We have put her living in the tomb!* Said I not that my senses were acute? I *now* tell you that I heard her first feeble movements in the hollow coffin. I heard them—many, many days ago—yet I dared not—*I dared not speak!* And now—to-night—Ethelred—ha! ha!—the breaking of the hermit's door, and the death-cry of the dragon, and the clangour of the shield!—say, rather, the rending of her coffin, and the grating of the iron hinges of her prison, and her struggles within the coppered archway of the vault! Oh whither shall I fly? Will she not be here anon? Is she not hurrying to upbraid me for my haste? Have I not heard her footstep on the stair? Do I not distinguish that heavy and horrible beating of her

heart? MADMAN!"—here he sprang furiously to his feet, and shrieked out his syllables, as if in the effort he were giving up his soul—"MADMAN! I TELL YOU THAT SHE NOW STANDS WITHOUT THE DOOR!" (295–96; Poe's italics and capitals throughout)

The reader encountering this passage cannot help but be struck by the profusion of italics, hyphens, exclamations, and capitals strewn throughout it. From a typographical perspective alone, Usher's discourse appears somewhat confused and disoriented. Add to this its myriad repetitions, insistent crescendo of rhetorical questions, and strange archaisms ("Oh whither shall I fly? Will she not be here anon?"), and it becomes difficult not to conclude that "the speaker" (296) of this utterance, as the narrator calls him, is not entirely in his right mind. It becomes apparent, more precisely, that the abrupt and disjointed words Usher utters from a virtually "unconscious" state once again belong to another context; that Usher speaks *somebody else's* mind; that his "whole person" has been overcome by a "strong *shudder,*" by the person who *shut her* mouth and *"dared not speak,"* by the "miserable wretch" who *"put her [secret] living in the tomb!"*: by the mad-lady-who-made-the-line. "The speaker," as the narrator's indefinite epithet underscores, is not just Usher but the lady who, "long—long—long—many minutes, many hours, many days" ago, buried alive the event of the rape and illegitimate birth. It is this archaic lady who *"now"* speaks through Roderick to tell her story. She is the one who now declares that to recite the sounds of the "Trist" is to "say, rather . . . her struggles within . . . the vault" or (bed)chamber and the rending of her shield. It is she, in sum, who, when Usher "shriek[s] out his syllables, as if . . . *giving up his soul,*" is this very "soul" or spirit expelled from within him, the (half of the) mad lady inhabiting this "*MADMAN,*" whose voice finally emerges to proclaim the secret haunting the line: "I TELL YOU THAT SHE NOW STANDS WITHOUT THE DOOR!" → "I TELL YOU THAT THE *LADY MADELINE* STANDS WITHOUT THE *USHER*!" (from *ustium* = "door") → "I TELL YOU THAT *THE LADY MADE THE LINE WITHOUT AN USHER*!"

Far from quieting the ghostly presence possessing Roderick, the narrator's reading aloud of the "Mad Trist" by (the fictional author) Sir Launcelot Canning functions by convoking it. In reciting the romance and allegorically voicing the lady's struggle, the narrator causes the secret haunting the Usher House to resonate. He becomes the instrument or sounding board of its articulation, the medium through which the centuries-old phantom inhabiting Roderick is made to echo and ultimately voice its content. He becomes, in essence, an exorcist. The effects of his exorcism go beyond conjuring the content of the secret hidden in the line, however. As the last paragraphs of the text reveal, the narrator's reading of the "Trist" also recalls from the dead the buried incarnation of that secret:

> As if in the superhuman energy of his utterance there had been found the potency of a spell—the huge antique panels to which the speaker pointed, threw slowly back . . . their . . . ebony jaws. It was the work of the rushing gust—but then without those doors there DID stand the lofty and enshrouded figure of the lady Madeline of Usher. There was blood upon her white robes, and the evidence of some bitter struggle upon every portion of her emaciated frame. For a moment she remained trembling and reeling to and fro upon the threshold, then, with a low moaning cry, fell heavily inward upon the person of her brother, and in her violent and now final death-agonies, bore him to the floor a corpse, and a victim to the terrors he had anticipated.
>
> From that chamber, and from that mansion, I fled aghast. . . . Suddenly there shot along the path a wild light, and I turned to see whence a gleam so unusual could have issued. . . . The radiance was that of the . . . blood-red moon which now shone vividly through that once barely-discernible fissure of which I have before spoken as extending from the roof of the building, in a zigzag direction, to the base. While I gazed, this fissure rapidly widened—there came a fierce breath of the whirlwind—the entire orb of the satellite burst at once upon my sight—my brain reeled as I saw the mighty walls rushing asunder—there was a long tumultuous shouting sound like the voice of a thousand waters—and the deep and dank tarn at my feet closed sullenly and silently over the fragments of the "HOUSE OF USHER." (296–97)

By reciting the "Trist," the narrator not only brings to (Roderick's) mind the secret of the lady so that it may be expelled; he literally brings her spirit back from the crypt. He awakens and conjures from the dead the buried objectification of the age-old drama possessing the race, the figure of the lady (who) Made(the)line of Usher. With the startling reappearance of Madeline the final curtain of this drama falls. As she collapses "inward upon the person of her brother," this now-exorcised ghost of the lady meshes with "the person" or (half of) the lady inhabiting Roderick. The twin spirits of the secret are brought out of the past and joined in the present. Brother and sister are reunited in a meeting of the (lady's) minds. And the phantom, like the "voice of a thousand waters," flows out in one final, tumultuous exhalation as its spirits, now expelled, go back underground whence they came, to be buried forever along with the House of Usher.[25]

Upon witnessing these catastrophic events, the narrator flees the mansion "aghast," his "brain reel[ing]" in confusion. Although his reading of the "Trist" has brought to (Usher's) mind the phantom and precipitated this scene of death and destruction, he has no awareness of having done so, no understanding of what he has caused to be reenacted. He only gazes upon the tumult before him, a confused, bewildered observer. In this respect, the narrator in Poe's tale is similar to the captain in *The Secret Sharer*, Xavier in *L'intersigne*, and the narrator in *Facino Cane*, all of whom recount their stories without comprehending what they signify or recognizing the role of their own haunting in their unfolding. In two crucial respects, however, Poe's narrator is different from Villiers's and Balzac's (the less complex nature of Conrad's text precludes extending the comparison to its narrator), two respects whose elaboration provides a new vantage point from which the concepts of narration, narrative framing, and haunting in fiction may be considered.

Unlike the case for the narrator's counterparts, whose narratives can be explained as an effect of their haunting by a phantom, nothing in Poe's story reveals why the narrator tells his tale. What is revealed is the change in roles he undergoes following his "infection" by the Usher secret, a change that adds an intriguing dimension to the notion of "narrator." Having gradually assumed the part of the lady Madeline, the narrator, upon reciting the "Mad Trist," leaves this role and takes on the function of what might be called an "unconscious analyst." He performs an exorcism without being aware, or making Roderick—the "patient" whose malady he has been summoned to alleviate—aware, of what he is doing. He makes a nonpresence speak but without himself understanding what it says or enabling Usher to understand.[26] In this second incarnation, Poe's narrator may be said to function as the inverse reflection of Alice Staverton in *The Jolly Corner*. Whereas Alice behaved as an "unanalytic listener," deflecting the effect of Spencer's haunting and thereby putting his phantom to sleep, the narrator in *The Fall of the House of Usher* functions as an "unconscious analytic speaker." By voicing the "Trist," he awakens the sleeping ghosts of the past and brings them out of hiding, without resolving or even remotely shedding light upon the psychic drama he has conjured.

A form of haunting different from anything yet seen is thus outlined in Poe's story. Not only is the phantom inhabiting the Usher race shared or divided between two heirs, but a figure outside the line is infected by it and transformed into the figure of an "analyst." The narrator's transformation is especially intriguing since it implicitly articulates a heretofore unexplored relationship between haunting and reading. It suggests that certain readings of texts may be the result of the reader's own haunting or "infection," that they may be driven by an unstated—and unrecognized—resonance or empathy between analyst and text (or analyst and fictive character). Poe's tale reflects, in other words, on the possible generative force of certain kinds of readings and on the way in which attempts to explain or account for a narrative's incongruities, contradictions, or "distress" may potentially bring about the obstruction or distortion of the literary-analytic process. Readers, the text tells us, may at times function like the narrator: as unknowing "voicers of things hidden" who successfully bring out, conjure, or "exorcise" dramas concealed within narratives but who are unable to hear the ciphered content of these dramas or articulate their significance. They may act as unwitting "sharers" of a text's secret, as co-symbols or fragments of a fiction whose distress they feel called upon to articulate, if not alleviate, but whose enigmas remain beyond their analytic grasp.[27]

A second distinction between Poe's narrator and his counterparts in Villiers's and Balzac's stories lies in the absence of evidence in Poe's tale to explain the narrator's susceptibility to the phantom's haunting. We noted in *L'intersigne* that Maucombe's failed effort to convey the fact of his paternity to Xavier was the reason for the secret's transmission as a phantom and that Xavier's identity as both addressee and subject of that transmission was the cause of his haunting. We saw in *Facino Cane* that the narrator's own unspoken search for his parents was the basis for his resonance with Facino Cane's unavowed quest for his origins and for his "adoption" of Cane's phantom. There are no such textual elements in *The Fall of the House of Usher* to establish why the narrator is infected by the Usher secret. The only clue provided in the tale, and it is a very small one, is the narrator's comment that he and Usher had been "intimate associates" (275) and "boon companions in boyhood" (274). If Usher summons the narrator to alleviate his malady (that is, to convoke the lady), it must be because this boyhood friend is for some reason able to bring back part of Roderick's past. It must be because, through their youthful association, the narrator came in touch with, resonated with, or in some sense shared an aspect of Usher's phantom that he is able to recall by his physical presence. Precisely what the narrator might have shared with Roderick, why he shared it, and how it may be linked to his ability to conjure or convoke the Usher secret remain enigmas. The path one might follow to find their solution is nevertheless suggested by the text: by the process of reading the tale inscribes within itself and that it eloquently, if discreetly, insists be retraced in any act of interpretation.

For *The Fall of the House of Usher* is not just concerned with how a secret may be shared between two protagonists. It elaborates how a secret can be shared between two (or more) texts; how texts, some of which may be autonomous and sufficient unto themselves and interpretable as such ("The Haunted Palace," "Le refus," and the works in Usher's library), can tacitly demand to be joined with their absent co-symbols and reunited in a *textual* dual unity. Poe's tale cannot be read without a constant back-and-forth motion or "to and fro," as the narrator might say, between and among the fictions embedded within it, fictions whose readings never merge or replicate one another but inform and renew one another. The difficulty of pursuing this perpetual shifting from one text to another, similar to tracking the subtle shifts among the various identities speaking from within Spencer Brydon in *The Jolly Corner*, is what makes Poe's story such a formidable one to interpret. The level of complexity in Poe's tale is even greater than that in James's text for the reason that the secret is tripartite (illegitimate heir, rape, madness), each part is fragmented, and each of these fragments is dispersed or disseminated throughout the texts encrypted within the tale. Nothing of the illegitimate birth, the drama of the rape causing it, or the mental conflict resulting from it in *The Fall of the House of Usher* can be determined without reading "The Haunted Palace," the "Mad Trist," the epigraph, and the books in Roderick's library in conjunction with each other. Each text continues in the others. Each text inhabits or haunts the others.

Indeed, part of the originality and significance of *The Fall of the House of Usher* lies in its concern with and demonstration of how texts can inhabit or haunt other texts. It does more than elaborate how a secret can be silently transmitted through a family line for centuries (a further development of what was seen in *Facino Cane*), how a relationship of doubling and duality can be both asymmetrical and complementary (a sharp contrast to the false, artificially created complementarity in *The Secret Sharer*), and how parts of a single identity can haunt or become lodged within several characters' minds (a major variation on what was developed in *The Jolly Corner*). Poe's story is, above all, about how one universe of discourse can communicate with another discursive universe seemingly absent but in fact present. It is about how reading means reading "beyond" the text, beyond its moment(s) of conflict, disorder, or inorganization to something outside its apparent limits that can nevertheless be decrypted and conjectured from within it.

This process of reading, in which the language of the text is understood as generated by a secret beyond the visible limits of the text yet inscribed within it, is quite different from the deconstructive view of the story outlined at the outset of this chapter. For Riddel the text, with its conflicting tendencies toward and away from decay, degeneration, and collapse, is an abyssal structure of fictions, each of which lies both inside and outside another and conceals the secret of its center: that the center is neither a presence nor an absence "but a place constructed to install a sign of presence or absence."[28] For Riddel *The Fall of the House of Usher* is an allegory of the text as hollow tomb, as a "crypt" whose center, when finally opened, is "revealed as the place of just another missing body, another simulacrum of a simulacrum."[29] He does not ask what might have led to the decay, degeneration, and collapse of the Usher house. His interest is in showing how this decay and degeneration are rhetorically articulated in the text and how the text as a work of fiction is sustained by the repeated displacement of its center.

My reading implicitly assumes as its starting point the problematic of decay, illness, and rupture that Riddel explores on a metaphorical level. It proceeds to ask what drama might have occurred that would result in a simultaneous tendency toward and away from decay, illness, interment, and cognition and why there is a zigzag, apparently hesitant or conflictual to-and-fro movement that engages all the works of fiction within the text and ends in collapse and annihilation. For this reason, the process of reading I have elaborated does not deny the deconstructive project but may be said to move toward its far side. It does not describe the rhetorical inversions by which signification is deferred but retraces the symbols in the text to a generative source of trauma that has been concealed. My interpretive approach is thus less concerned with showing how a text elaborates its moments of tension, conflict, and incoherence than with reconstructing from the symbol fragments that constitute it the hidden principles of coherence that can potentially dissolve its tension and render intelligible its conflicts. The texts in the tale—"The Haunted Palace," the "Mad Trist," the library books, the epigraph—are not viewed as part of an abyssal structure in which outsides become insides infinitely replicating each other. These texts are viewed as phenomena or symbols whose jagged edges can be read and rejoined to "transphenomena"[30] beyond perception and ready comprehension. They are viewed more precisely as what I will call "transtexts": as phenomena or symbols, generated specifically as a result of a phantomatic haunting, that we must read "transtextually" by carrying them back across a gap or silence in a family history that has been transmitted transgenerationally. While the reading process delineated is thus an infinite regress, it does not see the text's elements as conflating or collapsing upon themselves. The anasemic, transtextual analysis I perform allows the reader to construe the narrative as an unfolding story of survival in the face of past, unspoken catastrophes. Each catastrophe is different, each is transcended or survived differently, each marks a new shift in the ever-expanding, outward-moving boundaries of the text.[31]

Two questions left at the story's end point to the direction in which the borders of Poe's text need to be redrawn. Although the narrator's role as Madeline's replacement in the reenactment of the psychic struggle suffered by the lady-who-made-the-line has been delineated, we still do not know why the narrator is susceptible to assuming this role. By the same token, the discovery that the lady's secret involves a rape does not explain why this rape is also an "affair of the heart," as the text has indicated. In order to reconstruct the catastrophes whose transcendence resulted in these enigmas, we must ask what familial or potentially extrafamilial constellations would have had to exist for the narrator to be affected by the Usher phantom and for the lady-who-made-the-line to simultaneously experience an affair of the heart as a rape.[32] Although the text does not contain responses to these mysteries, it does signal where we might find them. It suggests that the reader look to another text, to a work of fiction—or even nonfiction, given the co-symbolizing, transtextual function of the *Directorium Inquisitorum* and Poe's letter to Griswold—written either by Poe or another author, that "haunts" and "is haunted by" the story. Whether this transtext might be the poem "Israfel," with its reference to a spirit "whose heart-strings are a lute," or "The Conqueror Worm," with its mention of phantoms, madness, and a horrifying intruder, or another of Poe's poems, short stories, or letters, or whether it might instead be one of Baudelaire's translations of Poe's fictions, a different poem by de Béranger, another narrative by Machiavelli, Tieck, or Holberg, another treatise by De la Chambre, or some other text by some other author, written before or even after *The Fall of the House of Usher*, remains to be discovered.

What can be stated now as a conclusion to this reading and as an introduction to the future research invited by the anasemic analysis here elaborated is that the possibility and implications of such a quest are inscribed within and allegorized by Poe's tale. A text itself generated by a perpetual co-symbolizing of disparate narrative elements inside as well as outside it, *The Fall of the House of Usher* expands the boundaries historically delimiting and defining the notion of text. It simultaneously alters notions of the formation and evolution of literary history since extant concepts of "authorial influence," "national" literatures, or literary chronology can no longer adequately describe the intertextual, transtextual relations it enacts or implies. A tale emblematic of the infinitude of the symbolic process, of the endless work of interpretation, and of the anasemic nature of literary history, *The Fall of the House of Usher* is a text that dramatizes its own haunting and, in so doing, suggests that other texts within the house of literature may themselves be haunted—by their own inhabitants.

Conclusion

THIS STUDY has aimed to show how the motivation of characters in certain works of fiction can be explained psychoanalytically. In the process, an interpretive methodology different from previous approaches to character analysis has been elaborated, along with an implicit response to structuralist and poststructuralist contentions of the illegitimacy of analyzing fictive characters. While the close reading of five literary texts is not a sufficient basis from which to draw sweeping conclusions of either a theoretical or methodological nature, the results of my interpretations do provide an opportunity to reflect upon specific questions concerning the generative force of secrets in texts, the origins and formation of phantom-narratives, the interrelation of psychic drama and narrativity, and the intersection between literary analysis and psychoanalysis.

The psychic constellation of the phantom, as it has been shown to organize the five stories in this study, allows us to consider thematic, behavioral, and linguistic elements of texts, ranging from obsessions, hallucinations, compulsive repetition, and fetishism to uncanniness, ghosts, and haunting, as possible signs or symptoms of unrecognized dramas that perturb a character because they have been concealed by someone in a preceding generation. This implies a major reorientation of commonly held views of character development. Psychoanalytic theories and methodologies, from Freud to the present, have tended to treat characters in literature as allegories of universal psychic truths. The transgenerational functioning of the phantom puts into question the hermeneutic validity of the more traditional forms this treatment has taken, such as Jones's Oedipal analysis of *Hamlet* discussed in chapter 1,[1] which explain characters' behavior in terms of predefined, generalized notions of incest drives and castration fears. It also questions the heuristic claims made for more recently delineated psycholinguistic paradigms through which characters' words and actions are evaluated in terms of inexorable dramas of phallically oriented desire. However sophisticated or nuanced, readings guided by these analytic models invariably find in texts triangular structures of rivalry, involving father-, mother-, and child-figures, or sagas organized by a subject's delusional desire for totality, the repeated metonymic displacement of that desire through a chain of signifiers resistant to appropriation, and the subject's assimilation of lack and entry into language (or failure to do so) via a drama of castration or its metaphorical equivalent.[2]

The phantom, by contrast, does not prescribe or hinge on any preconceived constellations or phases of identification or desire in a subject's development. Unlike stating that a tale is an Oedipal drama or that it recounts or allegorizes the subject's move (or inability to move) from the Imaginary to the Symbolic, calling certain texts "phantom-texts" prior to elaborating their interpretation (as I did in the Introduction to this study) does not necessarily bring to mind any specific scenarios, conflicts, or desires we can expect to find in them. It does not conjure a "story" that can be told, even schematically, apart from the narrative in which the phantom is lodged. Stating that *The Jolly Corner* contains a phantom, for example, does not allow us to deduce or infer anything about the contents of the drama that has been concealed, which character(s) or figure(s) concealed it, what interpersonal dynamics, desires, or conflicts caused it to be concealed, to whom it was transmitted, by what specific rhetorical configurations, whether the transmission was purely intra- or also extrafamilial, what kinds of symptoms the phantom's haunting presence has generated, what psychic scenarios it has caused to be acted out, how it structures or defines a character's existence, or how it organizes and propels the narrative. The phantom, in sum, is not a prescriptive model for interpretation that can be applied to a text. It is a conceptual possibility with implications for evaluating the behavior of certain fictive characters in narratives from a nondevelopmental, nonphallocentric, nonparadigmatic perspective that preserves intact the specificity of those characters and the distinctiveness of their narratives.

The phantom's uniqueness with respect to previous metapsychological concepts also provides a new vantage point from which to consider and delineate family histories in literature and from which to begin to conceive and elaborate a nonhegemonic relationship between psychoanalysis and literary analysis. Whether informed by Freudian, Lacanian, ego-psychology, or object-relations theories, psychoanalytic literary criticism has tended to speak about familial relationships and the evolution of fictive characters in literature in terms of the nuclear family, concentrating on parent-child interactions and the repression of conflicts within Oedipal or pre-Oedipal scenarios. The concept of the phantom widens the scope of psychoanalytic literary interpretation to include the possibility that a character's symptoms may not function as effects of psychic compromise driven by parental figures, or as objectified fantasies created to circumvent parentally erected barriers to the fulfillment of desires. Symptoms may instead be construed as cryptic traces of an unspeakable drama concealed by someone—anyone—in a character's (theoretically) infinitely regressive family history.

Reconstructing this family history involves an anasemic approach to reading in which the elements of a fictive character's behavior are identified and evaluated linguistically as both obstacles and clues to uncovering unspoken sagas, not readily visible within the text, that have been hidden by figures in an extended family past. The analytic movement back up toward these concealed sagas hinges on a new conception of the processes of symptom-formation. As the narratives examined in this study demonstrate, the phantom, unlike all other metapsychological formations, is radically heterogeneous to the subject it inhabits. Its disruptive presence in a character is a function of another's psychic topography. The symptoms it produces are thus not susceptible to modes of analysis aimed at exposing the disguised return of something the subject has dynamically repressed. The phantom's pathogenic work is the effect of a silencing or a preservative repression that obstruct attempts to perceive a character's words (or behavior readable as words) as tacitly referring to their unconscious portion because they cause those words (such as "shave the land" in *The Secret Sharer*, *manteau* and *tombeau* in *L'intersigne, or* in *Facino Cane*, "pince-nez" in *The Jolly Corner*, and "lute" in *The Fall of the House of Usher*) to be transformed into symbolic or cryptonymic traces of a gap in the speech of another. Reading in this context becomes a process of carrying these linguistic traces back to a transphenomenal source of the unspeakable situated in an ancestor's psychic history. It means construing a character's symptoms as the ciphered inscriptions of her or his unarticulated but ever-present prehistory.

This new conception of the relationship among family history, psychic history, silencing, and repression coincides with a radical shift in previous psychoanalytic views of "the Other" as a capitalized, generalizable notion. Anasemic analysis and the psychic configuration of the phantom allow us to identify the "other" in certain narratives as a specific entity, situated beyond the subject, who holds that subject in a pathological dual unity by virtue of having transmitted to him or her a silenced trauma. This de-capitalized "other" no longer functions as part of an ontology that invariably defines the speaking subject in terms of its inescapable otherness to itself, an otherness generated by the fundamental impossibility or inaccessibility of integration, understanding, the Phallus, the Unconscious, the Father, Death, and the like. The "other" is instead viewed as a text-specific identity whose concealment of a drama can be reconstructed from the particular, linguistically decipherable elements of a given narrative. The captain's obsessive hallucinations of sharing a secret in *The Secret Sharer*, his reckless maneuvering of his ship, and his near murder of a mate are viewed, within this optic, as symbolic stagings of a drama of murder the captain is unable to share because he has inherited it from someone else as that other's unspeakable legacy. Xavier's hallucinations in *L'intersigne* are linked to the specific silence erected by the priest, Maucombe, around his identity as Xavier's biological father. Facino Cane's obsession with gold is traced to the gap in his mother's speech that kept silent the Jewish identity of his father. Spencer Brydon's quest for his alter ego in *The Jolly Corner* is tracked to his grandfather's hiding of a trauma of cuckolding and illegitimate birth. And Madeline and Roderick Usher's acute mental and physical distress and their ultimate demise are carried back to the silencing, by an Usher wife centuries earlier, of a drama of rape and an ensuing intrusion into the family line of an illegitimate heir.

The anasemic process of deciphering a literary character's behavior in terms of a founding silence in the speech of a specific other also implies a radical departure from poststructuralist views of the subject as always already made inherently and inescapably "other" or excentric to him- or herself by the inevitable slippage of signifiers over inaccessible signifieds. The analytic concepts of symbol and cryptonymy enable us to understand certain characters' expressions of estrangement as symptomatic of their individual work of self-creation as "other" in response to their (unrecognized) need to preserve intact someone else's secret. Guardians or conservators of dramas or signifieds that have to be cut off from the signifying chain because they are too shameful to be revealed, characters haunted by phantoms transform themselves into symbolic or cryptonymic accounts of what could not and must not be said. Through speech and behavior unwittingly created to defy cognition, they become themselves ciphered sagas of how and why particular signifieds were hidden or made inaccessible and of the psychic topology that ensured these signifieds' continued concealment. The captain's feelings of self-estrangement, incompleteness, and dualness in *The Secret Sharer* are explained, from this perspective, not as symptoms of the unavoidable dividedness of his subjectivity but as symbols pointing to his separation from a drama of murder transmitted to him as a secret he cannot share. Spencer Brydon's profound sense of alienation in America, his feelings of being incomplete or divided from his "true" self, and his quest for his alter ego are understood not as effects of his inescapable ex-centricity to himself as a speaking subject but as symbols through which he recreates himself as the cryptic narrative of a drama of cuckolding and illegitimacy he inherits as his unrecognized legacy. Madeline Usher's inability to speak and Roderick's hallucinatory lapses and uncontrolled improvisations are not explained as signs of their innate otherness to themselves, produced by an unidentifiable deficiency in the Usher house and a perpetual decentering of signification. Their symptoms are construed as modes through which they create themselves as animated poems tacitly speaking of the hidden trauma of rape and illegitimacy preventing them from living their (fictive) lives as their own and leading ultimately to their demise.

The need to preserve intact while making unintelligible an unspeakable family drama can thus be said to propel the existences of the fictive characters in the five stories I have analyzed. This implies a new way of thinking about the driving forces of the narratives themselves. The connection among secrets, extended family histories, and the sagas enacted by the characters in each text suggests that the generative source or "authors" of the five texts are not simply Conrad, Villiers, Balzac, James, and Poe but the secret inscribed within each work. Were there no secret of murder concealed from the captain and haunting him as a phantom, he would not invent fictitious scenarios of secret sharing with Leggatt and his narrative of their adventure together would not exist in the form we see. Were nothing tacitly communicated between Maucombe and Xavier concerning the latter's birth, Xavier would not become the unwitting medium of Maucombe's message and would not narrate the cryptic tale of his paternity we read. If there were no veiled Jewish father in *Facino Cane,* the title character would not be in quest of gold, the narrator would not inherit this quest as his own, and we would not have before us his ciphered narrative of the origin and transmission of this quest. Were Spencer Brydon not haunted by the secret of an adultery and illegitimacy, he would not be in search of his alter ego, and the text, composed of his symbolic acting out of his grandfather's encounter with the adulterer and bastard offspring and of the transformation of the drama of cuckolding into a secret, would not exist. Finally, if Roderick and Madeline Usher were not both haunted by the unspeakable drama of a rape and resulting birth of an illegitimate heir, the encrypted saga of this drama and its concealment, which infects the narrator, which he helps to act out, and which we read as his narrative, would not have been produced. Each narrative flows forth from the secret it inscribes within itself as its founding silence or source. Each text hypothesizes its own point of origin—its own "author," we might say—but as a creation of the text itself.

This conception of authorship and of literary production expands upon modernist and postmodernist attempts to cast aside the notion of author as a nontextual entity and to dissolve the distinction between an inside and outside of the text. It is fundamentally different, however, from Lacanian views, which construe the infinite slippage of the inaccessible phallus and the metonymic proliferation of signifiers in its wake as generative of texts. It also diverges sharply from deconstructive approaches, of which Riddel's reading of Poe is but one example, which conceive the text's origins in terms of an infinite regress of deferred signification where "meaning" or the "center" is always only a hollow tomb of difference, "another simulacrum of a simulacrum." My analytic approach treats the text as incomplete and in need of being joined with its missing complement whose traces are contained within it. I presume, in other words, that the causative agent or origin of certain characters' behavior in certain texts can in fact be conjectured but as a cause or origin created in each instance by the text itself as its secret. Each phantom-text is understood to bear inscribed within it its own absent symbol fragment. Each is interpreted as being in a dual unity with itself, as sharing with itself its own secret.

Conceiving the text to be its own secret sharer makes possible a new articulation of the rapport between text and reader. From an anasemic perspective, viewing the text as bearing within it the traces of its own missing complement means that the text we encounter on the printed page is not yet realized as the text. What we perceive is a system of symbols created in response to a drama that had to be cut off from view. The task of the reader is to "complete" the text, to reconstruct from the visible text the symbol fragment estranged from it. This "completion" is never fully achieved since interpretation is understood as an infinite process. Uncovering a secret encrypted in a narrative and elucidating how its concealed presence motivates a character's behavior always brings to the fore still other enigmas or fragments that demand solution or "completion." Unveiling an unspeakable murder as the causative agent of the captain's obsessive fiction of sharing a secret with Leggatt, for example, leaves unanswered the questions of why a murder was committed, who was involved, and why it had to be kept secret. Although we have linked Xavier's hallucinations and feelings of spleen with the secret of his origins, we still do not know why the priest, Maucombe, committed an act of adultery or why he was unable to reveal his paternity to his son. Having accounted for Facino Cane's obsession with gold, we still cannot explain why his mother had an affair with a Jew or why this Jew became involved with the wife of an Italian nobleman. While we reconstructed the reason for Spencer Brydon's hunt for his alter ego, we have left unresolved the issue of why the grandfather did not confront the adulterer, why he transformed the drama into a secret, and whether or not he imagined that a bastard issued from the adultery. Finally, whereas we explained Roderick Usher's strange physical and mental symptoms, his sister's catalepsy, and the twins' catastrophic demise, we did not solve the mysteries of how a rape also came to be an affair of the heart, who the rapist was, or why he committed the act. Each resolved enigma exposes to view others whose solutions, while they cannot be determined from the material available in these texts, must be presumed to be inscribed in still other texts with which these narratives are joined in a "textual dual unity" or secret sharing.

The process of reading as it emerges from this study thus involves being aware of a narrative's potential susceptibility to transtextual analysis. It means recognizing that textual fragments or symbols in certain narratives have to be joined to their absent co-symbols across a disruption or discontinuity in a transgenerational saga which, while not readily apparent, anchors the unfolding of the narrative. The biblical story of Cain and Abel alluded to in *The Secret Sharer*, Saint Bernard's *Méditations* in *L'intersigne*, the *Super Flumina Babylonis* and the *Livre d'or* in *Facino Cane*, the references to the Book of Exodus and other portions of the Bible in *The Jolly Corner*, and "The Haunted Palace," the "Mad Trist," the epigraph, and the books in Usher's library in *The Fall of the House of Usher* all function as *transtexts*. They are traces readable not just anasemically but as part of the more specific transtextual process characteristic of phantom-texts in which their significance emerges as they are carried back across a gap or silence inherited by a character and are rejoined to a missing part of that character's unspoken family history. Reading transtextually is thus a process of bridging a "generation gap" embedded in a fictive narrative. It involves reuniting with their informing complements textual elements whose separation is the result of an ancestor's refusal to speak, and whose reunion makes it possible to hear what had to be silenced.

The perspectives on reading offered by the concepts of textual dual unity and transtextuality imply a shift from a hierarchical view of psychoanalysis as a body of knowledge to be applied to literature toward a view of psychoanalysis and literary analysis as two different contexts for the same approach to reading. Both psychoanalysis and literary analysis, as they emerge from this study, are concerned with understanding what causes a character (real or fictive) to reinvent him- or herself as an obstacle to interpretation and with elaborating how that obstacle can be transcended or made readable. In exploring the functioning of phantoms within the literary realm, my analyses expand upon Abraham and Torok's delineation of the forms and pathways a phantom may take, the potential symptoms its disruptive workings may provoke, and the manner in which its haunting presence can cause subjects to create themselves as cryptic poetic entities that implicitly demand to be deciphered. In the process, the readings demonstrate that the techniques of listening, the conceptual possibilities for investigating narrative structure and organization, and the interpretive (not therapeutic) goals of psychoanalysis and literary analysis—at least as far as the analysis of family secrets is concerned—are essentially the same. Both analytic modes aim to uncover within a seemingly unintelligible discourse elements of a poetic creation, the linguistic modes of concealment fundamental to its production, and the way in which that creation was generated in response to an unspeakable, unseen source of psychic turmoil. To what extent this identity between psychoanalytic and literary interpretation can be extended to the analysis of narratives not organized by encrypted secrets or to nonnarrative texts that may or may not involve secrets is just one of the several avenues of inquiry opened by this study.

The phantom-texts I have analyzed contain, to varying degrees, characteristics associated with the genres of the uncanny, the fantastic, the gothic, and the supernatural. While it would be false to assume that all works belonging to these genres have phantoms, there are doubtless many more texts traditionally included in these categories, by authors not treated in this study, whose enigmatic goings-on could be illuminated through analysis oriented by the concept of transgenerational haunting. Mérimée, Barbey d'Aurévilly, Hoffmann, Kleist, Wharton, Wilde, Verne, and Mary Shelley are only a few of those whose writings suggest themselves as subjects for future inquiry. Texts not belonging to these genres may also contain phantoms and may, as my ongoing research suggests, assume a variety of forms other than short stories, including novels, plays, and films. The fact that all five texts treated in this study are short narratives is not mere coincidence, however. While analysis of many more phantom-texts drawn from various literary forms would be necessary to confirm any explanation of this phenomenon, my suspicion is that succinct, abbreviated narratives may more readily, and therefore more frequently, sustain the elaboration of a psychic configuration determined by something that has been elided, left unstated, or removed from view.

Another area of investigation opened by my interpretations concerns the apparent preoccupation of at least certain authors of the nineteenth and early twentieth centuries with haunting secrets, adultery, and concealed illegitimacy. The flurry of scientific invention during this period may in part explain this. Innovations in the fields of medicine, psychology, and communications, including Mesmer's discovery of hypnosis, research on anesthetics, and the invention of the telegraph and the telephone—all of which involve "separating" the mind or the voice from the body—undoubtedly played a role in literature's orientation toward psychic phenomena and its emphasis on ghostly incarnations, the living dead, figures of disembodiment, and silent transmissions. Why the element of concealed illegitimacy might recur in texts is a more troubling question, especially since many works of this period dealt openly with the subject of bastards. A much larger study of many more texts would be required to determine whether the recurrence of this theme in four of the five stories in this book is purely coincidental or a sign of a much deeper and more widespread phenomenon. It would also be necessary to examine political, social, and economic developments of the period in which the works were written, particularly with regard to possible changes in laws of inheritance, attitudes toward birth control and abortion, and the status of women. This last area of investigation might prove especially significant since it is the wife in the family, not the husband, who has the affair in the four texts herein concerned with illegitimacy.

This observation in turn raises the question of the implications my readings hold for feminist scholarship. Feminist psychoanalytic critics have long sought alternatives to phallocentric models of interpretation for articulating and explaining the roles of women, gender, and the suppression of the female voice in literature. My analyses offer a new, nonphallogocentric perspective from which to address these issues. They invite the conjecture that conclusions about how social, cultural, historical, or gender issues affect a fictive character's speech and conduct may require supplementation or even reformulation to account for instances in which a secret haunts or "speaks through" a character and is transmitted by someone of a different sex, class, culture, or nationality. My readings oblige us to reconsider if not rethink entirely, for example, interpretations that might treat Facino Cane's passion for gold and Bianca in terms of gender-oriented notions of male-female relations or socially or culturally grounded ideas about masculine desires for power or possession, without taking into account the secret concealed by Cane's mother which speaks cryptically through Cane. They likewise compel us to reevaluate analyses of *The Fall of the House of Usher* oriented by social and gender perspectives that might construe Madeline's cataleptic state as representative of woman's muted, disembodied, disenfranchised position in nineteenth-century American society and literature and Roderick's verbal expansiveness and improvisation as emblematic of the empowered, dominant position of masculine discourse of the period, without considering that the speech and behavior of both brother and sister, male and female, are driven by a secret of rape and illegitimacy kept silent by a woman centuries earlier.[3] While I do not argue with the validity or usefulness of approaching these and other texts from socially, culturally, historically, or gender-oriented critical perspectives, these perspectives themselves may have to be reevaluated or at least broadened in light of the potential workings of the phantom to include the possibility that transgenerational, transsocietal, transcultural, transsexual configurations may influence or generate the language and behavior of fictive characters.

The phantom, along with the analytic concepts of symbol and cryptonymy, holds great potential for numerous other investigations. It offers an alternative to present modes of analyzing misogynistic portrayals of women in literature, which tend to hinge on notions of gender and of woman's socially or culturally determined inferiority. Images of women as living and speaking robots, dolls, or monsters created by men and portraits of women as witches or demon-possessed sorcerors may in some instances be traced to phantoms haunting male characters that have been generated by secrets concealed in an earlier generation by either a man or a woman.[4] The concept of transgenerational haunting also provides a new vantage point from which to interpret figures of human metamorphosis, ventriloquism, invisibility, and time travel in literature, as well as themes such as the disembodied voice, found not only in gothic and uncanny texts but in works ranging from Greek tragedy, with its emphasis on oracularly defined destinies, to science fiction. Outside of the literary realm, the phantom, which can arise in response to collective secrets and can haunt entire segments of society, may be used to analyze the emergence of various political, social, cultural, and intellectual institutions, including the institution of psychoanalysis itself.[5] It may also prove useful for interpreting the manifestation of certain group pathologies or ideologies that appear to emerge in response to traumatic political dramas.[6] Finally, the phantom potentially offers a new perspective from which to analyze the transmission and transformation of literary theories themselves as well as the resistance, within the literary/critical community, to certain approaches to interpretation.

Notes

Introduction

1. For an excellent overview of these and other psychoanalytic approaches to literature, see Elizabeth Wright, *Psychoanalytic Criticism: Theory in Practice* (New York: Methuen, 1984).

2. My concern is thus with secrets and not secrecy. In this it is clearly distinct from Frank Kermode's work in *The Genesis of Secrecy* (Cambridge: Harvard University Press, 1979) and from his examination of the relationship between the concealment of information and narrative organization in "Secrets and Narrative Sequence," *Critical Inquiry* 7, no. 1 (Autumn 1980): 83–101.

3. *Structuralist Poetics* (Ithaca: Cornell University Press, 1975), p. 230.

4. "The Idea of a Psychoanalytic Literary Criticism," *Critical Inquiry* 13, no. 2 (Winter 1987): 335.

5. *The Literary Use of the Psychoanalytic Process* (New Haven: Yale University Press, 1981), pp. 38–40.

6. As regards the characters in Shakespeare's plays, T. S. Eliot, along with many Shakespearean scholars, has articulated the problem in *Hamlet* precisely as the absence of an "objective correlative" in the play to explain Hamlet's hesitant behavior. This issue will be discussed in chapter 1.

7. "To Open the Question," *Yale French Studies*, nos. 55–56 (1977): 5–10.

8. Ibid., p. 6; Felman's italics.

9. *Studies on Hysteria*, 2: 160–61.

Chapter 1
For a New Psychoanalytic Literary Criticism

1. Paris: Aubier-Flammarion.

2. Trans. Nicholas Rand (Minneapolis: University of Minnesota Press, 1986). Hereafter cited as *The Wolf Man*.

3. Paris: Aubier-Flammarion, 1978. 2d edition, Paris: Flammarion, 1987. Henceforth cited as *L'écorce*. Page references are identical in both editions. The English translation is forthcoming in two volumes from the University of Chicago Press.

4. A significant amount of psychoanalytic criticism has consisted of what may be called deconstructive readings of Freud and Lacan. Notable examples include Jacques Derrida's "Le facteur de la vérité" and "Spéculer—sur 'Freud' " (both in *La carte postale: de Socrate à Freud et au-delà* [Paris: Flammarion, 1980]), Samuel Weber's *The Legend of Freud* (Minneapolis: University of Minnesota Press, 1982), and Luce Irigaray's *Speculum de l'autre femme* (Paris: Minuit, 1974). Such readings are extremely useful for identifying the interpretive power of Freud's and Lacan's theories as well as for exposing pivotal moments where their internal cohesion may break down or their heuristic

capacities may be deemed insufficient. This chapter, while not structured along deconstructive lines, also elucidates various strengths and problematic aspects of Freudian and Lacanian epistemologies. At the same time, it delineates several alternative metapsychological theories and interpretive methodologies that open heretofore unrecognized avenues for literary analysis.

In endeavoring to provide an extensive elaboration of major aspects of Abraham and Torok's work, this chapter may also be viewed as an expansion and, to a certain extent, a modification of prior expository accounts of some of their theories. See Jacques Derrida's foreword to *The Wolf Man*, entitled *Fors;* Peggy Kamuf's "Abraham's Wake," *Diacritics* 9, no. 1 (Spring 1979): 32–43; and Rand's "Translator's Introduction" to *The Wolf Man*, entitled "Toward a Cryptonymy of Literature." For a literary study informed by several aspects of Abraham and Torok's work, particularly symbol and cryptonymy, see Rand's *Le cryptage et la vie des oeuvres: du secret dans les textes* (Paris: Aubier, 1989).

5. The path followed by the female child is more complicated in Freud's view. It is determined by the girl's replacement of the renounced penis with a desire to bear the father's child. For the purposes of this study it is not essential to elaborate all the variations Freud proposed to account for the female child within the Oedipus structure. For a discussion of these highly debated variations, as well as an overview of some of the shifts and contradictions in Freud's writings pertaining to the Oedipus and castration complexes, see *Feminine Sexuality: Jacques Lacan and the école freudienne*, ed. Juliet Mitchell and Jacqueline Rose (New York: W. W. Norton, 1985). (Henceforth cited as Mitchell and Rose.) For a useful synopsis of the major reformulations of the Oedipus complex in Freud's work, see J. Laplanche and J.-B. Pontalis, *The Language of Psycho-Analysis*, trans. Donald Nicholson-Smith (New York: W. W. Norton, 1973). (Hereafter cited as Laplanche and Pontalis.) Major works by Freud in which the Oedipus complex is discussed include "Three Essays on the Theory of Sexuality," vol. 7; "Female Sexuality," vol. 21; "The Dissolution of the Oedipus Complex," vol. 19; and "Some Psychical Consequences of the Anatomical Distinction between the Sexes," vol. 19.

6. Jacques Lacan, "The Signification of the Phallus," *Ecrits: A Selection*, trans. Alan Sheridan (New York: W. W. Norton, 1977), p. 287. The collection henceforth cited as Sheridan.

7. Lacan makes no distinction between the boy- and girl-child at this point of development. His view of the specificity of woman's position as other emerges later and involves her relation to *jouissance*. For a discussion of woman's difference in Lacan see Mitchell and Rose, and also Jane Gallop, *Reading Lacan* (Ithaca: Cornell University Press, 1987).

8. Freud's theories concerning homosexuality and fetishism, for example, have as their underlying tenet the idea of an unresolved Oedipus complex (see "Fetishism," vol. 22, and "Some Neurotic Mechanisms in Jealousy, Paranoia and Homosexuality," vol. 18). An example of a Lacanian view of developmental fixation can be seen in his analysis of Melanie Klein's patient, Dick (in *Le séminaire I: les écrits techniques de Freud* [Paris: Seuil, 1975], pp. 75–103), which hinges on the idea of Dick's exteriority to the world of language and his inability to enter the Symbolic.

9. Lacan's equating of metaphor with condensation and metonymy with displacement has its origin in Roman Jakobson's influential work on aphasia: "Two Aspects of Language and Two Types of Aphasic Disturbances," *Fundamentals of Language* (The Hague: Mouton, 1956).

10. Elaborated by Abraham in "Notes du séminaire sur l'unité duelle et le fantôme" (Notes from the seminar on the dual unity and the phantom), in *L'écorce*, pp. 393–425. Hereafter cited as *Dual Unity*; all translations mine.

11. Abraham and Torok, both of Hungarian extraction, encountered the work of these two Hungarian psychoanalysts while pursuing their own analytic training in Paris in the 1940s and 1950s. In 1962 Abraham edited, annotated, and prefaced the French translation of Ferenczi's *Thalassa* (Paris: Payot, 1969). The preface is reprinted in part 1 of *L'écorce*, "Psychanalyse, science des sciences." Abraham also wrote a lengthy commentary on Hermann's theory of the "filial instinct" under the heading "L'enfant majuscule et l'unité duelle" (The dual unity and the anasemic concept of the child), in *L'écorce*. Torok has written on Ferenczi's concept of introjection and its relation to incorporation ("Maladie du deuil et fantasme du cadavre exquis" [Illness of mourning and the fantasy of the exquisite corpse]), *L'écorce*, on his notion of "catastrophe" ("Katasztrófák," *Cahiers Confrontation*, no. 7 [Spring 1982]: 149–51), and on the Freud-Ferenczi correspondence ("La correspondance Ferenczi-Freud: la vie de la lettre dans l'histoire de la psychanalyse" [The Ferenczi-Freud correspondence: The life of the letter in the history of psychoanalysis]), *Cahiers Confrontation*, no. 12 [Fall 1984]: 79–99).

12. In the article "The Shell and the Kernel," trans. N. Rand, *Diacritics* 9, no. 1 (Spring 1979): 27. (Henceforth cited as *Shell*; page references are to this translation.) The article first appeared in French in *Critique*, no. 249 (February 1969) and was republished in *L'écorce*.

13. "[C]es bouts-de-mère ... désigne[nt] des événements objectifs, c'est-à-dire, non grevés par l'Inconscient de la mère." *Dual Unity*, p. 414.

14. Abraham and Torok capitalize words such as Shell, Kernel, Core, Envelope, Unconscious, Ego, Child, and Mother to identify them as part of an "anasemic psychoanalytic discourse." The concept of "anasemia" will be discussed at the conclusion of this chapter.

15. The term "introjection" is used here in the sense defined by Maria Torok in her essay "Maladie du deuil et fantasme du cadavre exquis" (in *L'écorce*, pp. 229–51). It was introduced by Ferenczi in 1909 (in "Introjection and Transference") and subsequently adopted by Freud, Karl Abraham, and Melanie Klein, among others. In the process, the concept as originally defined by Ferenczi underwent significant alteration. Karl Abraham's introduction of the term "incorporation," which has since been used by analysts from Freud to Lacan, contributed to a growing confusion and overlapping of these two concepts. (For some idea of the extent of this confusion, see the entries headed "Introjection" and "Incorporation" in Laplanche and Pontalis.) By reiterating those aspects of Ferenczi's definition of introjection which have been overlooked or ignored, and by restoring the semantic specificity of "introjection" and "incorporation," Maria Torok makes a clear distinction between the two metapsychological concepts. She explains introjection as the process by which

libidinally charged objects are gradually included within the Ego, thereby enlarging and enriching it (see *L'écorce*, pp. 233–37). Incorporation, by contrast, occurs when the process of introjection is blocked by conflictual desires. The inaccessible object of desire is then installed or in-corporated as a "fantasy" within the body and hidden from the Ego. The implications of this distinction for Abraham and Torok's work are manifold and include new conceptualizations of psychic configurations such as melancholia, fixation, and fantasy and the discovery of heretofore unrecognized topographies such as "crypt" and "illness of mourning."

With respect to the dual unity, which Abraham and Torok discuss in several different contexts in their writings, care should be taken to distinguish between the roles played by repression and introjection in the child's emergence as an individual. (Incorporation does not enter into the normal, nonpathogenic evolution of the dual unity.) The analysts perceive the mother as the initial source of *both* the child's repressions and his or her introjections, thereby providing the substantive core of the child's Unconscious and Ego, respectively. As the process of individuation begins, the child receives from the mother objects bearing an unconscious charge that the child cannot make its own. The child absorbs these bound objects, effectively repressing what the mother has already repressed. This stock of repressions forms the basis of the child's Unconscious. As development proceeds, the child adds to it repressions produced from its own experiences. (Freud's theory of repression did not address this possibility of the child's actively repressing the already repressed of the mother. In this regard, Abraham and Torok's view of the formation of the child's Unconscious may be considered a significant extension of Freud's idea of dynamic repression. For their contribution of a theory of preservative repression, see the sections on the "phantom" in this chapter.)

Coincident with the formation of its Unconscious, the child introjects or assimilates objects (warmth, nourishment, love, etc.) given to it by the mother, making them its own property and transforming them into a part of itself. These introjections constitute the initial stock of the child's Ego. As the child grows more independent and "exhausts" what the mother can give it, it redirects the work of introjection to the outside world of "non-mother," expanding its Ego with introjections of its own experiences.

16. "*[N]ous sommes tous des mutilés de mère*, et cela indépendamment de notre histoire personnelle," *Dual Unity*, p. 399; Abraham's italics. The reader may sense a certain affinity between some of what has just been delineated and various aspects of object-relations theories. The emphasis on pre-Oedipal development and on the mother/child dyad are certainly areas of mutual concern. The term "individuation," also used by some object-relations theorists, suggests another potential area of overlap. While a detailed analytic comparison between object-relations theories and Abraham and Torok's work would be both revealing and useful, it is beyond the purview of this study and for the moment must be left for future pursuit. Three essays by Maria Torok may be suggested as a possible point of departure for such an investigation: "La signification de 'l'envie du pénis' chez la femme," *L'écorce*, pp. 132–71, rpt. from *La sexualité féminine, nouvelles recherches psychanalytiques* (Paris: Payot, 1964),

translated into English as "The Significance of 'Penis Envy' in Women," *Female Sexuality: New Psychoanalytic Views*, ed. Janine Chasseguet-Smirgel (Ann Arbor: University of Michigan Press, 1970), pp. 135–70, and just published in a new translation as "The Meaning of 'Penis Envy' in Women" in *Differences* 4, no. 1 (May 1992); with Abraham, "Qui est Mélanie Klein?" (Who is Melanie Klein?), *L'écorce*, pp. 184–99, rpt. from the introduction to the French edition of Melanie Klein's *Essais de psychanalyse*; and, with the participation of Barbro Sylwan and Adèle Covello, "Mélanie Mell par elle-même" (Melanie Mell by herself), *Géopsychanalyse: les souterrains de l'institution*, ed. René Major (Paris: Confrontation, 1981), pp. 211–42.

17. *Dual Unity*, p. 395; Abraham's italics.

18. In his essay "Le symbole ou l'au-delà du phénomène" (The symbol and beyond phenomena) in *L'écorce* (hereafter cited as *Symbol*), Abraham develops this thought along biological and physical lines through an inquiry into the process of cell division and the dyadic structure of the atom. The philosophical and literary implications of this inquiry will be discussed momentarily in the context of the symbolic operation.

19. One implication of this argument is the suggestion that we reassess how cultural codes originate and evolve. Abraham's reference to preexisting societal codes that the child uses in its quest to separate from the mother does not assume these codes to be ontological givens. On the contrary, these codes are to be understood as themselves emerging from a "symbolic process" occurring on a societal level. It may be proposed, in other words, that the threat of castration "originates" as a child's fantasy, that it is then used by society to explain the child's behavior, and that the child subsequently reappropriates it as a token of love for the mother.

20. "La source de signifiance du langage: communion dans le mensonge sur le désir anasémique de cramponnement" (The source of the signifying process in language: Communion in the lie about the anasemic desire of clinging), *L'écorce*, p. 386. Abraham's italics.

21. For a study of the female child's creation of pseudologies, the reader is referred to Maria Torok's essay "The Meaning of 'Penis Envy' in Women" in which she analyzes the meaning of the symptom of penis envy. The conclusions drawn in this essay, originally published four years before "The Shell and the Kernel" in 1964, run parallel to those in the later article and are clearly implied by Abraham's references to the child theories invented by "both sexes" (*Shell*, 27). To extrapolate from Torok's essay—penis envy may be understood as the correlative pseudology of the Oedipus complex for the female child. It is created by the child in response to the mother's prohibition (real or imagined) of masturbation. Torok views masturbation as a normal part of the process of individuation, involving the child's double identification with both parents in their sexual relationship (the girl's vagina is identified with the mother's, her hand is identified with the penis and attributed to the father). When this identification is blocked by a prohibition, the child's feelings of animosity toward the mother, who is perceived as withholding the child's desire (symbolized by the hand/penis), are repressed and return in the form of the myth of castration and the desire for the penis. This pseudology safeguards the

mother's love for the daughter by attributing the loss of the penis to someone else. The child invents a defensive fantasy—"I had a penis, but someone cut it off; that is why I want it back"—as a means of tacitly expressing her animosity toward the mother while preserving the stability of the mother-daughter relationship.

Torok's essay holds major implications for clinical psychoanalysis, psychoanalytic literary criticism, and feminist scholarship. It represents a radical departure from the Freudian and Lacanian views of penis envy, both of which take the girl's desire literally as the symptom of an anatomical lack. The lines of inquiry opened by Torok's position, particularly with regard to Freud's theory of the superego and Lacan's dictum, *La femme n'est pas toute* (Woman is not whole), remain to be elaborated in a future study.

22. Sheridan, "The Signification of the Phallus," p. 284.

23. His atypical use of the term "maternal instinct" notwithstanding (in "Propos directifs pour un Congrès sur la sexualité féminine," *Ecrits* [Paris: Seuil, 1966], p. 730), Lacan did not accept the Freudian theory of instincts but proposed in its place a "dialectic of desire." See in this regard, "Au-delà du 'principe de réalité,' " *Ecrits*, pp. 73–92; "La chose freudienne ou sens du retour à Freud en psychanalyse," *Ecrits*, pp. 401–36, and Sheridan, pp. 114–45; and "Subversion du sujet et dialectique du désir dans l'inconscient freudien," *Ecrits*, pp. 793–827, and Sheridan, pp. 292–325. For an excellent overview of Lacan's oscillations with respect to certain areas of Freudian theory, see Marcelle Marini, *Lacan* (Paris: Belfond, 1986), pp. 39–80.

Much has been written both critiquing and supporting Freud's and Lacan's views of human development and subjectivity from psychoanalytic, philosophical, and feminist perspectives. It is not necessary for the purposes of this study to restate these arguments here. For works from these perspectives specifically related to Lacan, see Derrida's "Le facteur de la vérité"; Jean-Luc Nancy and Philippe Lacoue-Labarthe, *Le titre de la lettre* (Paris: Galilée, 1973); Jane Gallop, *The Daughter's Seduction: Feminism and Psychoanalysis* (Ithaca: Cornell University Press, 1982) and her *Reading Lacan*; Mitchell and Rose's *Feminine Sexuality*; Shoshana Felman, *Jacques Lacan and the Adventure of Insight: Psychoanalysis in Contemporary Culture* (Cambridge: Harvard University Press, 1987); Juliet Flower MacCannell, *Figuring Lacan* (Lincoln: University of Nebraska Press, 1986); Ellie Ragland-Sullivan, *Jacques Lacan and the Philosophy of Psychoanalysis* (Urbana: University of Illinois Press, 1987); Lisa Jardine, "The Politics of Impenetrability," Joan Copjec, "Cutting Up," and Parveen Adams, "Of Female Bondage," all in *Between Feminism and Psychoanalysis*, ed. Teresa Brennan (New York: Routledge, 1989); Judith Butler, *Gender Trouble* (New York: Routledge, 1990); and Jane Flax, *Thinking Fragments: Psychoanalysis, Feminism and Postmodernism in the Contemporary West* (Berkeley: University of California Press, 1990).

24. Abraham first elaborated the concept of the phantom in 1974 in "Notes du séminaire sur l'unité duelle et le fantôme" and in "Notules sur le fantôme," the latter first in *Etudes freudiennes*, nos. 9 and 10 (Paris: Denoël, 1975), rpt. in *L'écorce* and published in English as "Notes on the Phantom: A Complement to Freud's Metapsychology," *Critical Inquiry* 13, no. 2 (Winter 1987): 287–92. (Hereafter cited as *Phantom*.)

Abraham's discovery led Torok to conjecture that phobias, in certain patients, might be traced to the haunting presence of a phantom. One result of this conjecture was her reopening of Freud's analysis of Little Hans and her discovery of a phantom at the origin of Hans's fear of horses. See "Histoire de peur. Le symptôme phobique: retour du refoulé ou retour du fantôme?" (A story of fear. The phobic symptom: Return of the repressed or return of the phantom?), in *Etudes freudiennes*, nos. 9 and 10 (Paris: Denoël, 1975), rpt. in *L'écorce*, pp. 434–46. Henceforth cited as *A Story of Fear*.

25. "Le fantôme d'Hamlet ou le VIe acte: précédé par l'entr'acte de la 'vérité' " in *L'écorce*, pp. 447–74; the English in *Diacritics* 18, no. 4 (Winter 1988): 2–19. Henceforth cited as *The Sixth Act*.

26. Freud himself discusses *Hamlet* very briefly in a footnote in *The Interpretation of Dreams* and in his paper "Psychopathic Characters on the Stage." The essence of his argument first appeared in a letter to Fliess dated October 15, 1897. It was left to Jones to do a comprehensive analysis of the play. In the 1919 edition of *The Interpretation of Dreams*, Freud refers the reader to Jones's study for an amplification of his ideas.

27. T. S. Eliot, "Hamlet and His Problems," *Selected Essays of T. S. Eliot* (New York: Harcourt, Brace, & World, 1950), rpt. in *Hamlet*, ed. Cyrus Hoy (New York: W. W. Norton, 1963), p. 176. Italics are Eliot's.

28. (London: Victor Gollancz Press, 1949). Page references are to this edition. Jones's essay was first published, in somewhat different form, under the title "The Oedipus Complex as an Explanation of Hamlet's Mystery" in *The American Journal of Psychology* 21 (January 1910).

29. This essay is a portion of Lacan's 1958–1959 *Séminaire VI* entitled *Le désir et son interprétation*. "The Seven Lessons on *Hamlet*" ("Sept leçons sur *Hamlet*") of which it is a part were edited by Jacques-Alain Miller and published in *Ornicar*, nos. 24, 25, 26–27 (Paris: Seuil, 1981–1983). The essay under discussion, translated by James Hulbert, appeared in *Yale French Studies*, nos. 55–56 (1977): *Literature and Psychoanalysis—The Question of Reading: Otherwise*, ed. Shoshana Felman. All page references are to this translation, henceforth noted as "Desire in *Hamlet*."

30. The concept of the dialectic of desire is delineated in "The Subversion of the Subject and the Dialectic of Desire in the Freudian Unconscious" (1960, in Sheridan). The essay's major lines of inquiry were elaborated in *The Seminar V* of 1957–1958, which immediately preceded the *Seminar VI* on *Hamlet*.

31. "[I]n the tragedy of Hamlet, unlike that of Oedipus, after the murder of the father, the phallus is still there. It's there indeed, and it is precisely Claudius who is called upon to embody it" ("Desire in *Hamlet*," p. 50).

32. Lacan puns frequently in his writings and seminars. The reader is alerted to this particular wordplay by references in the text to the *leurre de l'être* (the trap or deception of being).

33. Lacan alludes to the contingent relationship between murder and suicide in "The Mirror Phase as Formative of the Function of the I" (1949; the original, unpublished version written in 1936) and amplifies it in "Aggressivity in Psychoanalysis" (1948). Both works are in Sheridan. The latter, heavily influenced by Hegel and Melanie Klein, may be construed as a corollary to "The Mirror Phase." In it Lacan discusses the importance of aggressivity in the

formation of the ego and suggests that the subject's shattering of its narcissistic identification with its mirror image implies simultaneous symbolic gestures of murder (of the other) and suicide (the self identified with the other). Only by its own symbolic death can the subject enter language and "be" in the world: "[A]t every moment [man] constitutes his world by his suicide" ("Aggressivity in Psychoanalysis," p. 28).

34. "[Hamlet] says to Laertes, 'I'll be your foil.' And, sure enough, what will appear a moment later but the very foil that wounds him mortally and that also will permit him to complete his circuit and to kill both his opponent and the king, the final object of his mission. In this pun there lies ultimately an identification with the mortal phallus" ("Desire in *Hamlet*," p. 34).

35. Abraham and Torok's works also treat other forms of secrets. See "The Topography of Reality: Sketching a Metapsychology of Secrets," *The Oxford Literary Review* 12, nos. 1–2 (1990): 63–68. The original French published in response to Denise Braunschweig, "Psychanalyse et Réalité," in *Revue Française de Psychanalyse*, nos. 5–6 (Paris: Presses Universitaires Françaises, 1971), rpt. as "La topique réalitaire: notations sur une métapsychologie du secret" in *L'écorce*. Henceforth cited as *Topography of Reality*; page references are to the English translation.

36. "A Poetics of Psychoanalysis: 'The Lost Object—Me,' " *SubStance*, no. 43 (1984): 17n.1. Abraham and Torok's italics. The translation of the passage here quoted incorporates modifications made for the forthcoming English version of *L'écorce*. The original French, " 'L'objet perdu—moi': notations sur l'identification endocryptique," in *L'écorce*. (Hereafter cited as *The Lost Object—Me*.) This essay does not treat the theory of the phantom but the very different problem of "endocryptic identification." The note was added to distinguish between the metapsychological concept of the phantom, which Abraham and Torok elaborated in later essays, and their use of the term "phantom" on the second page of the essay, which represents "a specific malaise of the analyst" when faced with a "cryptophore," a patient carrying within him or her the psychic structure the analysts discovered and named a "crypt." The concept of the crypt will be discussed momentarily.

37. *Phantom*, p. 290; Abraham's italics. The translator's note explains: "OuLiPo (*Ouvroir de Littérature Potentielle* = Workshop for Potential Literature) is a research group of experimental writing founded in 1960 by Raymond Queneau and François de Lionnais. The aim of the group is to invent 'artificial' formal constraints (not unlike the traditional sonnet form or acrostics, for example) and to demonstrate that by applying them systematically, the potential scope of linguistic creation can be expanded. As in Queneau's *Cent Mille Milliards de Poèmes*, semantic coherence is virtually never pursued."

Abraham's literary allusion is typical of the suggestiveness of his and Torok's writings. In this instance, it invites a rereading, from the perspective of the potential haunting effects in language of the phantom, of the works of Raymond Queneau, who was himself interested in psychoanalysis and who wrote at some length about his own analytic experience. See in this regard, *Chêne et chien* (1937).

38. *Topography of Reality*, p. 65.

39. While an adequate elaboration of the etiology and the metapsychological and literary implications of the crypt would require a full-length study, a brief word about this psychic structure will help clarify its link to the formation of phantoms and its specificity with regard to previously articulated mental topographies. (Abraham and Torok discuss the crypt in *The Wolf Man* and in several essays: *Topography of Reality*, "Deuil ou mélancolie: introjecter—incorporer" [in English as "Mourning or Melancholia: Introjection—Incorporation," in *Psychoanalysis in France*, ed. Serge Lebovici and Daniel Widlocher (New York: International University Press, 1980), pp. 3–16], "Psychoanalysis lithographica," *The Lost Object—Me*, and "La maladie de soi-à-soi: note de conversation sur la 'psychosomatique' " [Self-to-self illness: Notes on the "psychosomatic"]. All were originally published in *L'écorce*.)

In *Topography of Reality*, the analysts outline a preliminary statement of the particularity of the crypt.

> The crypt . . . is neither the dynamic Unconscious nor the ego of introjections. Rather, it is an enclave between the two, a kind of artificial Unconscious, lodged in the very midst of the ego. Such a tomb has the effect of sealing up the semi-permeable walls of the dynamic Unconscious. Nothing at all must filter to the outside world. The ego is given the task of cemetery guard. . . . [W]e shall call the tomb and its lock *preservative repression*, setting it off from the *constitutive repression* that is particularly apparent in hysteria and generally called dynamic repression. The essential difference between the two types of repression is that in hysteria, the desire, born of prohibition, seeks a way out through detours and finds it through symbolic fulfillment; whereas for the cryptophore, a desire, already directly fulfilled, lies buried, equally incapable of rising or of disintegrating. Nothing can undo its having been consummated or efface its memory. . . . This reality cannot quite die, nor can it hope to revive. (65; Abraham and Torok's italics)

In hysteria, the psychic conflict which results when a desire comes up against a prohibition is "resolved" in the form of a symptom that effectively materializes the words of the prohibition, thereby articulating, however opaquely, the content of the repressed desire itself. When a desire is fulfilled or realized in a drama so shameful that it is both unspeakable and unknowable for the subject, the "solution" is the formation of a crypt. This unmarked tomb serves the double function of sealing "alive" within it the unutterable words constitutive of the secret drama and of denying, because it is unmarked and inaccessible to the dynamic forces of the return of the repressed, the very fact that a secret has been concealed. What "returns" from the crypt within which the scandal is incorporated are the linguistic remnants of a repression enacted upon the unutterable words themselves, remnants altered so as to void any perceivable lexical attachment to what must remain unspoken. Abraham and Torok call the process by which this alteration occurs *cryptonymy*. This concept will be discussed at length momentarily. An instance in which a crypt can be shown to lie at the origin of a phantomatic haunting is presented in chapter 6 on *The Fall of the House of Usher*.

With regard to the use of the term "incorporation" in the above explanation, it should be noted that, while all crypts involve the process of incorporation as Abraham and Torok have redefined it (see note 15 above), not all instances of incorporation result in the formation of crypts. For an example of the latter, see Torok's essay "Maladie du deuil et fantasme du cadavre exquis" in *L'écorce*.

It should also be noted that the few commentators who to date have referred to Abraham and Torok's work on the phantom have by and large not taken into account the theoretical modifications concerning its formation implied by *The Sixth Act*. They tend to state or imply that a crypt is always at the origin of a phantom. See, for example, Derrida's albeit brief discussion of the distinction between a crypt and a phantom (translated as "ghost") in *The Ear of the Other*: "[W]hen one is looking for a ghost or a crypt in a text [rather than in a patient], then things get still more difficult, or let us say more novel. I say a ghost *and* a crypt: actually the theory of the "ghost" is not exactly the theory of the "crypt." It's even more complicated. Although it's also connected to the crypt, the ghost is more precisely the effect of another's crypt in my unconscious." (New York: Schocken Books, 1985), p. 59; Derrida's italics. Originally published in French as *L'oreille de l'autre* (Montreal: V1b Editeur, 1982).

40. It is also different from Lacan's, which appears in his interpretation of Hamlet. "[*D*]*as Unheimliche*, the uncanny, . . . is linked not, as some believed, to all sorts of irruptions from the unconscious, but rather to an imbalance that arises in the fantasy when it decomposes, crossing the limits originally assigned to it, and rejoins the image of the other subject" (p. 22). Lacan seems here to link the uncanny with his explanation of Hamlet's hesitation as an identification with Claudius as the incarnation of his fantasy object: the phallus.

41. Critical commentaries on the "uncanny" are extensive. Noteworthy among them are Neil Hertz, "Freud and the Sandman," in *Textual Strategies*, ed. J. Harari (Ithaca: Cornell University Press, 1979), and Hélène Cixous, "La fiction et ses fantômes: une lecture de *l'Unheimliche* de Freud," in *Prénoms de personne* (Paris: Seuil, 1974). For this reason, these remarks are not meant to exhaust the subject but rather to suggest alternative directions for future study.

42. *Phantom*, p. 291.

43. 18: 36.

44. See chapter 2 on Conrad's *The Secret Sharer*, chapter 3 on Villiers's *L'intersigne*, and chapter 4 on Balzac's *Facino Cane*. References to demons and ghosts appear frequently in Freud's work and cannot always be reinterpreted in terms of the phantom. One reference to ghosts and the repetition compulsion that has invited such a reinterpretation appears in Freud's discussion of little Hans in "Analysis of a Phobia in a Five-Year-Old Boy," 10: 122: "[A] thing which has not been understood inevitably reappears; like an unlaid ghost, it cannot rest until the mystery has been solved and the spell broken. . . ." As noted earlier, Torok's essay, *A Story of Fear*, demonstrates how this famous case can be explained in terms of a phantom and how not only obsessive but phobic symptoms may be rethought in conjunction with this metapsychological concept. See also in this regard Barbro Sylwan, "Le ferd-ikt," *Etudes freudi-*

ennes, nos. 13–14 (1978). Sylwan's essay is based upon a particularly suggestive aspect of Torok's recent work concerning the presence of a secret in Freud himself and its transmission, as a phantom, to the "heirs" of the psychoanalytic tradition. See Torok's "L'os de la fin," *Cahiers Confrontation*, no. 1 (Spring 1979): 163–86.

45. *Phantom*, p. 290.

46. Ibid.

47. Ibid., pp. 290–91.

48. *Studies on Hysteria*, 2: 152.

49. *The Interpretation of Dreams*, 4: 105.

50. *The Wolf Man*, p. 32, quoted from Freud, 21: 152.

51. Torok pursues this question and its possible answer in the afterword to *The Wolf Man* entitled "What Is Occult in Occultism? Between Sigmund Freud and Sergei Pankeiev Wolf Man," and in other essays devoted to analyzing Freud and the institution of psychoanalysis. See "L'os de la fin" and, with Rand, "The Secret of Psychoanalysis: History Reads Theory," *Critical Inquiry* 13, no. 2 (Winter 1987): 278–92.

52. For Lacan, metonymy also includes the possibility of phonic association. The displacement from *les noms du père* to *les non-dupes errent*, for example, is by homophony, called by Lacan metonymy.

53. *Dual Unity*, p. 424.

54. Sheridan, pp. 147–78, and *Ecrits*, pp. 493–528.

55. One might argue that a Lacanian reading could also see "letters," "stamps," and "parcels" as signifiers pointing to "post," or that it could even arrive at "pillar" by what Lacan calls "metonymy" with "post." The operative distinction between such a signifying chain and the cryptonymic process I have outlined lies in the status of "post" and "pillar." In the Lacanian interpretation, "post" and "pillar" would be interchangeable, "empty" signifiers, above the bar of repression, functioning as substitutes for the absent, repressed phallus and pointing to the origin of the signifying chain: the threat of castration. In my example, "post" and "pillar" are signifieds whose traces are readable in the signifiers "letters," "dispatches," and "stamps." They do not automatically point to castration but are linked to a specific drama cut off from the signifying chain by repression enacted upon the words themselves.

56. "Le symbole ou l'au-delà du phénomène," *L'écorce*, pp. 26–76. Henceforth noted as *Symbol*.

57. Part of this passage is translated in Torok and Rand's "Paradeictic: Translation, Psychoanalysis, and the Work of Art in the Writings of Nicolas Abraham," *Diacritics* 16, no. 3 (Fall 1986): 24. The remainder of the passage and all following citations from *Symbol* are my translation.

58. See chapter 8 of *The Wolf Man*.

59. In "Le temps, le rythme et l'inconscient," a paper delivered in 1962 and collected in *Entretiens sur l'art et la psychanalyse* (The Hague: Mouton, 1968), p. 55. It was republished with modifications in *L'écorce* and translated into English as "Psychoanalytic Esthetics: Time, Rhythm and the Unconscious," *Diacritics* 16, no. 3 (Fall 1986): 3–14.

60. See *Dual Unity*, p. 394.

61. The psychoanalytic theory of catastrophe was introduced by Ferenczi and occupies a central place in his conceptual system. It was adopted and expanded upon by Abraham and Torok. See Torok's commentary in "Katasztrófák" in *Cahiers Confrontation.*

62. *Phantom,* p. 289; my italics.

63. See *Symbol,* chapter 1: "Le sens du symbole comme l'au-delà du phénomène" in *L'écorce,* pp. 26–41.

64. Abraham points to Freud's work on conversion hysteria as one of the inspirations for his anasemic project. A brief restatement, in anasemic terms, of the methodological steps Freud took in the case of Elisabeth von R. (discussed earlier in this chapter) will illustrate why Abraham viewed Freud's inquiry as fundamentally anasemic.

In retracing Elizabeth's leg pain and paralysis to linguistic expressions involving the impossibility of taking a step forward to escape a paralyzing family situation, Freud implicitly asked: what dynamic led to such a transformation? He responded by formulating the processes of censorship and repression. His inquiry continued by asking what lay behind these processes, what psychic topography would have to exist for such a dynamic to function? This led him to conjecture the existence of the unconscious/conscious system. From this theoretical reconstruction Freud was able to conclude that hysteria could no longer be thought of as a brain disease; rather it was a collection of somatic symptoms resulting from the conversion, accomplished by the unconscious, of an obstacle to being into a particular mode of being-despite-distress. The effect, anasemically speaking, was to de-signify "somatic" and "psychic," since these terms no longer meant exclusively corporeal and mental, respectively (See *Shell,* pp. 20–21).

A thorough discussion of the concept of anasemia would require a much lengthier study extending to all of Abraham's works on symbol, transphenomenology, temporality, and rhythm. (See in this last regard Abraham's "Psychoanalytic Esthetics: Time, Rhythm, and the Unconscious" and the commentary on this essay by Torok and Rand, "Paradeictic: Translation, Psychoanalysis, and the Work of Art in the Writings of Nicolas Abraham.") A further subject for future inquiry is the relationship between Abraham and Torok's work and Jacques Derrida's deconstructive project. Such an inquiry might take as its point of departure a discussion of the areas of convergence between the two projects, especially their shared concern with nonlogocentric, nonphallocentric signifying processes. Areas of divergence that would benefit from analysis include Abraham's idea of "differral" (*differement/différencement*) and Derrida's concept of *différance,* Abraham's view of temporality (including his work on "time" and "rhythm") as compared to Derrida's exploration of iterability and *espacement,* their differing perspectives on *trace,* the infinite regression of signification, intelligibility (including contrasts between the theory of symbol and the ideas of "undecidability" and "aporia"), and their dissimilar views of introjection and incorporation, which Abraham and Torok view as clearly separate and whose separation Derrida tends to blur. (See on this point Derrida's preface to *The Wolf Man,* "Foreward: *Fors*: The Anglish Words of Nicolas Abraham and Maria Torok," trans. Barbara Johnson, p. xvii and passim. Other useful works for this comparative study include Derrida's essays,

"Me—Psychoanalysis: An Introduction to the Translation of 'The Shell and the Kernel' by Nicolas Abraham," *Diacritics* 9, no. 1 [Spring 1979]: 4–12 and "Spéculer—sur Freud" in *La carte postale: de Socrate à Freud et au-delà* as well as the section of Rand's introduction to *The Wolf Man* entitled "Deconstructing and Decrypting: Jacques Derrida and *The Wolf Man's Magic Word,*" pp. lxvi–lxix.) A brief discussion of certain points of resemblance and difference between the deconstructive project and anasemia is included in chapter 6 of this book on Poe's *The Fall of the House of Usher.*

Chapter 2
The Ghost of a Secret

1. Joseph Conrad, *The Secret Sharer*, in *The Portable Conrad*, ed. Morton Zabel (New York: Penguin Books, 1975). Hereafter cited as *Portable Conrad*. Page references are to this edition.

2. Critics who view the narrative from an ethical vantage point consider it an allegory of the captain's quest to achieve moral courage and clarity of conscience, although opinion is divided as to which part of the captain's inner self Leggatt comes to embody in this struggle. Some judge Leggatt to be a criminal and the captain's decision to conceal him an act of poor judgment reflective of his weaker self and instincts. Others view Leggatt as an admirable figure for having transcended hollow forms of authority. They condone the captain's behavior for respecting the inner conscience by which all men must live. See Albert Guerard, "The Journey Within," *Conrad the Novelist* (Cambridge: Harvard University Press, 1958), pp. 14–33, rpt. in *Conrad's "Secret Sharer" and the Critics*, ed. Bruce Harkness (Belmont, Calif.: Wadsworth Publishing, 1962) (hereafter cited as *Harkness*); R. W. Stallman, "Conrad and 'The Secret Sharer,' " *Accent* 9 (Spring 1949): 131–43, rpt. in *The Art of Joseph Conrad: A Critical Symposium*, ed. R. W. Stallman (East Lansing: Michigan State University Press, 1960), pp. 275–88; and Daniel Curley, "Legate of the Ideal," *Harkness*, pp. 75–82.

Readers tending toward psychological or psychoanalytic explanations have drawn primarily from the theories of Freud and Jung to explain the captain's apparent identification with Leggatt, his decision to hide the fugitive, and his obsessive references to his "double" and "secret self." Some construe the relationship along Oedipal lines, attributing the captain's complicity with this "secret sharer of his thoughts" to his vicarious satisfaction, experienced via Leggatt's act of murder, of his own repressed desire to kill his father. Others use Jungian archetypal models to interpret Leggatt as the divided or "lost" portion of the captain's personality with which he is finally integrated. Works that pursue these lines of inquiry include Adam Gillon, *Joseph Conrad* (Boston: Twayne Publishing, 1982), p. 156; Albert Guerard in *Harkness*; Robert Rogers, *The Double in Literature* (Detroit: Wayne State University Press, 1970), pp. 42–44; Joan Steiner, "Conrad's 'The Secret Sharer': Complexities of the Doubling Relationship," *Conradiana* 12, no. 3 (1980): 173–86; Steve Ressler, "Conrad's 'The Secret Sharer': Affirmation of Action," *Conradiana* 16, no. 3 (1984): 195–214; and Donald Yelton, *Mimesis and Metaphor: An Inquiry into the Genesis and Scope of Conrad's Symbolic Imagery* (Paris: Mouton, 1967), pp. 272–98. A more recent contribution to psychoanalytic views of Conrad's text, Barbara Johnson and Marjorie Garber's "Secret Sharing: Reading Conrad Psychoanalytically" (*College English* 49, no. 6 [October 1987]: 628–40), offers a different perspective on the tale and is discussed at some length in note 11.

3. Mary Ann Dazey has aptly observed the ambiguity inherent in the title's singular noun "sharer" and has commented on the possibility of reading the word "secret" as either an adjective or a noun. See "Shared Secret or Secret Sharing in Joseph Conrad's 'The Secret Sharer,' " *Conradiana* 18, no. 3 (1986): 201–3. While agreeing with her statement of the problem, my analysis of the text will lead to a conclusion sharply different from the one she draws from this ambiguity, which she contends ultimately obliges the reader to identify "either the captain or Leggatt . . . as the sharer of the secret or as the concealed or hidden sharer" (203).

4. See the section in chapter 1 entitled "Unspeakable Secrets, Psychic History, and the Phantom of Hamlet."

5. Namely, that King Hamlet haunts young Hamlet in the form of a ghost and interferes with the prince's project of revenge by virtue of having taken with him to the grave the unrevealed, unshared secret that he murdered King Fortinbras in a rigged duel.

6. C. B. Cox, for example, states, "Land, sea and sky merge together in . . . a kind of dream-landscape . . . as the hero . . . seek[s] to find himself in his subjective consciousness. . . ." *Joseph Conrad: The Modern Imagination* (London: J. M. Dent & Sons, 1974), p. 144. See also Albert Guerard in *Harkness*, pp. 64–65, and Louis Leiter, "Echo Structures: Conrad's 'The Secret Sharer,' " *Twentieth Century Literature* 5, no. 1 (January 1960): 159–75, rpt. in *Harkness*, p. 135.

7. Once below, Leggatt's efforts to avoid detection can be understood in simple psychological terms. His discovery would not only expose him to court-martial but would jeopardize the career of the captain, who acts sympathetically with him. Having accepted the invitation to hide below, Leggatt has no choice but to stay out of sight until he can leave the ship.

8. A subject of debate among scholars, these passages have most frequently been viewed as belonging to the "moral dimension" of the story or as constituting part of a biblical allegory. See, for example, Porter Williams, Jr., "The Brand of Cain in 'The Secret Sharer,' " *Modern Fiction Studies*, no. 10 (Spring 1964): 27–30; and Louis Leiter in *Harkness*, pp. 143–47.

9. The overdetermined nature of the captain's references to "shaving the land" and "shaving his mate's whiskers" is reinforced by his many earlier descriptions of the mate's "terrible whiskers": "[My chief mate] raised sharply his simple face, overcharged by a terrible growth of whisker" (650); "the chief mate, with an almost visible effect of collaboration on the part of his round eyes and frightful whiskers" (651); "Goodness only knew how that absurdly whiskered mate would 'account' for my conduct" (654); "I thought suddenly of my absurd mate with his terrific whiskers" (658); "I watched [the mate] coming with a smile which . . . took effect and froze his very whiskers" (670); "It was, as it were, trifling with the terrific character of his whiskers" (671); "This was the sort of thing that made my terrifically whiskered mate tap his forehead with his forefinger" (684).

Cedric Watts has observed that the captain's shaking of his mate mirrors Leggatt's shaking of the insolent seaman aboard the *Sephora*, but he attributes this "uncanny yet relatively innocuous recapitulation" to part of the story's "dialectical force" which challenges our "normal moral presuppositions" toward allying ourselves with fellow workers (the crew) rather than a kindred spirit (Leggatt) and toward conforming to law or practicality rather than taking romantic risks. *The Deceptive Text: An Introduction to Covert Plots* (Sussex: Harvester Press, 1984), pp. 88–89. Others have noted certain structural parallels between the two passages without, however, reconstructing from them any concealed drama. See Louis Leiter in *Harkness*, p. 141, and Steiner, "Complexities of the Doubling Relationship," p. 181.

10. Other elements in the text support the hypothesis that the secret may have involved a conjugal affair between "mates." Whereas Leggatt kills his shipmate while trying to set his ship's sheets ("It happened while we were setting a reefed foresail. . . . He gave me some of his cursed insolence at the sheet. . . . It was no time for gentlemanly reproof, so I turned round and felled him like an ox" [658–59]), the captain symbolically "kills" his mate when the latter insolently criticizes his setting of the sheets:

> "My God!" [the mate exclaimed] recklessly. . . . "Where are we? . . . She will never get out. You have done it, sir. . . . She will never weather, and you are too close now to stay. She'll drift ashore before she's round. . . ."
> I caught his arm . . . and shook it violently. . . . (696–97)

Earlier, when Leggatt first arrives at the ship, the captain gives him a "sleeping suit" (657) to wear that is identical to the one he wears throughout the adventure. These allusions to sheets and shared sleeping suits, when heard in the context of Leggatt's sharing the captain's bed and the murder of a "mate," add to the impression (without, however, allowing us to affirm it conclusively) that the murder perturbing the captain involved a marital or extramarital drama in the "sheets."

It must be added that the captain's precise relationship to the "mate" or "mates" involved in this murder also cannot be established from the elements in the text. The secret may have been created and transmitted by a parent, grandparent, cousin, or other relative, or conceivably by someone in another family who, for reasons unavailable to the reader, transmitted it across genealogical lines. The other texts treated in this study will allow us to determine with greater precision the nature, origin, and participants of the familial dramas haunting their characters.

11. For a theoretical discussion of the "dual unity" and its relationship to the phantom, see chapter 1.

In their essay, "Secret Sharing: Reading Conrad Psychoanalytically," Barbara Johnson and Marjorie Garber offer a blueprint for various psychoanalytic approaches, including an allegorical one, that may be used to interpret *The Secret Sharer*. I refer to their article in particular and at some length not necessarily to question their readings, which are inspired primarily although not exclusively by Freudian and Lacanian theory, but to bring into relief the alternative results achieved by an approach that takes into account the possibility that a phantom may be at work in the narrative.

The authors begin their essay by asking how the relationship between concealment and doubleness may be articulated in the text. They respond by outlining five paradigms for reading the text psychoanalytically: the pathology of the author, the pathology of the protagonist, the pathology of the text, the text as a theory of a symptom or complex, and the text as an allegory of psychoanalysis. In the process they underscore the overdetermined nature of a narrative that can sustain a multiplicity of potential interpretations informed variously by Oedipal scenarios, floating signifiers, transitional objects and symptoms, and the Freudian concept of the uncanny. In their most fully developed reading, the story as an allegory of psychoanalysis, Johnson and Garber trace the moments of the analytic process as they see it unfold in the narrative. Restated in abbreviated form, their argument proposes that the captain is driven by unconscious, infantile desires and guilt associated with the fear of becoming an adult. Leggatt's appearance represents the return of the captain's repressed, the incarnation of the captain's "uncanny" state of being as a subject apparently whole but in fact divided or estranged from himself. Via transference, the captain casts Leggatt, the image of his doubleness, as both his unconscious and his analyst, sending him "below" (637) to "the room with the couch" (637). The actual analysis commences when the captain pretends to be deaf to Archbold's account of Leggatt's crime (a sign of his resistance to hearing about the ugly matter involving his other, unconscious self) and when Leggatt sits silently in the cabin, listening to what the captain "cannot hear." In the second phase of analysis, the captain's conscious and unconscious begin to commingle as thoughts of Leggatt come to mind while he tries to command the ship. Responding to his acute sense of self-estrangement, the captain transforms Leggatt into a "transferential symptom" (639) or "sharer" (639) of what the captain is afraid to lose: the (apparent) wholeness of his boyhood. Unsure whether he can "command alone, without being in a state of unbearable loss or guilt" (639), the captain transfers his turmoil onto Leggatt, "the sharer . . . he will [now] lose and feel guilty about" (639), a figure he can release or "lose" (639) on the island in order not to "lose himself" (639). "In the end, the secret remains, not solved but rather left behind" (639). This "letting go, made difficult as always by the element of transference, the subject's investment in the analyst" (639), is accompanied by the captain's offer of a gift: the hat Leggatt leaves floating on the water and that serves the captain as " 'a mark to help out the ignorance of [his] strangeness' " (630). The return of the hat, whose offering is designed to protect the departing symptom/analyst, marks the end of the analysis. No longer ignorant of the uncanny and indelible dividedness of his subjectivity and having at last "renounced both the potency and the terror of infantile omnipotence" (639), the captain seems finally "ready to recognize that control of his fate is neither his nor not his" (639) but is instead "somehow henceforth tied to the course of a floating signifier" (639).

Johnson and Garber's suggestion that the text is an allegory of psychoanalysis appears logical if one accepts Leggatt's role as a transferential symptom who shares or embodies part of the captain's unconscious. If one questions Leggatt's status as the object and receptacle of transference, however, the text can no longer be considered an allegory of the psychoanalytic process since it would contain only a patient, without an analyst. In my reading, Leggatt is not viewed as a symptom but as a vehicle for symptom-formation. He functions not by catalyzing assimilation of the subject's self-dividedness but by enabling the captain to sustain a hallucinatory state of doubling and sharing symptomatic of his haunting by someone else's unutterable secret. In this light, the captain's "uncanny" feelings of being a "stranger to himself" are not interpreted as signs of the return of something the captain himself has repressed or as ontological givens in the course of human development. They are understood as effects of a "preservative repression" in which the captain is estranged from a specific drama, too shameful to be spoken, that has been kept secret from him but is familiar to someone else. While not disputing Johnson and Garber's reading as the kind of interpretation that can result when the process is informed by certain analytic models, my reading allows for a more specific account of what drives the captain's speech and behavior. It enables us to see the captain's relationship with Leggatt as constituted by the creation of scenarios of artificial secret sharing that point to the haunting presence of a secret murder he cannot share. Rather than fulfilling an analytic function, Leggatt is perceived as an unwitting participant in the captain's reenactment of a trauma beyond his comprehension. The captain's feelings of self-estrangement are accordingly not explained in terms of a psychoanalytic model that defines the subject as an inexorably divided, alienated self; they are viewed as the effects of the unspoken drama of murder he unknowingly carries lodged within him.

12. In December 1909, Conrad sent a copy of his just-completed short story to his agent, Pinker, with a note including the following: "For titles I suggest—*The Secret Self* or *The Other Self, An episode from the sea*. It could be also *The Secret Sharer* but that may be *too* enigmatic. Pray select for me." (*The Collected Letters of Joseph Conrad*, vol. 4, ed. Frederick R. Karl and Laurence Davies [Cambridge: Cambridge University Press, 1990], p. 300, Conrad's italics.) Pinker made the final choice, which, while perhaps indicative of his own literary insight, suggests that Conrad may have been unaware of the phantom structure organizing his narrative and making *The Secret Sharer* the most appropriate title for the tale.

13. Edward Said, to cite only one example, sees the ending as a triumph in which Leggatt, "a direct reflection of the narrator," is sent off to live as a free man and the captain at last achieves "objective knowledge" and "reassured mastery" of his craft. *Joseph Conrad and the Fiction of Autobiography* (Cambridge: Harvard University Press, 1966), pp. 129–32.

14. The fact that the ship has no name and that the captain personifies her as a "trusted friend" (649–50) suggests that his references to the vessel as "she" may derive from more than mere nautical convention. The ship may somehow incarnate a woman "mate" (friend or wife) involved in the drama of murder. This conjecture, in the absence of textual evidence, has to remain purely speculative.

15. Mentioned in his preface to *'Twixt Land and Sea Tales*. *Conrad's Prefaces*, ed. Edward Garnett (London: J. M. Dent, 1937), p. 143.

16. See Keith Carabine, " 'The Secret Sharer': A Note on the Dates of Its Composition," *Conradiana* 19, no. 3 (1987): 209–13; and also Conrad's letter to Norman Douglas, December 23, 1909.

17. Critical attention paid to the relationship between *The Secret Sharer* and

Under Western Eyes has concentrated primarily on thematic, structural, and biographical similarities. See Gail Fraser, " 'The Secret Sharer' and *Under Western Eyes*" in *Interweaving Patterns in the Works of Joseph Conrad* (Ann Arbor: UMI Research Press, 1988), pp. 111–33; Gillon's *Joseph Conrad;* Carabine, " 'The Secret Sharer': A Note on the Dates of Its Composition"; and Ressler, "Conrad's 'The Secret Sharer': Affirmation of Action." The manner in which texts may be understood as complements that inform and "complete" one another is elaborated more fully in chapter 6 on *The Fall of the House of Usher*.

Chapter 3
The Interred Sign

1. For a reading of *L'intersigne* from a narratological perspective, see Ross Chambers, "Changing Overcoats: Villiers' 'L'Intersigne' and the Authority of Fiction," *L'esprit créateur* 28, no. 3 (Fall 1988): 63–77. Other noteworthy essays on Villiers's works include Lucette Finas, "Villiers de l'Isle-Adam: *Les Brigands,*" in *Le bruit d'Iris* (Paris: Flammarion, 1978), pp. 79–91; and Rodolphe Gasché, "The Stelliferous Fold: On Villiers de l'Isle-Adam's *L'Eve future,*" *Studies in Romanticism* 22 (Summer 1983): 293–327. See also A. W. Raitt's comprehensive comparative study, *Villiers de l'Isle-Adam et le mouvement symboliste* (Paris: Corti, 1965).

2. Villiers de l'Isle-Adam, *L'intersigne,* in *Contes cruels, Nouveaux contes cruels,* ed. Pierre-Georges Castex (Paris: Garnier Frères, 1968). (Hereafter cited as Castex.) Page references are to this edition. Two translations of *L'intersigne* to which the reader may refer exist, the first as *Intersignum* in *Sardonic Tales,* trans. Hamish Miles (New York: A. A. Knopf, 1927), the second as *The Sign* in *Cruel Tales,* trans. Robert Baldick (Oxford: Oxford University Press, 1985). The citations in English in the chapter make use of the earlier translation, which more accurately renders the vocabulary, style, and tone of the original French, but which I have nonetheless modified for accuracy.

3. Castex, p. 238.

4. Castex concludes that "Villiers claimed to show . . . that we receive, in our sleep, revelations from another world." Castex, p. 400. Jean-Paul Gourevitch proposes that in *L'intersigne,* "it is the limit between the universe and the world of mysterious correspondences that Villiers invites us to cross." *Villiers de l'Isle-Adam* (Paris: Seghers, 1971), p. 45.

5. "O toi, pensai-je, . . . pour qui la terre de Chanaan . . . n'apparaît pas . . . après avoir tant marché sous de dures étoiles" (223). ("You, I thought . . . for whom the land of Canaan . . . does not appear . . . after you have walked so far beneath the hard stars.")

6. "[J]e résolus . . . de m'éloigner de Paris [et] de me livrer à quelques salubres parties de chasse" (220). ("[I] resolved to . . . leave Paris [and] to indulge in some healthy hunting parties.")

7. In addition to "vigils for the dead," the word "veillées" can mean simply "the evenings." My insistence on the more mystical sense of the word is reinforced, in part, by the original version of the text, which specifies the subject of Xavier's conversation with Maucombe: "[J]e songe[ais] aux veillées que nous allions passer ensemble en causant de sujets *d'un intérêt mystérieux,*" Castex,

p. 465. ("I thought about the evenings we would be spending together talking about subjects *of a mysterious interest.*")

8. "Il me jeta le manteau sur les épaules [et] je fermais les paupières.... Ma foi, j'eus peur....

Donc ... j'ensanglantai les flancs du pauvre cheval, et les yeux fermés, [je m'enfuis, victime d'une] horreur superstitieuse dont je frissonais malgré moi." (235–36)

["He threw the cloak over my shoulders (and) I closed my eyelids.... Oh, how I was afraid....

And so ... I drew blood from the flanks of the poor horse and, my eyes closed, (I fled, victim of a) superstitious horror that made me shudder despite myself."]

9. "The essential role ... is played by a cloak that touched the tomb of Christ," Emile Drougard, ed., *Les trois premiers contes*, by Villiers de l'Isle-Adam (Paris: Société d'édition "Les Belles Lettres," 1931), 2:141. (Henceforth cited as Drougard.) "The last detail concerning the holy origin of the cloak was added," Castex, p. 464. "[A] sacred force is inherent in the cloak that touched Christ's tomb," B. Heidelberg, "Narrative Art in the *Contes cruels* of Villiers de l'Isle-Adam" (Ph.D. diss., University of Minnesota, 1972), pp. 177–78.

10. *Robert.*

11. Ibid. (*presser*: to squeeze so as to compress, deform, mark with an imprint).

12. Drougard, p. 264.

13. The appearance of the owl in Xavier's hallucination can be understood in this context of hearing what is seen. The word *hibou* is believed to be an onomatopoetic creation, a word born as an imitation of the sound made by an owl. It may also be mentioned that the owl plays a part in Hegel's *Introduction to the Philosophy of History*. Villiers was apparently familiar with Hegel, whose relationship to this and Villiers's other texts, although not dealt with in this study, is certainly worthy of further investigation.

The insistence of water in the text just noted can also be seen and heard in Xavier's frightening experience on the open road right before Maucombe offers him his cloak:

> Cinq minutes après notre départ, une *bruine pénétrante*, une *petite pluie* ... frappa nos mains et nos figures....
>
> —Mon vieil ami, dis-je à l'abbé, ... [v]otre existence est précieuse et cette *ondée glaciale* est très malsaine. Rentrez. Cette *pluie*, encore une fois, pourrait vous *mouiller* dangereusement....
>
> En ce moment la lune ... nous *baigna* ... de sa lumière [et j'entendis au loin des] funestes oiseaux.... (234)
>
> [Five minutes after our departure, a *penetrating drizzle*, a *fine rain* ... fell upon our hands and faces....
>
> —My old friend, I said to the abbé, ... (y)our existence is too precious and this *icy downpour* is too dangerous. Go back. This *rain*, I say again, could give you a dangerous *soaking*....
>
> At that moment the moon ... *bathed* us ... in its light (and I heard far off some) sinister birds....]

14. The word *nature* is stressed several times in the text, either by italics or capitalization, and serves to reinforce this idea of a "natural" (in both the French and English sense of "illegitimate, bastard") son. In describing the subject of Xavier's tale at the beginning of the narrative, for example, the narrator associates the word *nature* with something stupefying, out of the ordinary, and unknown: "la conversation tomba sur un sujet des plus sombres: il était question de la *nature* de ces coïncidences extraordinaires, stupéfiantes, mystérieuses, qui surviennent dans l'existence de quelques personnes" (219; Villiers's italics). ("the conversation turned to an extremely sombre subject: it had to do with the *nature* of those extraordinary, astounding, and mysterious coincidences that occur in the lives of some people" [Villiers's italics].) Later, recounting his third vision, Xavier himself establishes a connection between the blood-red, familial stain now readable as a sign of his tainted origins and the question of "nature": "Une chose me paraissait surprenante: la *nature* de la tache qui courait sur ma main" (229; Villiers's italics). ("One thing struck me as surprising: the *nature* of the stain that ran over my hand" [Villiers's italics].)

15. The reading of Maucombe's name as *mot incombe*, "the word weighs or is incumbent upon," is reinforced by the priest's comment to Xavier upon his arrival: "nous sommes ici pour témoigner,—par nos oeuvres, nos pensées, nos paroles et notre lutte contre la Nature—pour témoigner *si nous pesons le poids*" (226; Villiers's italics). ("we are here to bear witness,—by our works, our thoughts, our words and our struggle against Nature—to bear witness as to *whether we have what it takes*" [literally, *whether we bear the weight*"] [Villiers's italics].) Not only is Maucombe linked to a weight that is carried or borne, but this weight is connected to a battle against *Nature*, to what can now be read as a struggle involving a "natural" or illegitimate son.

16. The most complex example of this is contained in *L'Eve future* in which the robot speaks the words of great philosophers that have been recorded on a phonograph encased within her frame. For a brief outline of this research, see my essay, "1886—Auguste de Villiers de l'Isle-Adam Publishes His Last Novel *L'Eve future*: The Phantom's Voice," in *A New History of French Literature*, ed. Denis Hollier (Cambridge: Harvard University Press, 1989), pp. 801–6. My work in this area has thus far concentrated on Villiers's prose works. There is evidence to suggest, however, that some of his dramatic works, including his most famous play, *Axël*, may also be interpreted from the perspective of the disembodied voice and the phantom.

Chapter 4
Legacies of Gold

1. Honoré de Balzac, *Facino Cane*, in *La comédie humaine*, ed. Pierre-Georges Castex (Paris: Librairie Gallimard, 1977), vol. 6. French citations are to this edition. Translations throughout the chapter are based on Sylvia Raphael's *Facino Cane* in *Selected Short Stories of Balzac* (New York: Penguin Books, 1977) and have been modified by me.

2. *Grande Dizionario della lingua italiana* (Turin, Italy), 1961.

3. These two admittedly schematic readings are meant to be exemplary of the kinds of interpretations of the text that might be done using Freud's and Lacan's theories. They do not preclude other analyses, emphasizing different aspects of these theories, that might yield different results. For an example of a Freudian interpretation of *Facino Cane* that does follow lines somewhat similar to my own sketch, see Janet Beizer, *Family Plots: Balzac's Narrative Generations* (New Haven: Yale University Press, 1986).

4. P. 1028. The presence of Arabic in the text is emphasized by two references to *The Arabian Nights*. The first is made during Facino Cane's attempt to convince the narrator to accompany him to Venice: "Voulez-vous me mener à Venise . . . ? vous serez . . . riche comme *Les Mille et Une Nuits*" (1025). ("Will you take me to Venice . . . ? You will be . . . rich like the heroes of the *Arabian Nights*.") The second is made by the narrator in describing his ability to inhabit other people: "Chez moi l'observation . . . me permetta[it] de me substituer à [un individu] comme le derviche des *Mille et Une Nuits* prenait le corps et l'âme des personnes" (1019; Balzac's italics). ("This power of observation enabled me to . . . substitute myself for [the individual], just like the dervish in the *Arabian Nights* who took on the body and soul of people.")

5. P. 1024: "—Ici [on m'appelle] *le père Canet*. Mon nom n'a jamais pu s'écrire autrement sur les registres. . . ." ("—Here . . . they call me *father Canet*. They never could write my name any other way on the registers"); p. 1024: "—Allons, en avant, *père Canard*, dit le flageolet." ("—Come on, get going, *father Canard*, said the flageolet player"); p. 1030: "[J]e me cachai dans Madrid; puis . . . je vins à Paris *sous un nom espagnol*. . . ." ("[I] remained in hiding in Madrid. Then . . . I came to Paris, *using a Spanish name*. . . .")

6. The multilingual ambiguity surrounding Facino Cane's name is heightened by the narrator's description of him as both Dante and Homer: "Figurez-vous le masque en plâtre de *Dante*. . . . Quelque chose de grand et de despotique se rencontrait dans ce *vieil Homère* qui gardait en lui-même une Odyssée condamnée à l'oubli" (1022–23). ("Imagine *Dante's* death-mask. . . . There was something great and despotic in this *old Homer* who kept within himself an Odyssey condemned to oblivion.")

7. "—Comment vous nommez-vous donc? [dit le narrateur.]

— . . . en italien, c'est *Marco Facino Cane, principe de Varese*.

—Comment? vous descendez du fameux condottiere Facino Cane dont les conquêtes ont passé aux ducs de Milan?

—*E vero*, me dit-il. Dans ce temps-là, pour n'être pas tué par les Visconti, le fils de Cane s'est réfugié à Venise et s'est fait inscrire sur le Livre d'or. Mais il n'y a pas plus de Cane maintenant que de livre." (1024; Balzac's italics)

["—What's your name then? (said the narrator.)

— . . . in Italian, it is *Marco Facino Cane, principe de Varese*.

—What? You are descended from the famous condottiere, Facino Cane, whose conquests passed to the Dukes of Milan?

—*E vero*, he said. At that time, Cane's son took refuge in Venice to escape being killed by the Visconti and had himself inscribed in the Book of Gold. But now neither Cane nor the book exists any more." (Balzac's italics)]

8. Cane mentions the Rothschilds in trying to convince the narrator to

accompany him to Venice: "—Voulez-vous me mener à Venise . . . vous serez plus riche . . . que les Rothschild" (1025). ("—Will you take me to Venice . . . you will be richer . . . than the Rothschilds.")

9. Hearing the homophony between French and Hebrew is suggested by the text's numerous references to Semitic languages and contexts and by Facino Cane's insistence that, while in prison, he was able to "hear the sound of gold" ("j'entendais le son de l'or" [1028]). The text also contains another interlinguistic rhyme in the play on Facino Cane's name: le père *Canet*.

10. ". . . en 1770, je vins à Paris sous un nom espagnol, et menai le train le plus brillant. . . . Au milieu de mes voluptés, quand je jouissais d'une fortune de six millions, je fus frappé de cécité" (1030). (". . . in 1770 I came to Paris, using a Spanish name, and lived in the most brilliant style. . . . In the midst of my pleasures, when I was enjoying a fortune of six million, I was struck by blindness.") Cane offers three conflicting explanations for this event, underscoring its enigmatic and highly determined origin: "—[Je suis aveugle] par accident, . . . une maudite goutte sereine" (1023). "Je ne doute pas que cette infirmité ne soit le résultat de mon séjour dans le cachot, de mes travaux dans la pierre, si toutefois ma faculté de voir l'or n'emportait pas un abus de la puissance visuelle qui me prédestinait à perdre les yeux" (1030). ("—[I became blind] by accident, . . . a cursed atrophy of the optic nerve. . . . I have no doubt that this affliction was the result of my stay in prison and of my labors in the stone, unless my power of seeing gold constituted an abuse of the power of vision that predestined me to lose my sight.")

11. "[J]'avais mis ma confiance en [une] femme [qui] me conseilla de consulter un fameux oculiste de Londres: mais, après quelques mois de séjour dans cette ville, j'y fus abandonné par cette femme dans Hyde-Park, elle m'avait dépouillé de toute ma fortune sans me laisser aucune ressource" (1030). ("I had put my trust in [a] woman [who] advised me to consult a famous London oculist. But after a stay of some months in London, she deserted me in Hyde Park, having robbed me of all my fortune and leaving me without resources.")

12. *Or* is an interlinguistic cryptonym. It functions by interlinguistic homophony between *or* and OR (אור) and by "allosemy" (see *The Wolf Man*, p. 19) or variant meaning of "light" as "enlightenment." The question might be raised as to whether Balzac knew the word OR in Hebrew. On a purely biographical level, it is likely that he knew at least some words of Hebrew, especially words associated with mysticism or the spiritual. Balzac was fascinated by occultism and cabalism and carried with him a talisman from the Arab emir Bedouck, which can be seen in the Balzac museum in Saché, France. In the chapter of *La peau de chagrin* entitled "Le talisman," he quotes a text written in Sanscrit that is engraved on the back of the magical skin. It is also conceivable that Balzac unwittingly "inherited" some knowledge of Hebrew as a phantomatic transmission, for reasons we can only imagine. The emphasis in his writings on gold and the frequency with which clearly identified Jewish characters appear suggests these are not idle speculations.

This, however, is not the primary issue in this interpretation. Of consequence for the reading is that the text itself, through its lexical allusions, omissions, and encryptings, leads us to the Hebrew word OR, and that this word in turn leads us to conjecture Cane's quest for his Jewish origins.

It is noteworthy that Balzac's modification of the first version of the text corroborates the idea that a Jewish identity is unspeakable in the text. In the original version, the prisoner who engraved the Arabic inscription on the wall of Cane's cell is identified as a Jew. "[J]e parvins à déchiffrer . . . une inscription arabe par laquelle un juif, auteur de ce travail, avertissait ses successeurs qu'il avait détaché deux pierres de la dernière assise, et creusé onze pieds de souterrain" (in Castex's notes, p. 1541). ("I managed . . . to decipher an Arabic inscription in which a Jew, author of this work, informed his successors that he had dislodged two stones from the last row of masonry and dug eleven feet underground.") Balzac elided this sole explicit reference to a Jew in the tale from the final version of the text: "[J]e parvins à déchiffrer . . . une inscription arabe par laquelle l'auteur de ce travail avertissait ses successeurs" (1028). ("[I] managed . . . to decipher an Arabic inscription in which the author of this work informed his successors.")

13. This structure in which the metal gold is a substitute for the word *or* leads to a reconsideration of the notion of fetishism. Both Freudian and Lacanian readings of the text view gold as a substitute for the true object of Facino Cane's passion: the mother or the phallus. In the reading just elaborated, Facino Cane's fetish is linked to language; the object of his desire is not the object gold but the French word *or*, with its connection to Hebrew origins and enlightenment. If Cane experiences pleasure in touching and fondling the metal, it is because this act puts him in touch with the sequence *or* → OR → (en)light(enment) about Hebrew origins. The metal gold is thus not the fetish object in the text but a substitute for the "fetish-word" *or*.

Abraham and Torok introduce the idea that fetishism can be determined by and manifested in language, and that it no longer depends (as it did for Freud) on the substitution of an object for the nonexistent penis of the mother or (according to Lacan) for the absent phallus, in their analyses of the Wolf Man and "The Man of Milk" (the latter in "A Poetics of Psychoanalysis: 'The Lost Object—Me,' " in *SubStance*, no. 43 [1984]: 3–18). In each of these cases, a specific word (the Russian verb *teret* and the Spanish noun *leche*, respectively) hides a system of meanings and associations that provides the true source of pleasure for the subject.

14. See n. 5 above. The previously noted references to Facino Cane as Dante and Homer also suggest he embodies more than one identity in the text.

15. *Grande Dizionario della lingua italiana.*

16. "J'ai eu de grands plaisirs, j'ai vécu à la cour de Louis XV parmi les femmes les plus célèbres; nulle part je n'ai trouvé les qualités, les grâces, l'amour de ma chère Vénitienne" (1027). ("I have enjoyed great pleasures; I have lived at the court of Louis XV among the most celebrated women; nowhere have I found the virtues, the charms, the love of my adored Venetian.")

It should be clear that Bianca is totally unaware of acting out a part in Cane's psychic drama. Her role as "adulterous wife" is entirely a function of the phantom haunting Cane and of his re-creation of the scene of adultery kept secret by his mother.

17. "[Q]uand je m'en rapprochai [de Facino Cane], . . . ma curiosité fut excitée au plus haut degré, car mon âme passa dans le corps [de ce] joueur de

clarinette" (1022). ("[W]hen I got close to [Facino Cane], . . . my curiosity was excited to the highest degree, for my soul passed into the body of this clarinet player.")

18. "J'ai adressé des notes au premier consul, j'ai proposé un traité à l'empereur d'Autriche, tous m'ont éconduit comme un fou!" (1031). ("I wrote to the First Consul, I proposed an agreement with the Emperor of Austria, they all dismissed me as a madman.")

19. The cause of Facino Cane's death from a "catarrh" (from the Greek *katarrhein* meaning "to flow down") may be seen as a metaphor of the transmission of the phantom, which "flows down" from Cane to the narrator.

20. Albert Béguin, Diana McCormick, and Pierre-Georges Castex have emphasized the autobiographical elements of the text. Castex prefaces the story in his earlier edition of *La comédie humaine* (Paris: Seuil, 1966) by noting that it is "of value above all for its autobiographical details: Balzac did in fact live, in 1819, in a garret on the rue Lesdiguières; he did in fact have a housekeeper named la mère Vaillant; above all, the page where we see the narrator accustom himself to penetrating, by his thoughts, into the inner being of passersby, is one of the most precious confessions we have about the imaginative and creative powers of the novelist" (6:257). Béguin and McCormick elaborate upon this idea in their respective works *Balzac lu et relu* (Paris: Seuil, 1965), p. 154, and *Les nouvelles de Balzac* (Paris: Librairie Nizet, 1973), pp. 215–16.

21. The English title of the short story is always rendered as *The Girl with the Golden Eyes*. My translation of the French title is more literal. Interpretation of the story with the insights gained from this reading of *Facino Cane* would potentially reveal whether it is more accurate.

22. See in particular Shoshana Felman, "Rereading Femininity," *Feminist Readings: French Texts/American Contexts, Yale French Studies*, no. 62 (1981): 19–44.

Chapter 5
In the Mind's I

1. Henry James, *The Jolly Corner*, in *The Complete Tales of Henry James*, ed. Leon Edel, vol. 12 (London: Rupert Hart-Davis, 1964). Page references are to this edition.

2. See Leon Edel, "The Americano-European Legend," *Tales of Henry James*, ed. Christof Wegelin (New York: W. W. Norton, 1984), and Louis Auchincloss, *Reading Henry James* (Minneapolis: University of Minnesota Press, 1978).

3. See, among others, Annette Larson Benert's Bakhtinian interpretation in "Dialogical Discourse in 'The Jolly Corner': The Entrepreneur as Language and Image," *Henry James Review* 8, no. 2 (Winter 1987): 116–25. The idea that Brydon's residence in Europe has saved him from becoming a monstrous American is expressed in various ways by numerous critics, among them F. O. Matthiessen, *Henry James: The Major Phase*, (New York: Oxford University Press, 1963); Edmund Wilson, "The Ambiguity of Henry James," *The Triple Thinkers* (New York: Harcourt, Brace, & Co., 1938), rpt. in *The Question of Henry James*, ed. F. W. Dupee (New York: Holt and Co., 1945), hereafter cited

as Dupee; and Marius Bewly, *The Complex Fate* (New York: Gordian Press, 1967). For a different perspective on the relationship between cultural context and identity, see Russell J. Reising, "Figuring Himself Out: Spencer Brydon, 'The Jolly Corner,' and Cultural Change," *The Journal of Narrative Technique* 19, no. 1 (Winter 1989): 116–29.

4. "The Ghost of Henry James: A Study in Thematic Apperception," *Character and Personality* 12 (December 1943): 79–100.

5. The legitimacy of such an enterprise would, I believe, depend upon a methodological approach yet to be elaborated: one that would eschew using predetermined formulas of psychic organization as models for analysis.

6. In *Henry James: une écriture énigmatique* (Paris: Aubier-Montaigne, 1982) Jean Perrot proposes that the emergence of the alter ego in the story through movements of "erection," "drops," and "protrusions" dramatizes Spencer Brydon's libidinal force and signals an ultimately victorious autoeroticism in which the forces of the id triumph over the ego. For different but related views see Floyd Stovall, "Henry James's 'The Jolly Corner,'" *Nineteenth-Century Fiction* 12, no. 1 (June 1957): 72–84; Edmund Wilson's "The Ambiguity of Henry James" in Dupee, pp. 186–87; Martha Banta, *Henry James and the Occult* (Bloomington: Indiana University Press, 1972); Quentin Anderson's preface to *Henry James: Selected Short Stories* (New York: Rinehart Editions, 1950); Peter Buitenhuis, *The Grasping Imagination: The American Writings of Henry James* (Toronto: University of Toronto Press, 1970); and Donna Przybylowicz, *Desire and Repression: The Dialectic of Self and Other in the Late Works of Henry James* (University: University of Alabama Press, 1986).

7. Trans. Richard Howard (Ithaca: Cornell University Press, 1977) from the original *La poétique de la prose* (Paris: Seuil, 1971).

8. Ibid., p. 187.

9. Ibid., p. 188. Todorov's italics.

10. Todorov has justifiably called *The Jolly Corner* the densest of James's short stories.

11. The military link can be seen in the horns that have traditionally adorned the helmets worn by warriors of various countries.

12. The legitimacy of finding the linguistically embedded *cornu* (horn) in "corner" is of course reinforced by Spencer's quest to find the (Latin) *alter ego* in the jolly corner.

13. In Exod. 34:29, 30, 35. "Cumque descenderet Moyses de monte Sinai, tenebat duas tabulas testimonii, et ignorabat quod *cornuta* esset facies sua ex consortio sermonis Domini. Videntes autem Aaron et filii Israel *cornutam* Moysi faciem, timuerunt prope accedere. . . . Qui videbant faciem egredientis Moysi esse *cornutam*, sed operiebat ille rursus faciem suam, si quando loquebatur ad eos" (*Biblia Sacra Vulgatae Editionis* [Italy: Marietti, 1965]). The word in the original Hebrew Bible is קרן (karan), which has the two senses of "to protrude as horns" and "to shine or give off rays of light." The translators of the Vulgate, for reasons still debated by biblical scholars, chose a word in Latin that communicated only the first of these meanings. One of the ramifications of this choice can be seen in the representation of Moses, in a statue by Michelangelo, with what have been called two "horns" emanating from his head.

14. *Cornard,* in common usage by 1608, comes from the French *corne* (horn), which, like the English "corner," comes from the Latin for "horn": *cornu* (*Robert*).

15. *Pince-nez* offers an excellent example of the potential complexity and variety of the cryptonymic process. It is composed of two distinct cryptonyms that, when joined, yield one cryptonym whose meaning or archeonym is *fraudulent heir.* It may be diagramed as follows:

Pince-nez: *Pince* → hand (by synonymy between French and English) → palm (by *allosemia* or variant meaning) → palming → imposter + *nez* → *né* (by homophony) → born (by further synonymy between French and English) = *imposter* + *born* = *fraudulent heir.*

This cryptonymic configuration is of course itself dependent on the prior decrypting of the hidden narrative of "hands" in the text, without which it could not be deciphered.

The authoritative *Dictionnaire historique des argots français,* ed. Gaston Esnault (Paris: Larousse, 1965) identifies "pince" as the popular word for "hand" in common usage by 1857. There can be little doubt that James was aware of this word in 1908, particularly in view of his years spent living in Paris and his excellent knowledge of colloquial as well as polite French. For a recent study on the frequency and importance of French in James, see Edwin Fussell, *The French Side of Henry James* (New York: Columbia University Press, 1990).

16. *Robert* confirms *coucou* (translatable as the English "yoo-hoo") as an interjection used by children playing hide-and-seek in use by 1660. It also confirms, along with the *Dictionnaire étymologique de la langue française,* eds. Block and Wartburg (Paris: Presses Universitaires de France, 1975), that *cocu* is a variant form of *coucou,* via onomatopoetic formation, in use since the fourteenth century to mean "cuckold."

The connection between a cuckold and the alter ego inhabiting Spencer is further reinforced by Spencer's comparison of the alter ego to a "full-blown flower" (204) and by his reference to not being noticed, not even by a "fat Avenue 'officer' " (208), as he sneaks out of the jolly corner in the early morning. The quotation marks around " 'officer' " and the resonance between "full-blown" and "fat" lead us to put "flower" and " 'officer' " together and to translate them in a Romance context (suggested by *alter ego*). We read the French: *primevère officinale,* a flower that blooms in the spring, known in English as a "mountain primrose," and whose common name in French is *coucou.*

17. The reason for James's use of an anonymous third-person narrator to tell the story can be addressed in terms of what has just been elaborated. This narrative device permits the multiplication, fragmenting, and evacuating of identities in Spencer to be articulated. If the text were a first-person narrative told by "Spencer," it would take the form of a fragmented, chaotic, or even "psychotic" discourse that would render the reader's attempts to unravel the identities within it extraordinarily difficult, if not impossible.

18. We can hear pressed within Brydon's name itself the bare elements constituting this imagined scene: his "bride" or wife, the "don" or gentleman ("another agent" → another, a *gent* → a gentleman) with her, and the procreation or "breed[ing] on" that occurs in his absence. The text, moreover, legitimizes and indeed encourages whatever slight deformation in pronunciation

this reading entails in the passage where Mrs. Muldoon, the caretaker of the house, expresses her reticence to enter the jolly corner after dark and frankly tells Miss Staverton that no lady could be expected to like " 'craping up to thim top storeys in the ayvil hours' " (199). The possibility of altered pronunciation is further legitimized by the narrator's reprise of this deformation in recounting Spencer's adventure: "He had begun some time since to 'crape' " (199).

19. Alice Staverton has been regarded by some critics as a framing character in the story. See Mary Doyle Springer's *A Rhetoric of Literary Character: Some Women of Henry James* (Chicago: University of Chicago Press, 1977), pp. 113–26. Others have attempted to draw autobiographical parallels with James's sister and sister-in-law, both named Alice. The first view is given an alternative by this reading; the second remains a possibility worthy of investigation.

20. Motes → specks (by synonymy) → specks (by homonymy) → spectacles (by synonymy).

21. "Brydon . . . retraced his steps . . . [and] knew himself at the other side of the house. . . . He came down . . . the last flight . . . [and] saw . . . the prodigy of a personal presence" (219–24).

The identification of Spencer's uncle as the fraudulent offspring is sustained by another encrypted bilingual narrative in the text. Throughout the story, Spencer's alter ego is associated with large sums of money. When Spencer refuses to renovate the jolly corner so that he may hunt for his "other self," he tells Miss Staverton that there is no logical reason for his refusal to make a deal, except money: "There are no reasons here *but* of dollars" (202; James's italics). When he speaks of what he would have been like if he had not become an expatriate in Europe, Spencer acknowledges he would have been "a billionaire" (205). And at the end of the story, when Spencer and Alice Staverton describe the figure they have both seen, Spencer "lucidly" adds, "He has a million a year" (232). If we connect this insistence on the alter ego's wealth, the emphasis on Spencer's long residence as a citizen of "Europe" (in quotation marks in the text), the presence of French in the narrative, and the conflation of all three of these elements in the expression, *pour deux sous* ("I was too young . . . to judge, *pour deux sous* [for two cents worth], whether it *were* possible [to stay here]" (204; James's italics), we can hear the encrypted French locution that refers to a wealthy relative, emigrated from France to America, who leaves his heir back in "Europe" an unexpected inheritance. We hear *mon oncle d'Amérique*, "my rich *uncle*" (literally "my uncle in America").

22. It is possible that an answer lies in another text by James. *The Sense of the Past*, a text begun shortly after *The Jolly Corner* and left unfinished at James's death, might be examined from this perspective as a possible complement or co-symbol of *The Jolly Corner*.

23. The best example of a psychoanalytic interpretation that views the narrative as a complex allegory of reading remains Shoshana Felman's "Turning the Screw of Interpretation," in *Literature and Psychoanalysis: The Question of Reading Otherwise, Yale French Studies* nos. 55–56 (1977): 94–207. For an essay outlining how a reading of the story as a phantom-text might proceed, see Elisabeth Simon, "Le tour d'écrou 1981," *Cahiers Confrontation*, no. 8 (Fall 1982): 51–74.

Chapter 6
A Meeting of the Minds

1. *The Fall of the House of Usher* was first published in *Burton's Gentleman's Magazine* in September 1839 and republished, with revisions, in 1840 and 1845. All references to the story are to the final, 1845 version contained in the standard edition, *The Complete Works of Edgar Allan Poe,* ed. James A. Harrison (New York: AMS Press Inc., 1965), vol. 3.

2. Marie Bonaparte, to cite the classic example of its genre, considers Madeline a substitute for Roderick's mother toward whom the son allegedly had "infantile incestuous wishes." *The Life and Works of Edgar Allan Poe: A Psycho-Analytical Interpretation* (New York: Humanities Press, 1971). Translated by John Rodker from the original French, *Edgar Poe: étude psychanalytique* (Paris: Denoël et Steele, 1933), p. 249. Leo Spitzer states that the siblings are helpless inheritors of the "degeneracy of th[eir] race," whose members, ruled by the "law of sterility and destruction . . . , must exterminate each other," in "A Reinterpretation of 'The Fall of the House of Usher,' " *Essays on English and American Literature,* ed. Anna Hatcher (Princeton: Princeton University Press, 1962), pp. 51–66. Originally published in *Comparative Literature* 4 (1952): 351–63; rpt. in *Twentieth Century Interpretations of "The Fall of the House of Usher,"* ed. Thomas Woodson (Englewood Cliffs, N.J.: Prentice-Hall, 1969), p. 60. (Hereafter cited as Woodson.) For some others who share, to varying degrees and for not always the same reasons, this interpretation of incest, see D. H. Lawrence, *Studies in Classic American Literature* (New York: Thomas Seltzer, 1923); rpt. in *The Recognition of Edgar Allan Poe,* ed. Eric Carlson (Ann Arbor: University of Michigan Press, 1966), pp. 121–27 (henceforth cited as Carlson); Allen Tate, "Our Cousin, Mr. Poe," *Collected Essays,* 1960; rpt. in *Poe: A Collection of Critical Essays,* ed. R. Regan (Englewood Cliffs, N.J.: Prentice-Hall, 1967); John March, "The Psycho-Sexual Reading of 'The Fall of the House of Usher,' " *Poe Studies,* no. 5 (1972): 8–9; Daniel Hoffman, *Poe, Poe, Poe, Poe, Poe, Poe, Poe* (Garden City, N.Y.: Doubleday, 1972); Renata Mautner Wasserman, "The Self, the Mirror, the Other: 'The Fall of the House of Usher,' " *Poe Studies,* no. 10 (1977): 33–35; and Sybil Wuletich-Brinberg, *Poe: The Rationale of the Uncanny* (New York: Peter Lang, 1988).

3. Darrel Abel's opposition of "life-reason" and "death-madness" is among the most famous of these. See his "A Key to the House of Usher," *The University of Toronto Quarterly* 18 (1949): 176–85; rpt. in Woodson, pp. 43–55. Among others with similar concerns are Barton Levi St. Armand, "Poe's Landscape of the Soul: Association Theory and 'The Fall of the House of Usher,' " *Modern Language Studies* 7 (1977): 32–41; and J. Gerald Kennedy, who views the tale as the enactment of Roderick's horror and denial of death in *Poe, Death, and the Life of Writing* (New Haven: Yale University Press, 1987).

4. Richard Wilbur, "The House of Poe," in Carlson, p. 265. Originally presented as a Library of Congress Anniversary Lecture, May 4, 1959 and printed in *Anniversary Lectures* (Washington, D.C.: Library of Congress, 1959). See also Yvor Winters, "Edgar Allan Poe: A Crisis in the History of American Obscurantism," Carlson, p. 193. Originally published in *American Literature* 18 (January 1937): 379–401.

5. James Cox, "Edgar Poe: Style as Pose," *The Virginia Quarterly Review* 44 (Winter 1968): 67–89; rpt. in Woodson, p. 115.

6. Abel in Woodson, p. 53. Other perspectives on the short story range from considerations of vampirism to the idea that Roderick is a metaphor of the artist and that the critic is an entrapped figure within the story. For an essay on the latter see Terry Heller, *The Delights of Terror: An Aesthetics of the Tale of Terror* (Chicago: University of Illinois Press, 1987).

7. See note 11 in chapter 2.

8. *Boundary 2* (Spring 1979): 117–44. The following citations are from this article. (Cited in subsequent notes as Riddel.) See also Dennis Pahl, *Architects of the Abyss: The Indeterminate Fictions of Poe, Hawthorne, and Melville* (Columbia: University of Missouri Press, 1989), for a view of the text as an "allegory of unreadability." Pahl himself admits that his reading has "much in common with Riddel's" (p.11 n. 22), but he also draws from Lacan and Freud, among others.

9. Although the deconstructive concerns of Jacques Derrida were specifically referred to in chapter 1 of this study, and although Riddel's approach is fundamentally Derridian, I do not mean to limit discussion to the deconstructive methodology and concerns of Derrida. Paul de Man's deconstructive project, in particular his reflections on the dialogic nature of narrative, could be very fruitfully discussed in conjunction with anasemic analysis, transphenomenology, and the symbolic operation. For a critical commentary on deconstructive readings of other Poe works in the context of a discussion of Americanist versus deconstructionist approaches to reading, see R. C. Prospo, "Deconstructive Poe(tics)," *Diacritics* 18, no. 3 (Fall 1988): 43–64. My reading of *Usher* and my comments on Riddel may also be applied, mutatis mutandi, to Prospo's commentary on Gide's analysis of the *mise en abîme* structure of the "Mad Trist" and to Louis Renza's brief comments on Usher in his article, "Poe's Secret Autobiography," *Psychoanalysis and the Question of the Text*, ed. Geoffrey Hartman (Baltimore: Johns Hopkins University Press, 1978), pp. 58–89. While Renza's approach and concerns are quite different from my own, his Bloomian reference to *The Jolly Corner* as a text that embodies the return of James's repressed relationship with Poe as predecessor suggests a sensibility to the potential for "haunting" in the works of both Poe and James that is not entirely unaligned with my own.

10. Whereas most readers have glossed over this admittedly rare word (the *OED* cites only Poe for usage although there are numerous references under the following entry "porphyrogenite"), others have been confused by it: " 'Porphyrogene' is . . . a puzzler. Porphyry is a kind of rock; its connotations of stolidity don't seem appropriate to the ruler of this still happy palace. Or the word might refer to Malchus Porphyrius or Porphyry . . . , a neo-Platonic philosopher, in which case 'Porphyrogene' might imply 'like a great philosopher.' " *The Short Fiction of Edgar Allan Poe*, ed. Stuart and Susan Levine (Indianapolis: Bobbs-Merrill, 1976), p. 105.

11. The penultimate line of the poem in fact reads: *Mon coeur est un luth suspendu* (My heart is a suspended lute). A possible explanation for Poe's substitution of *son* (his/her) for *mon* (my) will be offered later in this analysis.

12. One could add that the syllable "red" in Ethelred is a sign that something has to be read or interpreted in his name.

13. Many critics have wondered why Poe used the English rather than the French spelling (Madeleine) of Madeline's name, given his penchant for French protagonists and settings in his short stories and the presence of French in this particular tale. This interpretation may be considered a response.

14. This analysis demonstrates how archeonyms (original words) and allosemes of a secret that has to remain concealed must be banished from the narrative. Here the archeonym of the rape, *viol* in French, is excluded from the text, as are the allosemes—"viol" in English, "violin," "viola," etc.—that link its cryptonyms to it. Only the cryptonyms of the secret such as "stringed instruments" and "guitar" can appear.

15. This reading is reinforced by Poe's footnote, appearing just prior to the passage cited, in which he specifies the other men who have shared Roderick's "train of thought" regarding the sentience of vegetable things: "Watson, Dr. Percival, Spallanzani, and especially the Bishop of Landaff. —See 'Chemical Essays,' vol. V" (286). Richard Watson, a chemist, was the bishop of Landaff and shared with Lazzaro Spallanzani, a professor of natural history, an interest in the generation and reproduction of species and in natural and artificial fertilization. Spallanzani is the author of a treatise entitled "Histoire de la génération." Usher's "train of thought" is thus linked to ideas of artificial or cross-fertilization and inquiries into reproductive histories.

16. It may be noted that the cryptonym *Vigilæ Mortuorum secundum Chorum Ecclesiæ Maguntinæ* is unlike any seen thus far since its decrypting not only depends on a previously uncovered cryptonym (*coeur* → *luth* → *lutte* → struggle) but involves four different languages combined in different ways: two interlinguistic synonyms (*Maguntinæ* → *Mainz* + *Chorum* → *choeur*) followed by either interlinguistic paranomasia (*Mainz* → minds) or a homophone and another cryptonym (*choeur* → *coeur* → *luth* → etc.). This example helps demonstrate the potentially infinite variety and complexity of cryptonymic formations.

17. The correspondence established here between "The Haunted Palace" and a human head differs from that claimed by Richard Wilbur and Ivor Winters, cited earlier, not just because it involves the lady's head instead of Roderick's (as they maintain). More important is the fact that this correspondence is not founded on an assumed equation between two symbols (equating a pearl-adorned door with a mouth full of teeth, for example, or yellow banners with golden hair) but on the unraveling of a symbolic operation in which elements or co-symbols of "The Haunted Palace" complement and complete textual fragments pertaining to the House of Usher.

18. "River" and "door" reinforce the equating of "throng" with the line of Usher, since "usher" comes from the Latin *ustium, ostium* meaning "door, entrance, mouth of a river" (*Webster's*). Hearing Latin in the text is legitimized by the *Directorium Inquisitorum* and the *Vigilæ Mortuorum secundum Chorum Ecclesiæ Maguntinæ*.

19. This "loss of head" is itself allegorized in the "Trist": "And Ethelred uplifted his mace, and struck upon the head of the dragon, which fell before him" (294).

This reading of "The Haunted Palace" reveals that the distinction postulated earlier between *The Fall of the House of Usher* and the other phantom-texts in this study has to be nuanced. The references to mental illness, malady, and disorder in Poe's tale cannot be viewed solely as a thematization of madness or as a vague commentary on the mental state of Usher family members. "Madness," "discord," "mental inorganization," like "guitar," "stringed instruments," and "lute," and like "*manteau*," "*tombeau*," "*or*," "pince-nez," and "monocle" in their respective texts, are cryptonyms, words that simultaneously hide and mutely voice part of the secret haunting the House of Usher. At the same time, "madness," "mental inorganization," etc. have an additional function in Poe's text that distinguishes it from the other texts in this study. These lexical entities allow us to deduce that the secret transmitted as a phantom throughout the Usher line originated in a *crypt* formed by the lady-who-made-the-line. (For more on the "crypt" see the subsection "The Phantom" in chapter 1.) The lady, we can conjecture, was caught in a psychic double bind as a result of the rape and illegitimacy. She could either tell the truth of the fraud and thereby ruin the family, or she could hide the truth, thereby saving the family for appearance sake but in fact ruining it, since the infiltration of the bastard would mean its de facto demise.

Whereas in hysteria psychic conflict occurs when a desire comes up against a prohibition, here the conflict results from the need to choose between two equally impossible because literally unspeakable alternatives. The response is the formation of a crypt, a living tomb in which the unutterable drama constituted by words ("I have lost the head") is removed from consciousness and buried intact, its content neither affirmed nor denied. Preserved from the forces of dynamic repression, what returns from the crypt are symptoms or symbols whose cryptonymic formation aims to defy telling and obstruct cognition but that nonetheless obliquely refer to what has been obstructed. Through her madness and mental inorganization, in other words, the lady reinvents her existence as a cryptic narrative that simultaneously conceals and reveals the catastrophe she has buried alive and that she will unknowingly transmit as a phantom, a narrative that can be decrypted to say: I am mad → I have lost my head → I have lost the head of the family.

Poe's tale is thus unique among the five stories analyzed in this study. None of the others provides the textual evidence for reconstructing an internal conflict or "psychic aporia" that would have necessitated the formation of a crypt in the "originators" of the phantoms (Maucombe, Facino Cane's mother, or Spencer Brydon's grandfather). We cannot know whether the phantoms in these earlier narratives began as crypts or, as in *Hamlet*, as consciously created secrets "wrapped in silence" and taken knowingly to the grave.

20. Usher's verbal improvisation has already been shown to speak eloquently if cryptically to reveal the fraudulent heir in the line. His one painting, described by the narrator as a "phantasmagoric conception" (283) of the "interior of an immensely long and rectangular vault or tunnel [lying at an] exceeding depth below the surface of the earth" (283), may also be heard to speak of a buried or hidden "conception." Along with the references to "crypt" and "encrypting" in the text, it can be understood as one of the means through which Poe's text suggests the presence within it of a structure analogous to the psychic formations of the crypt and the phantom in which a secret is buried or encrypted and then displaced or transmitted.

21. Poe's substitution of *son* (his/her) for *mon* in the epigraph can be understood in terms of this secret sharing as a sign that the heart resonating with a struggle in the text belongs both to him and to her, to Roderick and Madeline together.

22. The reading of "malady" as "my lady" is not based purely on homophony but is contingent upon the correspondences already established between malady, illness, madness, and the lady's internal conflict.

23. The narrator's infection by this struggle is also evident in the insistent repetition (eleven times in the text's first paragraph just partially cited) of the word "upon," which may be heard as a cryptic reference to the rapist who got "up on" the lady, and in the narrator's impression that there hung about the mansion "an atmosphere which had no affinity with the air of heaven, but which had reeked up from the *decayed trees* . . . a *pestilent and mystic vapour*" (276). The "sensations which oppress" (276) the narrator, he implicitly reveals, have to do with a diseased, secreted air → heir that hangs suspended around the House.

24. The narrator's "replacement" of Madeline is foreshadowed in the text when he first sees Roderick's sister. "While [Usher] spoke, the lady Madeline . . . passed slowly through . . . the apartment. . . . I regarded her with an utter astonishment not unmingled with dread—and yet I found it impossible to account for such feelings. A sensation of stupor oppressed me, as my eyes followed her retreating steps" (281).

25. Roderick can be heard to announce this departure in his last, "archaic" words: "Oh whither shall I fly?" → "Oh *with her*, with her spirit shall I fly."

26. To cite only a few of the numerous examples in the text supporting this idea: "*I know not how it was*—but, with the first glimpse of the building, a sense of insufferable gloom pervaded my spirit" (273); "Much that I encountered . . . contributed, *I know not how*, to heighten the vague sentiments of which I have already spoken" (277); "Shaking this off with a gasp . . . , I uplifted myself upon the pillows, and, . . . hearkened—*I know not why* . . . to certain low and indefinite sounds" (290).

27. We could say that *The Fall of the House of Usher* warns of the possibility, in literary analysis, of what psychoanalysis calls "countertransference," and it implicitly calls upon the analyst/reader to be aware of this dynamic and its potential to obstruct the course of interpretation.

28. Riddel, p. 129.

29. Ibid., p. 130. Riddel's use of the word "crypt" is a metaphorical one and not related to its metapsychological sense elaborated by Abraham and Torok.

30. See the seventh section of chapter 1: "Symbolic Operation, Trauma, and Anasemia."

31. This commentary could be added to the subjects enumerated in note 64 of chapter 1 that would form part of a lengthy elaboration of the differences between Derrida's deconstructive project and the process of anasemic analysis described by Abraham and Torok and extended into the literary realm by my readings. Some recent commentaries on Abraham and Torok's work have tended to subsume anasemia within deconstruction and to articulate its concerns accordingly. This admittedly very brief comparison of Riddel's reading

of Poe with my own may at least begin to clarify in what way these two projects, while not antithetical, are nonetheless quite different.

32. The circumstances that could lead to this apparent contradiction are not hard to imagine. It is conceivable, for example, that the adulterer was indeed loved by the lady but forced himself upon her, leaving her with conflicting feelings of love and rage. It is equally plausible that a loving and beloved relative—a father, uncle, grandfather—committed the rape, a drama that could understandably lead to feelings of rage in conflict with natural feelings of love for a family member. A trauma of incest, in other words, could conceivably lie behind the lady's "struggle of the heart." In the absence of textual evidence, these hypotheses must remain untested.

Conclusion

1. See also my outline of a Freudian reading of *Facino Cane* in chapter 4.

2. The use of psychoanalytic theory as a model for interpretation is of course not limited to Freudian and Lacanian approaches but extends to conceptual systems elaborated by others including Klein and Jung.

3. For a gender-oriented reading of Poe's text, see Cynthia Jordan, *Second Stories: The Politics of Language, Form, and Gender in Early American Fictions* (Chapel Hill: University of North Carolina Press, 1989). See also Leland Person, *Aesthetic Headaches: Women and a Masculine Poetics in Poe, Melville, and Hawthorne* (Athens: University of Georgia Press, 1988), in which the author considers Poe's tale a dramatic account of the "male's self-destructive repression of women."

4. My research suggests that *L'Eve future,* Villiers's science fiction novel about a man's creation of a speaking, "living" robot in the image of a woman, is a text in which the male protagonist's misogyny can be explained in terms of his haunting by a phantom.

5. Maria Torok's current work is devoted to analyzing Freud and the emergence of the institution of psychoanalysis.

6. The collective concealment of secrets by the government of Argentina during the "Dirty War" is one example of a potentially phantomogenic situation. Evaluation and analysis of the now well-documented increase in psychopathology among the surviving children, grandchildren, and relatives of the "disappeared" might be facilitated if pursued with the theory of the phantom in mind.

Index

Abbreviations for works by N. Abraham, Torok, and Lacan appear in parentheses following full titles.

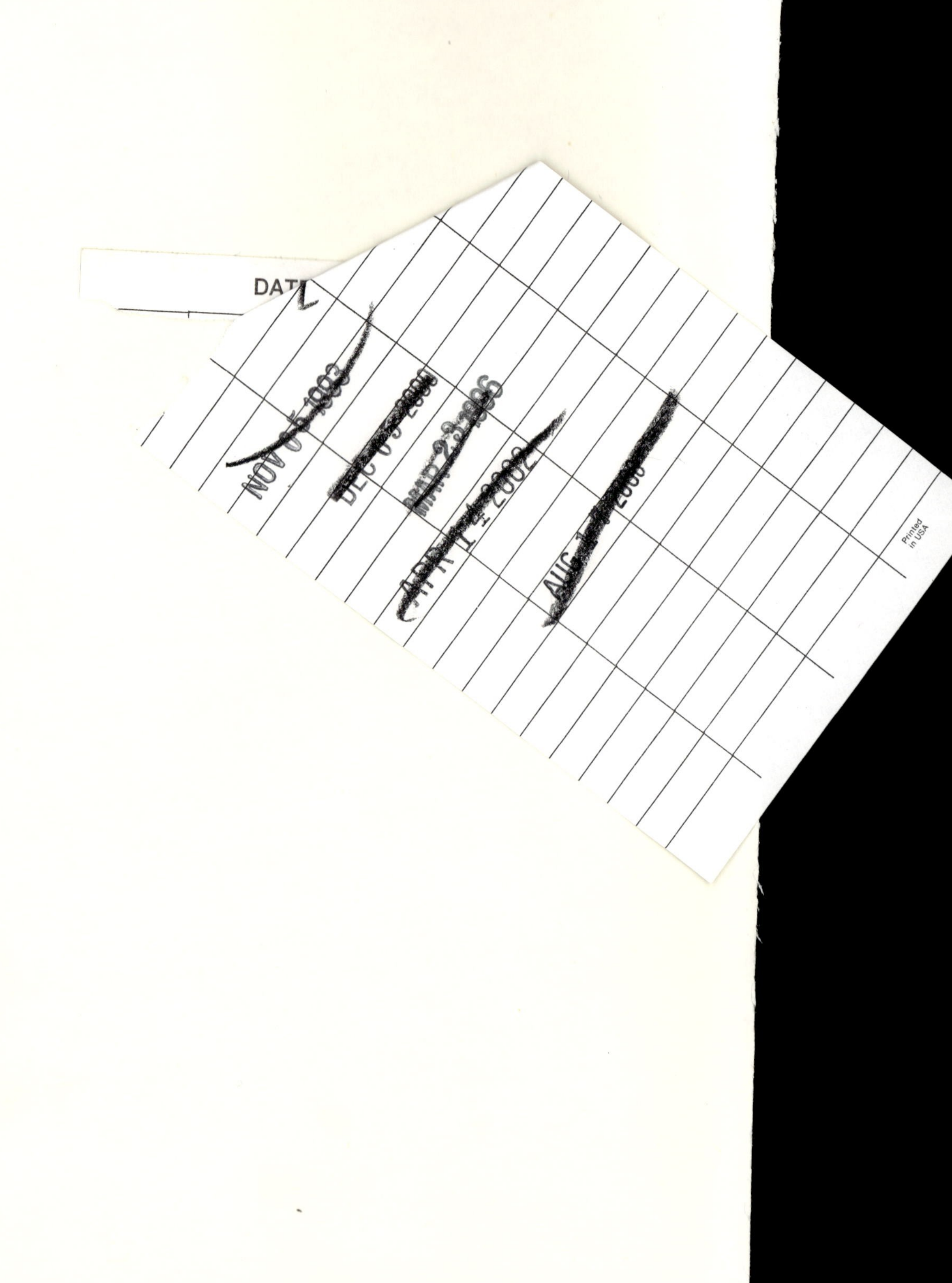